Turbulent Times

Turbulent Times

The British Jewish Community Today

Keith Kahn-Harris and Ben Gidley

continuum

Continuum International Publishing Group

The Tower Building
11 York Road
London SE1 7NX

80 Maiden Lane
Suite 704
New York NY 10038

www.continuumbooks.com

British Library Cataloguing-in-Publication Data
A catalogue record for this book is available from the British Library.

ISBN: HB: 978-1-8470-6316-8
          PB: 978-1-8471-4476-8

Library of Congress Cataloging-in-Publication Data
Gidley, Ben.
  Turbulent times : the British Jewish community today / Ben Gidley and Keith Kahn-Harris.
    p. cm.
  ISBN 978-1-84706-316-8 — ISBN 978-1-84714-476-8 1. Jews—Great Britain—History—21st century. 2. Jews—Great Britain—Politics and government—21st century. 3. Jews—Great Britain—Social life and customs. 4. Judaism—Great Britain—History—21st century. 5. Great Britain—Ethnic relations. I. Kahn-Harris, Keith, 1971- II. Title.

  DS135.E5G525 2010
  305.892'4041—dc22

                              2009051348

Typeset by Free Range Book Design & Production
Printed and bound in India by Replika Press Pvt Ltd

Contents

Acknowledgements   vii

Introduction   1

1   Jewish Community and Jewish Leadership in the UK   15

2   Research and the 'Reflexive Turn' in Anglo Jewry   38

3   The Continuity Consensus   56

4   From Jewish continuity to Jewish Continuity   71

5   The Renewal Agenda   94

6   From Renewal to Renaissance   117

7   New Antisemitism, New Insecurity   136

Conclusion   163

Notes   177

Bibliography   207

Glossary   225

Index of Names and Institutions   229

Acknowledgements

In conducting the research for this book, we conducted a small number of interviews with key Jewish leaders involved in the developments we discuss. We have reproduced some extracts from these interviews in the book and the others provided background material that has informed our analysis. We would like to thank the following interviewees for their time and for their valuable insights: Jonathan Ariel, Rabbi Tony Bayfield, Simon Caplan, Henry Grunwald, Jonathan Kestenbaum, Professor Barry Kosmin, Clive Lawton, Rabbi Dr Tali Loewenthal, Jeremy Newmark, Winston Pickett, Rosalind Preston, David Rosenberg, Chief Rabbi Jonathan Sacks, Michael Sinclair, Jonathan Woocher, Rabbi Saul Zneimer and one senior lay leader who wished to remain anonymous. Roy Graham and Mathew Kalman also shared their time and important insights with us. We are conscious of the fact that we only interviewed one woman – a reflection of the male dominance in the most senior ranks of the British Jewish communal leadership.

The research and writing for this book was completed with the assistance of grants from the Rothschild Foundation Europe, the Memorial Fund for Jewish Culture and the Economic and Social Research Council. Both of us were employed at the Centre for Urban and Community Research at Goldsmiths College. We would like to express our thanks to the Director of the CUCR Professor Caroline Knowles, her predecessor Professor Michael Keith and other colleagues, in particular Professor Les Back, for their support and mentorship. We would also like to thank Professor Geoffrey Alderman for his assistance at key stages in our research and writing. We are grateful to Joel Schalit, who provided invaluable assistance in commenting on the final drafts of the book.

Finally we would both like to thank our families for their love and support. We dedicate this book to them.

Introduction

There are around 270,000 Jews in the UK, less than 0.5 per cent of the population; smaller than the British Muslim, Hindu or Afro-Caribbean populations. The Jewish community may be small, but it is well established. Jews have lived openly in Britain since the seventeenth century, and the number of Jews expanded significantly with immigration from Eastern Europe at the turn of the nineteenth and twentieth centuries. At its height in the 1950s, estimates suggested there were somewhere between 400,000 and 500,000 Jews in Britain.[1]

Modern British Jews have suffered none of the large-scale pogroms to which Jews elsewhere were subject. 'Scientific' antisemitism never achieved the foothold in Britain that it did elsewhere in Europe. In the nineteenth century, most legal barriers to full Jewish participation in civic and political life were removed. In the twentieth, the remaining unofficial barriers to participation in social and cultural life fell away. In the post-World War II period, British Jews took full advantage of the expansion of the universities and of other sources of social mobility to become a community that today, as the 2001 census showed, is generally better off materially than the general population.[2]

This book critically examines the history of concerns for Jewish communal survival amongst the British Jewish communal leadership in the late twentieth century and beyond. Our argument is that there has been a transition from a dominant communal agenda preoccupied with the nurturing of communal *security* against the perceived threat of persecution to one that is concerned about an *excess of security* and complacency amongst British Jews. Crucial to understanding this shift, we suggest, is the relationship between debates about community within British Jewry and wider debates about community and multiculturalism in Britain. How have the Jewish community and its leaders responded to such debates and helped to shape them? How have they drawn on ideas about the place of the Jewish community stemming from other contexts, such as Israel, America and Europe?

As one of Britain's oldest minority groups, British Jews provide an important case study in minority communal leadership. This book is the first to investigate communal leadership in the British Jewish community in the contemporary period. This book, based on detailed sociological research, is intended to contribute both to the sociological literature and to the Jewish community's ability to understand itself. It is the first large-scale attempt to contextualize British Jewry into contemporary debates about multiculturalism, and we hope both to feed a Jewish perspective into these debates and disseminate learning from these debates within the Jewish community. We suggest that the shift from a communal strategy of security to one of insecurity relates to the transition from a monocultural Britain to a multicultural one. At the same time, with multiculturalism under attack in the post-9/11 period, we believe that the story we tell here is a resource for a more robust defence and renewal of British multiculturalism.

The Anglo Jewish community

The unbroken Jewish presence in Britain for over three centuries has allowed British Jews to build an extensive and sophisticated network of institutions. Through the eighteenth and nineteenth centuries, what had been a tight-knit, largely Sephardi[3] community was gradually transformed into a diverse, largely Ashkenazi community. The Chief Rabbinate, initially the rabbi of the Ashkenazi Great Synagogue in London, became the most significant Jewish religious authority in the UK. If the Chief Rabbinate was, as is sometimes argued, modelled on the Archbishop of Canterbury, then Anglo Jewry's Church of England was the United Synagogue. Formed in 1870 by an act of parliament through the alliance of the three main London Ashkenazi synagogues, the United Synagogue remains the largest British Jewish umbrella body, with over sixty member and affiliated synagogues. The United Synagogue is an orthodox organization in that its rabbis and synagogues cleave to orthodox practice and theology. However, it is widely understood that the majority of its membership, and indeed many of its lay leaders, do not practise orthodoxy in the strict *halachic* sense.

The United Synagogue has never had a monopoly of Jewish affiliation. The Sephardi community has its own structure. The more conservative Federation of Synagogues is an orthodox body founded in the late nineteenth century to cater for Eastern European immigrants who did not care for the Anglican trappings of the United Synagogue. It survives to this day as a more conservative body than the United Synagogue. The Union of Orthodox Hebrew Congregations (UOHC) was founded in 1926 as an ultra-orthodox umbrella body and now represents over a hundred congregations in the rapidly growing Haredi community. Reform Judaism grew in the UK following the formation of the West London Synagogue in 1841 and in the post-war period developed its own umbrella body, now known as the Movement for Reform Judaism; it has over forty affiliated synagogues. A separate non-orthodox synagogue grouping developed in the early part of the twentieth century through Lily Montagu and Claude Montefiore's Jewish Religious Union, which gave rise to the Liberal Jewish Synagogue. Now known as Liberal Judaism, it has over thirty congregations and tends to be more radical in its theology and religious practice than Reform Judaism. The smallest umbrella body is the Assembly of Masorti Synagogues, dating from the early 1960s, whose twelve congregations are similar to American Conservative Judaism in practice.

A 2006 study showed that 68 per cent of UK Jewish households were affiliated to a synagogue.[4] Fifty-five per cent of affiliated households belonged to United, Federation or similar centrist orthodox synagogues, 34 per cent to a non-orthodox synagogue and 11 per cent to a UOHC synagogue. Since 1990, United and Federation membership had declined slightly whereas UOHC membership had almost doubled. Non-orthodox percentages had all increased with Masorti nearly doubling in size to 3 per cent. There appears to be a process of polarization in which the non-orthodox and ultra-orthodox Jewish populations are growing at the expense of 'mainstream' orthodoxy.

Synagogues and their umbrella bodies are only one part of the Anglo Jewish institutional story. As we shall see in the next chapter, the Board of Deputies, Anglo Jewry's representative body, has its origins in the eighteenth century and has evolved into a quasi-parliamentary body in which 'deputies' represent individual synagogues. The Board has traditionally been the principal mechanism through which the concerns and interests of Anglo Jewry are represented to the British state and the British public. It survives despite continual questioning of its ability truly to represent Anglo Jewry, with criticisms at various points of the non-inclusion of progressive Jews, Haredi Jews, secular Jews, Zionists and anti-Zionists.[5]

Zionism has been both a unifier and divider in the British Jewish community. As we shall see in chapter 1, pre-1948, Zionism was viewed with deep suspicion by many communal grandees. However, post-independence, Zionism rapidly became a source of consensus in the community, with the high watermark being the demonstrations of solidarity during and following the 1967 Six Day War. The Joint Israel Appeal (later renamed the United Jewish Israel Appeal), the Jewish National Fund and other Israel charities became the focus of communal philanthropy. Zionism is also the focus for Jewish youth work, with a network of Zionist youth movements providing the infrastructure for tours to Israel and youth clubs. In recent decades though, as chapter 7 demonstrates, Israel became a source of controversy in the community, with questions of how and whether Jews should criticize Israel becoming a subject of debate.

As we shall see in chapter 5, education has become an increasingly important communal priority in recent decades. Jewish schools, which for most of Anglo Jewish history only reached a minority of Jewish children, have been a feature of British Jewish communal life since the eighteenth century. The community has also built and sustained an extensive network of welfare institutions. While much of the Jewish welfare sector has its origins in the assistance of poor immigrants from Eastern Europe, it has endured into the period of Anglo Jewry's upward mobility. In 2008, Jewish Care, the principal Jewish welfare body, had an income of over £50 million and over nine hundred employees. A 2000 study found that there were over 2000 Jewish voluntary organizations in the UK with a combined income in 1997 of over £500 million.[6] This is 3 per cent of the total UK voluntary sector income of that year – roughly six times what would be expected given the size of the UK Jewish community.

British Jews in public life

For a modestly sized Jewish population, many Jews have reached prominent positions in most spheres of British life. The nineteenth century saw the development of a small, wealthy group of Jewish communal grandees that joined the ranks of the English upper classes. Their main interest, as we shall see in the next chapter, was in demonstrating to the Jewish and non-Jewish community that it was possible to be a good British citizen in public and a Jew in private. The desire to demonstrate closeness to British hierarchy has not diminished in the present era. Chief Rabbi Jonathan Sacks was ennobled in 2009 by Gordon Brown, and his predecessor was ennobled by Margaret Thatcher. Jews have held most major offices of state, most recently providing the first Jewish Speaker with the election of John Bercow in June 2009. Today's Jewish oligarchy is made up largely of businessmen/philanthropists rather than the nobility. What has not changed is the closeness of this oligarchy to the British state with the likes of Lord Michael Levy, Lord Stanley Kalms and Sir Trevor Chinn being high-profile supporters of party political causes.

In addition, some of the country's leading intellectuals and academics have been Jews (many, but not all, European émigrés), among them Isaiah Berlin, Zygmunt Bauman, Martin Gilbert, George Steiner, Ludwig Wittgenstein and Karl Popper. In the UK today, there are acclaimed writers such as Howard Jacobson, internationally renowned actors such as Sacha Baron-Cohen, Matt Lucas and Maureen Lipman, major TV personalities such as Sir Alan Sugar, musicians such as Amy Winehouse, and journalists such as Melanie Phillips and Jonathan Freedland.

For all the presence of Jews in the most prominent positions in British cultural life, few have been centrally concerned with Jewish issues in their work. For example, Isaiah Berlin's Jewish origins and the influence of the antisemitism that brought his family to the UK were central in the development of his *oeuvre*, but he was a secular Jew, ensconced in Oxford for most of his life, rarely writing about explicitly Jewish issues. Harold Pinter's upbringing as an East End Jew was clearly important in his development, but it was rarely reflected in his plays as an overt theme. While there have been Jewish politicians who have been publicly identified with Jewish causes, such as Greville Janner MP, who served as president of the Board of Deputies in the 1980s, most have been relatively uninvolved in Jewish communal life apart from occasional efforts made on Jewish issues such as Israel. The successful comedian Matt Lucas may have been involved in Jewish youth groups growing up, and occasionally raises funds for Jewish causes today, but his comedy very rarely deals with Jewish themes. Significantly, there is no Jewish equivalent of the successful British Asian TV comedy *Goodness Gracious Me*.

The simultaneous ubiquity of Jews and absence of Jewishness in British public life is paralleled by the absence of Jews in social scientific research in the contemporary United Kingdom. While there have been many prominent Jews in the social sciences in the UK, there has been little social scientific research on Jews. Zygmunt Bauman is the only living world-renowned Anglo Jewish social scientist who has discussed Jews explicitly and extensively (and he spent much of his early career in Poland). Since the 1970s there has been an explosion of interest in immigrant groups in Britain. For example, some of the most influential social scientific scholarship has concerned the sociology and culture of British Asians and Afro-Caribbeans. Yet there is no Jewish Stuart Hall or Paul Gilroy to demonstrate how the British Jewish experience might reveal the hidden dynamics of British society and culture. Even if there were Jews such as Stanley Cohen at the heart of British cultural studies as it developed in the 1970s, this tradition too has little to say about Anglo Jewry.[7] Neither has there been much sociological research on contemporary Jewry itself, at least within the academy. It is ironic that at a time when diaspora is a 'hot' topic in the social sciences in the UK,[8] the venerable Jewish Diaspora is neglected.

Contemporary research on minorities in Britain tends to emphasize racism and material disadvantage, a paradigm into which the largely prosperous contemporary Jewish community does not appear to 'fit'. Partly as a response to this, as Mitchell Hart has argued,[9] contemporary Jewish historians such as David Cesarani, Tony Kushner and Geoffrey Alderman have all tried to show how the history of Anglo Jewry was actually more fraught than earlier British Jewish historians portrayed, with their concern to demonstrate the loyalty and success of Anglo Jewry.[10] For many scholars of British Jewry, then, the apparent 'success' of British Jewry is a 'problem' to be resolved through emphasizing the dark side of the Jewish relationship with the UK.

Jews and multiculturalism

Even if Jews now appear to 'fit' economically and socially into British society, then, they do not 'fit' into the major categories through which minorities are generally defined in contemporary Britain: they are a 'faith' but many Jews, including those who observe numerous Jewish rituals, do not see belief in God as central to their Jewish identity or observance; they are a 'religion' but many Jews observe no rituals at all; they are a 'race' or an 'ethnicity' but they do not all share the same background and some are converts to the Jewish religion; they are a 'nation' but most are not citizens of Israel, the Jewish state. In chapter 1, we discuss how historically the Jewish community was defined principally as a religion, while more recently Jews have been defined as a race/ethnicity for the purposes of anti-discriminatory legislation.[11] Perhaps the best way to define Jews is as a 'people',[12] but this category has no relevance in dealing with the British state and so Jews are forced to define themselves using various categories – never entirely satisfactorily – according to specific needs.

Because Jews have become associated with 'whiteness',[13] they do not fit into dominant paradigms of multicultural research. As Eric Goldstein has argued: 'Ironically, in an atmosphere that purports to value and encourage "difference", Jews are stymied ... by the tendency of American culture to make blackness and whiteness the critical categories of group life.'[14] Similarly, Sander Gilman argues that: 'the Jews, now seen as the ultimate victims of inhumanity, an inhumanity to be answered by the multicultural, are now excluded from the multicultural as too successful, too white and too Jewish'.[15]

The lack of Jewish voice at the heart of social and cultural research in the UK is reflected in the lack of Jewish voices in public debates about multiculturalism and racism. Both the previous Chief Rabbi, Immanuel Jakobovits,[16] and the current Chief Rabbi[17] have been critical of multiculturalism. Historically, communal leaders have been extremely concerned about the public image of Anglo Jewry, disowning or repressing anything that seems to endanger the security of the community.[18] Whereas in previous times, in a monocultural society where antisemitism was never far from the surface, minorities were expected to be well-behaved and discreet, in recent decades this concern had become increasingly anachronistic. The post-war immigrant minorities were often more assertive about their public presence. An event like the Notting Hill Carnival, which began in 1958 partly in response to racist violence against London's migrant citizens, has become an occasion where the Afro-Caribbean community publicly celebrates itself, exemplifying a multicultural willingness publicly to declare one's existence and one's pride in it. The Jewish community, despite the lessons its diasporic story might have for a multicultural nation, failed to get a place at the table of multiculturalism; the communal leadership's stress on secure British belonging meant it has often been seen by other minorities as simply part of the white mainstream.

The problematic position of Jews in the UK

We suggest that the paradoxical position of Jews in the UK as both ubiquitous and marginal has had deleterious consequences for the British Jewish community. Anglo Jewry has successfully created conditions where it is safe and comfortable to be Jewish in the UK. This is no small achievement. However, the historical reticence of Jews to articulate their Jewishness publicly has fostered a damaging cultural invisibility that over time has undermined much of the vitality of Anglo Jewry. A situation was created in which most Jewish intellectuals and cultural figures tend to shun not only public expressions and discussions of Jewishness, but also even private engagement with the Jewish community.

What do we mean here by 'community'? While we recognize that the term is problematic and can be used in several different ways, in this book we focus on community as a self-conscious though by no means unified entity whose members interact in Jewish institutions. The Jewish community cannot be understood apart from Jewish communal institutions, even if some members of the community interact rarely or not at all with those institutions. For better or worse, this institutionally anchored community forms the 'mainstream' of Anglo Jewry, although to a certain extent more radical and marginalized Jews also have their own institutions. We make the distinction between 'Anglo Jewry', the collectivity of Jews in the UK, and the Jewish community in order to emphasize how not all British Jews are involved in Jewish institutional life or even see themselves as Jewish and as having anything in common with other Jews in the UK.

It is precisely the distinction between the Jewish community and Anglo Jewry that is responsible for some of the historical failings of the community. The institutions that constitute the Jewish community have developed largely without the input of the most creative and innovative minds in Anglo Jewry. Further, the lack of engagement with other British minorities has meant that the cultural vitality that has come to be associated with multiculturalism has often passed the Jewish community by. Consequently, the British Jewish community has, for all its 'success', little reputation for explicitly *Jewish* achievement. The community has produced few world-renowned Jewish scholars, Louis Jacobs, the founder of Masorti Judaism, being the most notable exception – and he was disowned by a key section of the communal leadership. Assessments of UK Jewry by writers and intellectuals have often been damning. One American Jewish academic wrote in 1986:

> Anglo-Jewish organizational life altogether remains notably pedestrian. There are seemingly unlimited societies and programs – actually, some three hundred different ones – revolving around synagogues, Zionism, or welfare ... Except for the waning mystique of Zionism, however, there is little of solid Jewish cultural content in their programs. Large numbers of Jewish charity committees function as hardly more than disguised matrimonial clubs ... The religious establishment is a bore ... The writers and academicians offer Anglo Jewry meagre intellectual fare compared to the feast that presently enriches American Jewish life and education. There are capable professionals in the Jewish organizations, but they enjoy little of the status and influence of their counterparts in the United States or even in France.[19]

The British journalist Stephen Brook was equally scathing in his book *The Club* in 1989:

> it's hard to envisage a generation of Jewish intellectuals that could restore the cultural vitality of the community – and I'm not talking about Israeli dancing and baking Purim cakes.
>
> ...
>
> philistinism and intolerance within the fold have persuaded countless gifted Jews to direct their energies away from the community; and British Jews loyal to their religious and cultural tradition have always sought to adopt the lowest possible profile. It is certainly respectable to be Jewish in Britain, but it's neither exciting nor chic.
>
> ...
>
> the Jewish Establishment in Britain is not only mediocre in itself, but revels in its mediocrity, shallowness and philistinism, and as long as such attitudes prevail, Anglo Jewry may survive, may be more intensely Jewish, but it will never thrive and enrich the nation as a whole.[20]

In their 1991 book *A Sense of Belonging*, based on their 1990 Channel 4 TV series of the same name, Howard Cooper and Paul Morrison describe:

> an Anglo Jewry enclosed, provincial, obsessed by its committees and communal institutions; busy, dynamic and apparently empty.
>
> ...
>
> The very defensiveness and insularity of large parts of Anglo Jewry, its very desire to hold onto its young, was strangling them. Many of the brightest and most creative began to drift away, and still do.[21]

These books describe Anglo Jewry just before a 'tipping point', where a variety of internal and external factors generated a wide-ranging process of renewal. Whereas once such denunciations of the British Jewish community were made from outside the community, from the late 1980s they increasingly came to be made from *within* the community. These denunciations were effective and set in train a process of change that meant that the UK Jewish community in 2009, when this book was completed, was very different from the UK Jewish community in 1990 (from where we date the start of the process of change).

From 1990 the UK Jewish community became more publicly assertive, more self-confident, more innovative, more educated, more culturally creative, more efficiently led, more self-critical. The changes we are describing since 1990 were *not* part of a 'normal' incremental process of development, although some changes have roots that go back decades. Rather, they demonstrate a sea change in how the community and particularly its leadership positioned itself in the context of multicultural Britain. While we are positive about many of the changes we describe, we are not claiming that every change was a positive one, nor that every aspect of the community that needed change *was* changed. We are claiming, however, that the willingness of British Jews and British Jewish institutions to innovate and to be more visible in their Jewish expression has the potential to produce a community that may at last transcend some of the historic dullness and quietism of Anglo Jewry. If the paradox of Anglo Jewry's simultaneous ubiquity and marginality may still persist, there are grounds for optimism that for an emerging generation the desire to be successful in the UK will not necessarily be accompanied by reticence about publicly affirming and engaging with Jewishness.

Turbulent times

The title *Turbulent Times* reflects the fact that the changes that have taken place in Anglo Jewry have frequently been accompanied by controversy, insecurity and fear. One theme that runs through the book is how what we call a 'strategy of insecurity' was used by Jewish leaders to motivate change. Fears that Anglo Jewry would disappear through assimilation or that it would be imperilled by antisemitism have been loudly and publicly expressed. At the same time, the process of change was often enmeshed in fundamental debates about what being Jewish was about, sometimes leading to bitter disputes between different parts of the community. The wider context surrounding Anglo Jewry could also be described as turbulent. Since the 1980s, the UK has seen both the consolidation of multiculturalism and a backlash against it following the 9/11 and 7/7 attacks. The UK Jewish community has also been affected by the changing situation in the Middle East, with the Al-Aqsa Intifada and the 'War on Terror' having a direct impact on Anglo Jewry.

More generally, the changes that the Jewish community underwent took place against the background of a modernity that was ever more unstable. From their inception in the nineteenth century, the social sciences have emphasized the difficulties of living in modernity: the rapid and bewildering process of change, the alienating quality of capitalist labour, the anomic isolation of urban life, the erosion of tradition. In the last decades of the twentieth century, these changes were intensified and speeded up in a process that is sometimes known as postmodernity.[22]

Insecurity has become a dominant theme in the social sciences in the last two decades. As Gabe Mythen writes:

> the latter half of the twentieth century has been described as an epoch of flux, uncertainty and social change ... We are living in a 'runaway world' stippled by ominous dangers, military conflicts and environmental hazards ... increasing portions of our everyday lives are spent negotiating change, dealing with uncertainty and assessing the personal impacts of situations that appear to be out of our control.

This is exacerbated post-9/11 when politicians talk about us living in a 'post-secure' world.[23] As Jasanoff comments: 'Just as a century ago, the idea of "progress" helped to define an optimistic era, so today "risk", by its very pervasiveness, seems to be the defining marker of our own less sanguine historical moment.'[24] Bill Clinton described our world as 'a world in which risk is endless'.[25] For Zygmunt Bauman, the 'liquid modernity' of our age means living 'under the constant condition of anxiety', prone to become 'neurotic about matters of security'.[26]

Many of the sociologists of the 'classic' period, particularly Max Weber,[27] foretold the decline of religion. In the twentieth century it was often argued that modernity engendered a process of 'secularization' in which religion lost its central place in the world. The decline in church attendance and the political power of churches in many 'western' societies seems to bear this thesis out. However, in the last few decades, the work of sociologists of religion such as Peter Berger[28] has demonstrated that spiritual beliefs have a more tenacious hold on individuals in modernity than the classic sociologists predicted, and have even grown in salience in America and the global South. Grace Davie has argued that in modernity it is common for people to 'believe without belonging' to a religious institution.[29] The future of religion is, in short, much more complex and unpredictable than sociologists at one time thought.[30] Nonetheless, it is certainly true that for religious communities this unpredictability can provoke insecurity surrounding their long-term survival.

Just as modernity can undermine religious institutions and beliefs, so it can undermine group distinctiveness and belonging more generally. Globalization and the mass media make it more difficult for groups to maintain secure boundaries from their surroundings. Further, as Robert Putnam has influentially argued,[31] the very possibility of community can

be undermined in fast-moving modernity. Even if pessimistic characteri-
zations of modernity may underestimate the possibilities for new forms of
community and the resilience of older types, there is no doubt that the lack
of stability may make community members insecure about their future.

The 'project' of maintaining Jewish community in Britain in the late
twentieth century and beyond inevitably encounters some of modernity's
most difficult and complex trends. In a fast-moving, turbulent world, to
wish for the Jewish community to continue is to expose oneself to
challenges that are intimidating and disquieting.

The structure of this book

This book recounts and explains the changes that have taken place in the
British Jewish community since 1990. As sociologists, we place these
changes in the context of shifts in British society and in modernity more
generally. The focus in the book is on Jewish institutions and their leaders
and generally not on the 'grassroots' of the Jewish community. While such
a study would be interesting and useful, the breadth and complexity of
the changes that have occurred in Jewish institutions is such that they
deserve an entire book. This is not a comprehensive history of the British
Jewish community since 1990. We do not look closely at the changes in
the Jewish welfare sector or at the growth in the Haredi Jewish
community. We are principally concerned with those leaders and institutions that set themselves the task of responding to the challenge of
'renewing' Jewish life in the UK. We seek to tell the story of a complex
set of changes in as clear a way as possible; if we do not discuss certain
institutions extensively, it is not necessarily because they did not change
but because other case studies illustrate our points more clearly.

In chapter 1, we outline the historical background to the shift we
discuss in the book. We argue that the predominant aim of the leadership
of Anglo Jewry has, for most of its history, been to ensure the security of
British Jews by stressing to non-Jews the loyalty and civility of British
Jewry, and by stressing to Jews the necessity of living up to this description.
This *strategy of security* developed in a monocultural Britain, where
difference was viewed suspiciously and acceptance as British citizens
could not be guaranteed. In the post-war period, as Britain became
progressively multicultural, this strategy became anachronistic. Events
such as 1967's Six Day War encouraged the emergence of a new generation of Jewish leaders who were more prepared to be publicly assertive
about their Jewishness.

In chapter 2, we show how the strategy of security was replaced in the early 1990s by a *strategy of insecurity* in which the threats facing Anglo Jewry were publicly stressed, both to Jews and non-Jews. An important factor in the widespread adoption of this strategy was the induction of the new Chief Rabbi Jonathan Sacks in 1991. Sacks argued that Anglo Jewry was facing a crisis of 'continuity', in which intermarriage and assimilation were endangering the long-term survival of Jewish life in Britain. We show that the strategy of insecurity drew on and helped to engender a 'reflexive turn' in the British Jewish community in which social research was used to help to diagnose the problems of Anglo Jewry.

Chapter 3 examines the development of the 'continuity consensus' that took hold across much of the communal leadership in the 1990s. We look at the sources and inspirations for this consensus in Jewish thought and practice across the Jewish world. The continuity consensus held that long-term Jewish survival could not be guaranteed and that action was required to bolster Jewish families, communities and identities against the threat of disappearance.

In chapter 4, we look in detail at one of the most ambitious attempts to ensure Jewish continuity, the organization Jewish Continuity founded by the Chief Rabbi in 1993. As we shall see, the organization's over-ambitiousness, together with major ambiguities and problems in relation to management and pluralism, meant that it did not last long. However, it did place Jewish continuity at the heart of communal concerns and helped to generate a climate of change and innovation that proved influential. In chapter 5 we show how, despite the problems of Jewish Continuity, the project ensuring Jewish continuity was gradually transformed into a 'renewal agenda' that took hold across the community in the late 1990s. Unlike the continuity consensus, the assumptions behind the renewal consensus engendered a more concrete and achievable programme of change. We focus on the changes produced in the Jewish education sector and within the synagogue movements as examples of the renewal of the Jewish community in the 1990s and 2000s.

Chapter 6 shows how the changes brought about by the renewal consensus were accompanied by and often related to a broader series of changes in the 'atmosphere' of Jewish life in the UK. The 1990s and 2000s saw a dramatic growth in Jewish cultural and educational provision, sometimes seen as a 'Jewish renaissance' in the UK. Much of this was brought about by an increasingly vital and educated Jewish populace, sometimes acting outside of institutional frameworks. We also note that there were some aspects of the community that had hardly changed since

1990, such as the more intractable issues of denominational difference and political representation.

Chapter 7 provides a contrast with the upbeat argument in chapter 6. Here we examine how the strategy of insecurity generated concern amongst Jewish leaders at what came to be called the 'new antisemitism' following the outbreak of the Al-Aqsa Intifada in 2000. This concern produced a new set of institutions and institutional changes designed to defend Israel and protect Jews against antisemitism. These changes have been controversial and raise complex questions about the representation of British Jewry.

In the conclusion, we return to the core arguments made in the introduction. We contend that the challenge of communal survival is here to stay, demographic trends that marginalize the Anglo Jewish community will continue, and renewing the Jewish community will require persistence and hard work. Representation will continue to be a challenge, as the Jewish community can and should never be homogeneous. Different views on Israel and contesting definitions of antisemitism, for example, need to be aired. We argue for a community in conversation, a *dialogical* community. In turn, this has lessons for British multiculturalism more generally, as Anglo Jewry has, in significant ways, been damaged by the assimilationist ideology which dominated it for so long.

Chapter 1

Jewish Community and Jewish Leadership in the UK

Modern British Jewish communal history begins with the Resettlement in 1656, when Oliver Cromwell, after considerable public debate, tacitly gave permission for Jews to practise Judaism in private in the country.[1] Sephardi Jews arrived from the Low Countries, settling predominantly on the eastern edges of the City of London. They were later joined by Ashkenazi Jews, particularly from the Rhineland. Although there were poorer Jews, involved mainly in trade, in crafts and in textiles, the majority of the population was reasonably wealthy and concentrated in the mercantile and financial sectors.

Formal institutions of communal governance began to emerge almost immediately after Resettlement, in some ways echoing and in some ways departing from the medieval modes of communal leadership. In the first half of the eighteenth century, the Sephardi community occasionally appointed *Deputados* – Deputies – to deal with political matters that concerned Jews. The year 1760 saw the formation of 'a standing committee to convey suitable expressions of devotion to the new king, George III, and to deal thereafter with any urgent political matters'.[2] This prompted the formation of an Ashkenazi equivalent: the 'German Secret Committee of Public Affairs'. This held joint meetings from the end of the year, from which grew the London Committee of Deputies of British Jews. These structures echoed the intercessionary role of the older *shtadlanim*, the Jewish diplomatic representatives in premodern times, but, with its formalized and almost parliamentary structure, it mimicked emerging and specifically modern forms of leadership in wider British society.

Meanwhile, relative social buoyancy was achieved despite deeply embedded antisemitism in British culture, as well as a legal order that formally denied Jews the same civil rights as Anglican gentiles. The eighteenth and especially the nineteenth centuries saw a series of legislative changes that gradually conferred on Jews most of the same rights as other citizens, including the right to sit in Parliament. This gradual initiation of formal equality has come to be known as the Emancipation.

By the mid nineteenth century, the Anglo Jewish communal leadership was thoroughly culturally assimilated in its public behaviour, while continuing to follow Jewish religious law in the private sphere. It was also upwardly mobile, as signalled by migration out of East London to places such as Bayswater and the West End.[3] This westward shift indicated a new-found security and self-confidence, coinciding with the slow process of Emancipation. Anglo Jewry in this moment was characterized by a self-conception as 'English citizens of the Jewish faith'; that is, they identified as a *community of faith*, not as an ethnic or cultural collectivity. This notion was already embedded in the terms of Resettlement: Jews had petitioned Cromwell that they 'may therewith meete at our said *private devotions in our Particular houses* without fear of molestation either to our persons famillys or estates'.[4] The presence of Jews in Britain was negotatied on the basis of Judaism as a *private* religion; only in this dimension would Jews be different from their fellow citizens.

Mark Levene and others have described this conception of citizenship, this notion of 'English citizens of the Jewish faith', as '*the Jewish liberal compromise*', in which:

> One's Jewishness was henceforth not a collective interest … but purely a matter of individual religious choice … [T]his view argued that being Jewish in no way cut across one's identification with the British nation, nor could it be deemed to cut across one's loyalty to or ability to serve the British state.[5]

The Jewish liberal compromise in politics was matched by an assimilationist orientation in culture; Israel Finestein has called this a 'behaviourist acculturation, largely concerned with a search for indistinguishability out of doors and in club and market-place'.[6] Difference was kept indoors; public identity was focused entirely on demonstrating sameness and loyalty with the national mainstream. In the public statements of the communal leadership in this period, we can see a constant repetition of declarations of secure belonging and citizenship. To give one example, here is an extract from a *Jewish Chronicle* editorial from the 1880s: 'We are Englishmen and the thoughts and feelings of Englishmen are our thoughts and feelings.'[7]

The Jewish liberal compromise can only be understood in the context of a Britain which imagined itself as fundamentally *monocultural*. As Cesarani has written:

> Jews were not welcomed into a diverse, pluralistic society. On the contrary, the message was: Jews can live freely amongst us if they conform to our values. The 'antisemitism of tolerance' conditioned Jewish life in Britain. It induced Jews to minimize their differences, privatizing Judaism and shedding many aspects – especially those most visible – of Jewish culture and tradition.[8]

Communal leadership operated in general on the basis of behind-the-scenes interactions with the British state. Eugene Black writes that the Board of Deputies:

> rarely took political initiatives. The executive preferred discreet negotiations ... Judicious discussions, as far removed from the glare of publicity as possible – so ran leadership thinking – best served the community.[9]

Alderman similarly notes that 'there was felt to be a need ... for Anglo Jewry to maintain a low profile'.[10] This low-profile politics manifested, for example, in early responses to antisemitism, as in relation to the anti-Jewish riots of 1911 and 1917, when official responses downplayed the role of antisemitism, highlighted the role of random hooliganism, and portrayed the Jewishness of the victims as incidental.

The Cousinhood

Behind the formal institutions of communal leadership lay an informal kin-based network of leaders that tended to hold the majority of offices in the community. Chaim Bermant defined this 'Cousinhood' as 'a compact union of exclusive brethren with blood and money flowing in a small circle which opened up from time to time to admit ... anyone else who attained rank or fortune, and then snapped shut again'.[11] As Gutwein notes, 'the Cousinhood's rule was a function of its wealth [which was] translated into community power by means of philanthropy' – its donations gave it 'operative control' over communal institutions. It was part of a wider British economic elite – integrated into it and accepting of its ethos.[12]

The Cousinhood was a 'mediating agent between the community and the state' – in the 'tradition of Jewish intercession of older generations'.[13] Its practices were based on *noblesse oblige*: what Endelman calls an 'ethos of voluntarism', giving as 'a family habit'.[14] The overlaying of family-based leadership with formal institutions meant that political authority operated in a paternalistic way. As David Cesarani summarizes:

> Their power structure was ... characterized by oligarchy and plutocracy: they were dominated by a small number of men, scions of an interlocking network of illustrious families which had been present in the British Isles for over one and a half centuries.[15]

While the Cousinhood in its cultural practices mimicked the behaviour of the British ruling classes, this form of leadership, family and wealth based, has been typical of modern Jewish communal leadership globally. Hal Lewis characterizes this form of leadership as 'secular oligarchy'.[16] For him, wealth is central to its formation, both as a route to prominence in the outside world and hence prestige within, but also as a source of communal authority in itself. Financial power is important when all funds are voluntary – communal projects depend on financial contributions; the piper plays the tune of those who pay, and in turn power incentivizes philanthropy.[17] Formal democracy often covers the fact that the leadership in communal organizations is rarely elected through open, competitive elections. Instead, leadership is often achieved through what Roseman calls 'vertical mobility' – promotion, 'moving through the chairs', without the requirement of skills or charisma – or 'horizontal mobility' – parachuting in due to celebrity status or leverage power.[18]

The Cousinhood and its poor relations

Starting in the 1870s, persecution and economic hardship in Central and Eastern Europe led to mass migration to the UK, concentrated geographically in East London and a handful of other urban quarters. The Jewish population leapt from 40,000 to around 130,000 in the decades between 1870 and World War I. The conspicuously 'un-English' culture of the new migrants presented a major challenge to the Anglo Jewish settlement and the liberal Jewish compromise. However, the discourse of secure British citizenship and belonging still remained the dominant motif for the communal leadership in this period.

The response of the leadership to the new migration was threefold. The leadership reasserted its assimilationist cultural orientation, taking vigorous steps to encourage or if necessary force the migrants to abandon their publicly distinct ways and embrace English ways; Bill Williams calls this 'deferential anglicisation'.[19] It took a representational or intermediary role, placing itself in between the migrants and the British state. It reasserted its paternalistic mode of authority, developing new institutions and agencies to deliver services to the migrants, encourage their acculturation and ensure their loyalty.

The new diversity of the Jewish population, and in particular internal class differences, underlined the importance to the Anglo Jewish leadership of emphasizing loyalty to the Jewish community at the same time as encouraging assimilation. The tension between communal unity and cultural assimilation was expressed in the forms taken by the institutions and agencies of acculturation created by the Anglo Jewish elite: charities based on mimicry of English social forms – e.g. the Jewish Lads' Brigade on the Church Lads' Brigade, the Jewish Working Men's Club on the 'rational recreation' movement, the Jewish Board of Guardians on the emerging 'scientific philanthropy' – and not on Judaic traditions. The paternalism that had characterized Anglo Jewish leadership in the previous period continued to soak through these agencies.

There were myriad ways in which communal authority and deferential anglicization were resisted by the immigrants. There were the socialist, anarchist and other radical movements that flourished in the immigrant areas, actively refusing the authority of the Cousinhood and promoting class conflicts within the community.[20] There were the noisy, informal spaces of worship and organizations of self help in the immigrant quarters: the *khevres* and *shtiblekh* in attic rooms above sweatshops, carrying the 'democratic tradition'[21] of Jewish life in the Pale and, in Alderman's words, often at odds with 'the cold formalism and cathedral-like structures' of the United Synagogue.[22] And there were emerging forms of ultra-conservative religious practices, epitomized by the Machzikei Hadas synagogue in East London, a schismatic institution set up in explicit opposition to the official orthodoxy of the United Synagogue, initially challenging the Chief Rabbi's right to authorize kosher butchers, but growing into a full-blown confrontation over theology and assimilation.[23] Despite these instances of refusal, however, the Anglo Jewish leadership had great success in enrolling the immigrants and their children into the project of assimilation. Each new generation of Anglo Jewry, increasingly socially mobile and increasingly suburbanized, was palpably more 'British' in language, cultural behaviour and identifications.

Learning citizenship: the Jews' Free School

The Cousinhood were opposed to Jewish day schools for the children of middle class Jews, but approved of them for the children of the immigrant poor. They saw the working class Jews as having to be culturally anglicized before they could belong in English society, before they would be eligible for political participation. Jewish day schools, like the Jews' Free School (JFS), originally established in 1732, were a method for anglicizing them.

This way of thinking was clearly expressed by the headmaster of JFS, Moses Angel. In 1871, he told the London School Board that the parents of JFS pupils were 'the refuse population of Europe ... until the children [were] Anglicised or humanised it was difficult to tell what was their moral condition ... [They] knew neither English nor any intelligible language'.[24] The *Jewish Chronicle* wrote in 1888 that 'the great majority enter [the JFS] practically foreigners; leave it potential Englishmen and women, prepared to take their part in the struggle of life in the spirit of English citizens'.[25] A Board of Trade report in 1894 was hopeful about the progress of that anglicization/humanization process: 'They enter the school Russians and Poles and emerge almost indistinguishable from English children.'[26]

In 1903, the headteacher at the JFS, Louis Abrahams, gave a speech to parents, exhorting them:

> Strengthen the effort of the teachers to wipe away all evidences of foreign birth and foreign proclivities, so that [your] children shall be identified with everything that is English in thought and deed ... that [your] boys and girls may grow up to the flag which they are learning within these walls to love and honour, that they may take a worthy part in the growth of this great Empire, whose shelter and protection ... will never be denied them.[27]

In his speech, Abrahams also called for the throwing off of Yiddish, 'that miserable jargon which is not a language at all' in order to 'become English – truly English'.[28] The headteachers were very keen to indicate the difference between the children and their parents. In school, only English could be spoken, and it was hoped that in the home 'they would be teaching their parents English'. The private space of home, then, was positioned outside the public space of citizenship, with the school on the borderline between them. This fits in with the liberal conception of citizenship to which the Anglo Jewish community subscribed: Jews could be Jewish in the home, but men or citizens on the streets.

Zionism and the communal revolutions of the twentieth century

The Jewish liberal compromise was reconfigured in the twentieth century as a result of the assertion of an emergent immigrant elite under the twin banners of Zionism and the democratization of the community. This resulted in what has been described as a 'communal revolution' in 1917, when the Board of Deputies had a substantial Zionist voting bloc, which censured the elite Anglo Jewish Association's (AJA) anti-Zionist statements, a revolution consummated in 1943 when Zionists achieved control over the Board, severing ties with the AJA.[29] However, what remained consistent was an emphasis on the secure citizenship and belonging of British Jews.

The first half of the twentieth century saw the Cousinhood contending with what Yiddish journalist Abraham Cahan termed the 'alrightniks': the nouveau riche entrepreneurs or immigrant parvenus who made up a nascent eastern European middle class. This was a suburban population, concentrated in newly built neighbourhoods such as London's Stoke Newington or Manchester's Hightown and High Broughton.[30]

The period around World War I was structured by what Williams calls 'a dynamic interrelationship between the three main social elements in communal life – the established middle class, the immigrant mass and the alrightniks'.[31] The alrightniks dominated an emerging layer of communal organization: the new synagogues that immigrant *khevres* moved into, a network of Benevolent Societies practising a form of small-scale charity based on Talmudic precepts rather than English middle-class philanthropy, and the Jewish Friendly Society movement. There was a growing resentment of London, Anglo Jewry's traditional centre of power, from provincial Jewry, marked by the emergence of Jewish Representative Councils (JRCs) in Manchester, Glasgow and Leeds. These new institutions emerged from immigrant milieux, but they tended to function in English rather than Yiddish. For Williams, they suggest an alternative, less formal, path to anglicization, a source of status for a new aristocracy within the immigrant society, and a culture of aspiration within that society.[32]

There is a paradox here. In one sense, the new Jewish middle class played a role in legitimating the Cousinhood by embracing and proving the success of what Gutwein calls a 'bourgeois-emancipationist ideology' based on social mobility tied to suburbanization and anglicization. At the same time, though, the middle class, with the *Jewish Chronicle* as its main mouthpiece, began to demand inclusion in leadership, 'albeit under Cousinhood auspices whose right to ultimate control it did not challenge'.

If the Cousinhood's authority had been based on a plutocratic principle which equated wealth with the right to power, why should the alrightniks not have access to power too, now that they had made it under the terms set by the Cousinhood?[33]

The conflict between the new alrightnik institutions and the older Cousinhood came to a head in 1917. In that year there was panic around the military service of foreign-born Jews, with many Russian-born Jews refusing to either join the British army or return to serve with Britain's ally, Russia.[34] At the same time, the Zionist movement was clamouring for a declaration by the British state in favour of a Jewish homeland in Palestine.[35] The most traditionalist elements of the Cousinhood, represented by the League of British Jews and the AJA, lobbied against a pro-Zionist statement and called for the statutory exclusion of non-naturalized foreign-born Jews.[36] The immediate topic of contention was Zionism. The alrightniks dominated the Zionist movement, providing it with both leadership and financial patronage, and this placed it in increasing conflict with the pure assimilationism of the existing oligarchs. Zionism challenged one of the key tenets of the Emancipation contract: the notion of exclusive loyalty to the country of settlement and consequent exclusion of loyalty to Jewish nationhood.[37]

However, it would be wrong to say that the Zionists, the immigrant middle class or provincial Jewry overthrew the oligarchy in 1917; rather, as Cesarani put it, 'the 1920s were marked by the persistence of the *ancien régime*'. The Board of Deputies was reformed, but cautiously: there were new seats for the friendly society movement (fifteen seats), but this was more than balanced by enlarged representation for the old guard; the United Synagogue Council acquired twelve deputies, the Federation two and the AJA's allocation rose to nine. Only seventeen out of 100 places on Board committees were represented by non-London deputies – and of these nine places were taken by Nathan Laski and his son Neville.[38] Louis Samuel, second Lord Swaythling, one of the most recalcitrant of anti-Zionists, continued to hold significant offices in the community. Zionists grumbled at this throughout the 1920s, and unsuccessfully attempted to take control of the United Synagogue, but the general picture was of communal stalemate.[39]

Williams similarly suggests that the old elite responded inconsistently to the communal challenge, resorting, at different times, to both conflict and conciliations, but, most often, to co-optation. The alrightniks moved into positions of communal management, while the old elite began to patronize the institutions of the alrightniks. 'As a result,' Williams continues, 'the community of 1920 was already a complex amalgam of

East and West, its leadership – its new elite – now drawn as much from the immigrant as from the native bourgeoisie: now only the socialists were excluded.'[40] Massive contributions to Jewish charity bought Zionist immigrants such as Bernhard Baron, Simon Marks, Israel Sieff and Harry Sacher positions of communal power in a polity 'whose voluntary organizations depended upon princely donations, where authority and wealth were inter-mingled'.[41] Consequently, the 1920s and 1930s saw what Cesarani calls 'a virtual system of "dual power"' between Zionists and assimilationists.[42]

Any change in personnel within the communal leadership brought about by this 'communal revolution' masked a deeper continuity. The new leadership, like the old, emphasized the same discourse of secure English citizenship and belonging. The new leadership thus failed to challenge anti-alien legislation, or, conversely, build on the 1917 Balfour Declaration. These failures were the inevitable result of the communal strategy of stressing secure belonging and citizenship and dismissing threats to Anglo Jewish security. This structural failure was played out in the 1930s and 1940s, as the Anglo Jewish leadership, despite the inclusion of the new immigrant middle class, failed to rise to the challenges of fascism in Britain and Nazism on the continent.

Anglo Jewry and fascism

The 1930s saw the unprecedented rise of antisemitism, culminating in the 1940s in the annihilation of millions of European Jews. Yet, throughout this decade, the Anglo Jewish leadership consistently downplayed its threat. In 1933, the year of Hitler's election as chancellor of Germany, Neville Laski was elected president of the Board of Deputies. Laski stood firmly with the AJA (whose president was the Cousinhood's Leonard Montefiore) in rejecting all calls to act publicly against domestic fascism and German Nazism. In Britain, there had been a resurgence of antisemitic violence from 1932, when the British Union of Fascists was formed. Laski called for restraint, berating Jews for their 'ostentation' which allegedly stirred up antisemitism and for their 'invasion' of certain professions.[43]

The *Jewish Chronicle* initially saw antisemitic attacks as 'isolated and indeed unique' and 'deplored by the vast majority of non-Jews', although voices for action grew stronger as the threat grew.[44] In line with the communal leadership's stress on secure British citizenship and belonging, fascism was designated as something foreign that might grow on the continent but would not take root in British soil.[45] The response the leadership called for drew deeply on the tradition of deferential angli-cization. Jews should remain dignified and exercise restraint, because self-defence and direct action would bring blame upon Jews and thus justifi-cation for the fascists.

In response to Hitler's rise in Germany, Laski similarly fought sponta-neous anti-Nazi protests by the Workers Circle and trade unions. He fought the emergence of anti-Nazi organizations like the Youth Emergency Council and United Jewish Protest Committee, and he fought all proposals to boycott Nazi Germany.[46] However, a major current in Anglo Jewry demanded action. The Central Jewish Consultative Committee was formed as a 'clearing house' for alternative opinions in Jewry; the Anglo Jewish Council of Trades and Industry was set up to advocate for a boycott, followed by the Jewish Representative Council for the Boycott of German Goods and Services.[47]

There was widespread disquiet in the Jewish community, particularly from working-class East Enders bearing the brunt of fascist violence, at the Board's quiescence. One letter to the *Jewish Chronicle* concluded:

> The growth of antisemitism in this country requires an overhauling of our communal machinery. The present Board of Deputies no longer represents the Jewish community. It is out of touch with the rank and file.[48]

There were calls for the Board to include representation from Jewish trade unions, for example, but this was seen as 'too political' by the Board's leadership.[49] The leadership's quiescence propelled the East End working class, especially the youth, towards the left, and especially the growing Communist Party. An anti-fascist movement emerged to challenge the leadership: the Jewish Labour Council, formed in 1934 on the initiative of the Workers' Circle, and its successor, the Jewish People's Council (JPC), was formed in 1936.[50] Although labour Zionists were involved in this movement, the growth of the left was seen as a severe threat by the Zionist movement, whose social base was the much smaller middle class, and stimulated the Zionists to seek the invigoration, rather than destruction, of the communal authorities. In response to the JPC, the Board of Deputies finally launched an anti-defamation campaign, aimed at countering the myths about Jews peddled by the fascists, intended to appeal to the mainstream British public opinion whose common decency could ultimately be relied upon – a response 'consistent with an under-standing of antisemitism informed by the self-image of an optimistic and secure community within a tolerant and fair-minded society'.[51] The dominant strategy from the communal leadership in the 1930s, then, was a continuation of the pre-1917 policy: remaining quiet in public and conducting politics in private. During the Holocaust, there was heavy lobbying from Jewish leaders towards the rescue of European Jewry, but this was, on the whole, kept to behind-the-scenes activity and only within the rubric of the loyalty of the Jewish community to the war effort. While the *Jewish Chronicle* consistently published reports of Nazi persecution to a solely Jewish audience, 'the Jewish leadership ... criticized it for exaggeration'.[52]

In 1943, against the perceived background of the failure of the community leadership to take a strong position on Nazism, there was what has been called the 'second communal revolution': consolidating its 1917 gains, the Zionist movement effected the 'capture' of the Board of Deputies at its triennial elections of June 1943, forcing the Board to dissolve its conjoint arrangement with the AJA at the next meeting in July.

However, while 1917 opened up a fissure in the community, leading to the proliferation of rival organizations (the League of British Jews on one side, a Zionist 'party' on the Board on the other), 1943 did not. The issue died down after the events; the Zionists became the dominant voice in the community, the anti-Zionists 'relegated to the status of a bunch of die-hards wistfully recalling happier days'.[53] In 1943, the individuals involved in the communal strife were reluctant opponents, keeping channels of communication open and delaying the confrontation.[54] What this meant was that the Zionists did not:

> conquer the community; rather ..., it was Anglo Jewry which conquered the Zionists. Their enthusiasms, their energies and their organizational abilities (not the least of which was their persistent ability to raise enormous sums of money) were harnessed to other communal causes – in all of which the older patrician families continued to constitute essential vertebrae.[55]

In other words, while Anglo Jewry underwent a shift in orientation in the first half of the twentieth century, the emphasis on fostering secure British citizenship and belonging remained. As our story moves into the contemporary period, however, we believe that there has been a significant change. We argue that there has been a shift from a politics of security to one of *insecurity*. The remainder of this chapter examines the post-war period more closely, charting the contours of this shift.

Insecurity and the problem of Jewish continuity

In the post-war period, we believe, there has been a shift from a politics of security to one of *insecurity*. Instead of stressing the secure belonging of British Jews, communal leaders increasingly resort to a discourse of *crisis*, emphasizing the community's insecurity. Where perceived threats were once responded to by nurturing communal security, there is now a concern about the dangers of an *excess* of security and complacency amongst British Jews.

It is not our task here to suggest that the new agenda is unfounded – we share many of these concerns. What we are interested in, instead, is how the crisis discourse – the emphasis on insecurity – has been used to renew the legitimacy of Jewish communal leadership under changed circumstances, constituting, we suggest, something of a 'third communal revolution'.

Central to this shift has been a twin concern, with antisemitism and with Jewish continuity. Jewish continuity has always been threatened by antisemitism. In the post-Enlightenment period, Jewish continuity was also threatened by assimilation. As we have seen, the dominant strategy in the assimilationist period was publicly to emphasize Jewish sameness with mainstream society and Jewish security in this society. Jewish difference and Jewish insecurity were relegated to the sphere of the private. From early in the assimilationist period, there have been Jewish voices critical of assimilation, just as there have been Jewish voices against antisemitism. The 1920s, for example, had seen the emergence of concern about 'secularization'. As early as 1919, the *Zionist Review* bemoaned the young's declining synagogue attendance; 1919 saw the formation of the Sinai League to 'preserve and protect' Jewish tradition, and of the Reconstruction movement; in 1928 B'nai B'rith held a symposium on the question; and there were regular articles in the *Jewish Daily Post, Jewish World* and other Jewish periodicals to this effect throughout the 1920s.[56] However, until 1967, these sorts of voices were relatively marginal, and generally expressed only in internal Jewish contexts. The dominant mood began to change in 1967, with the Six Day War.

The Six Day War was experienced in the community as a turning point in a long history of Jewish concerns for Jewish continuity.[57] The war was seen as underlining threats to Jews – but also as a 'miracle' that finally ensured Jewish survival. It deepened a perception of the common fate of Jewish people. The Board of Deputies, for example, had resisted joining the World Jewish Congress since 1936, but finally joined in the wake of the Six Day War, in 1974.[58]

The year 1967 also marked the moment at which it became possible to say that 'deferential anglicization', the strategy of assimilation promoted by the communal leadership, had largely succeeded. By 1967, London's Jewish East End was being heavily depopulated and the centre of gravity of the community was very much in the suburbs. In London and in the provinces, Yiddish was no longer passed on to the younger generations and became a marginal object of nostalgia and even shame. The secure sense of belonging, of whiteness and Britishness that the Cousinhood had long promoted, was now the reality for most English Jews.[59]

After 1967, we hear an increasing voicing of concern at a crisis in 'the cultivation and retention of a transmissible, distinctively Jewish, identity',[60] exemplified by a Board of Deputies conference session on 'The Challenge of Secularisation' in 1977. Paradoxically, then, Jewish security, a secure sense of belonging engendered by the success of the assimilation project, provoked a need to reinforce communal identification, prompting and making possible a new strategy of communal authority, a 'strategy of insecurity'. *Private insecurity, public security* was transformed into *public insecurity, private security*. That is, in the 1970s, we do not necessarily see a rise in British Jews *being* insecure, but rather a deliberate, growing enunciation of insecurity as *strategy* of communal leadership in the post-1967 period, becoming dominant in the 1990s. It is important to stress that the strategy of insecurity we describe here is only one strategy: it does not totally replace other strategies. It is also important to differentiate between different levels of 'public' and 'private'. The novel development post-1967 is not that Jews felt insecure, or that they articulated this feeling, but that they began to express it publicly, out loud, outside the Jewish community. In the remainder of this chapter, we will show how the period from the Six Day War in 1967 up until the end of the 1980s (which coincided with Immanuel Jakobovits's term as Chief Rabbi) was a *transitional* period, during which an official emphasis on secure belonging continued to be articulated by the communal leadership, while voices stressing insecurity began moving closer and closer to the mainstream.

Jews out loud? The rise of multiculturalism

An index of the fact that the emphasis on secure belonging was still dominant – if weakening – in the 1980s can be found in the preface to historian Geoffrey Alderman's 1983 study of Anglo Jewish politics:

The major conclusions of this research – that, far from being totally assimilated within British political culture, Jewish voters in Britain have already been capable of independent political behaviour, sometimes in marked contrast to national or regional trends – is also one which runs counter to the most cherished beliefs of Anglo Jewish leaders.[61]

These 'cherished beliefs' had been weakening in the 1970s and 1980s, with the development of public political campaigns in the UK Jewish community over Soviet Jewry and Israel. The community had to *feel* secure to be politically active in this way, even as the political action responded to sources of insecurity, such as antisemitism and Palestinian terror. The increasing reality of the 1970s and 1980s was a Jewish community acting politically for the first time *as Jews*. This reality was denied by the communal leadership, even as it participated in many of the movements. As Cesarani notes:

> In their political behaviour the official communal organizations were insistent that Anglo Jewry was only a denominational group in spite of all evidence to the contrary – such as its voting behaviour and its commitment to Israel and Soviet Jewry – and the enticements which multi-culturalism now offered to a more confident, assertive ethnic Jewish identity.[62]

We can perceive signs that the Jewish community was starting to respond to the challenge of multiculturalism from the period immediately after the Six Day War, which was also a period of rising political activism among black British people[63] and of Enoch Powell's racist interventions in the immigration debate.[64] A significant moment in this shift was the establishment in 1968 of a Working Party on Race Relations by the Board of Deputies. The Working Party collated information on communal activities around race relations. They noted, for example, a 'teach-in' on the topic at the Association of Jewish Ex-Servicemen and Women (AJEX), the publication by the Institute of Jewish Affairs of its *Patterns of Prejudice* journal, and work done by local Jewish Youth Voluntary Service groups in bringing communities together for social activities.[65] This shows the reflection within the community of the emergence of a public conversation about 'race relations' and 'integration' in the late 1960s.

Nonetheless, these examples were only indicative of the beginnings of a shift. As Shalom Charikar wrote in 1985, looking back on Enoch Powell's incendiary 'Rivers of Blood' speech:

The *Jewish Chronicle* in its editorial condemned it. Labour MPs, including Jewish Labour MPs, also condemned the speech ... But a *specific* Jewish response? There was none. And to me and other Black Jews, this silence by the Jewish leadership was audible. For an official Jewish reaction we had to wait a month. The question was raised at a meeting of the Board of Deputies of British Jews ... – not as part of its agenda, but from the floor. A statement was issued condemning the speech adding that the *lack of restraint on immigration* was an excuse for provocation and racist attacks.[66]

From the late 1960s, other groups in Britain were increasingly asserting their right to difference; non-indigenous cultural heritage was no longer an object of shame, something that must stay indoors, but rather an opportunity for celebration. Britain was no longer seen as a monocultural entity into which immigrants must assimilate. The dominant policy that cohered in this period was 'integration', defined by then Home Secretary Roy Jenkins in a landmark May 1966 speech 'not as a flattening process of assimilation but as equal opportunity, accompanied by cultural diversity, in an atmosphere of mutual tolerance'.[67] This shift undermined the core tenets of the liberal Jewish compromise and its policy of deferential anglicization.

By the 1980s the policy of integration had itself begun to give way to versions of multiculturalism, stressing cultural diversity more strongly, and had moved beyond mere mutual tolerance to a celebration of cultural difference. Although this took many forms, a certain version became deeply embedded in education policy and municipal governance, a version which strongly emphasized differences between 'ethnic cultures' defined as discrete and homogeneous.[68] This version of multiculturalism was strongly influential in London, for example in the policies of the Greater London Council (GLC) under its leader Ken Livingstone, and was strongly associated with left-wing criticism of Prime Minister Margaret Thatcher (to whom then Chief Rabbi Immanuel Jakobovits was close).

The importance of this issue, and an index of the persistence of the strategy of security, can be seen in the debates around the rise of British fascism in the late 1970s and in Jakobovits' intervention in the politics of race. The 1970s saw the rising presence of the far right racist and antisemitic National Front, manifested both electorally and on the street. Many Jews were individually involved in the campaigns against this, most notably in the Anti-Nazi League (ANL). There was behind-the-scenes intelligence and lobbying work, including support for *Searchlight* magazine (refounded in 1975) and the Board of Deputies Defence Committee, which were both funded by Jewish philanthropists, including Gerald Ronson. However, much of the leadership of the Jewish community was slow to add its voice, and the anti-Zionist far left groups, particularly the Socialist Workers Party, who led the ANL, were seen as dangerous allies for the community.[69]

The Archbishop of Canterbury's Commission on Urban Priority Areas, resulting in the report *Faith in the City* at the end of 1985, took a fairly social liberal view of problems in the inner city, relating them to the inequalities of the free market. Lord Jakobovits's response, *From Doom to Hope*, criticized this social liberalism, and strongly asserted the importance of ethnic minorities fitting in. *From Doom to Hope* perpetuated the myth that the Jewish community has always had good relationships with the British state and certainly the police. Jakobovits wrote: 'on arriving here we had cultivated trust in and respect for the police, realising that our security as a minority depended on law and order being maintained' – a claim belied by the reality of the 1917 anti-Jewish riots (and Jewish self-defence in response), of Cable Street and of the many Jews who were involved in the Anti-Nazi League in the late 1970s. *From Doom* also perpetuated the myth of swift Jewish anglicization: 'we did not gate-crash into our Gentile environment; we made ourselves highly acceptable and indispensable by our industrial, intellectual and moral contributions to society'.[70]

These myths were challenged at the time within the Jewish community, for example by Greville Janner, Geoffrey Alderman, Louise Ellman and Edie Friedman, who all argued that Anglo Jewish history did not conform to the rosy vision the Chief Rabbi suggested. They were also sharply critical of his negative attitudes to other minorities.[71] Chaim Bermant later noted that Jakobovits was representative of a powerful assimilationist tendency in the community that did not want to see Jews as a minority group, and that the association of Jews with other minorities disturbed them. Bermant commented: 'one can possibly become too English too soon'.[72] Perhaps significantly, Jakobovits himself was an immigrant, born in East Prussia in 1921.

The dissenting views, expressed by Janner and others, suggest the influence of a multicultural understanding of Englishness. This influence manifested itself particularly powerfully in the 1980s in the Jewish Cultural and Anti-Racism Project:

'A slap in the face to the Jewish community'. This was the eloquent greeting from Dr Gerwitz of the Board of Deputies to the Jewish Socialists' Group which enabled the Jewish Cultural and Anti-Racist

Project (JCARP) to be set up. A year later we can look back on our efforts and see that we have indeed given a slap in the face – not to the community – but to the self-proclaimed leadership who are now very much on the defensive on the major issue of Jewish defence and responses to racism in Britain today.[73]

JCARP was formed in response to the rise in antisemitic violence from the late 1970s, a rise recorded by *Searchlight* but not publicized by the communal leadership.[74] It was launched in early 1984, with a twofold agenda: to fight racism and fascism (whether aimed at Jews or at others) but also to insert Anglo Jewry into the emerging narrative of multicultural Britain. That is, JCARP saw British Jews as something other than 'a community of faith', as in the liberal Jewish compromise, but as an ethnic or cultural community, who had the right to take its seat with Afro-Caribbean, Asian and other minority communities at the multicultural table.

JCARP argued that deferential anglicization had led large numbers of British Jews to internalize the racism of the dominant culture:

Many committed anti-racists organise around the slogan, 'Yesterday the Jews, today the Blacks' – a view mirrored in the Jewish community by those who believe that racism no longer affects Jews, and by those who have increasingly adopted white Anglo Saxon attitudes towards Black people ...[75]

Fitting in well with the period's multiculturalist politics, JCARP promoted Jewish ethnic culture, in particular the popular culture of the Eastern European Jewish masses from whom most British Jews were descended: Klezmer music, Yiddish language and literature, institutions like the Bund and the Workers' Circle. JCARP was funded by the Greater London Council, and strongly supported by Ken Livingstone, despite extensive lobbying efforts from the Board of Deputies. Its promotion of Yiddish culture, something which has become mainstream and uncontroversial in twenty-first-century Anglo Jewry, was more bitterly opposed within the Board than its questioning of Zionism.[76]

The shift from monocultural Britain to multicultural Britain undermined the assimilation project; it took some time for Anglo Jewry to adjust to this, as shown by the resistance in the 1980s to Anglo Jewish activity under a multicultural rubric. The success of the assimilation project and the power of the strategy of security were precisely what made this transition difficult.

With the success of the project of assimilation, the Jewish communal leadership had less and less need internally to police the behaviour of the community. The focus was increasingly turned outwards, towards issues such as Israel and Soviet Jewry. In this, Anglo Jewry followed a pattern recurring across the liberal democracies. Hal Lewis, in a global survey of Jewish leadership in this period, has written that the ability of the communal infrastructure to raise money and assert leadership 'is directly related to its facility for maintaining a sense of crisis'. The organizations 'intuitively understood the linkage between crisis and fund raising'.[77]

> While no longer pre-occupied with the internal governance and administration of the *kehillah*, as those functions had now been adopted by the state, Jewish leaders turned their attention to the defense and advocacy of external, polity-wide matters, such as Jewish nationalism, combating anti-Semitism, and building meaningful Jewish institutions ... Thus, while post-Emancipation Jewish political leadership was forbidden on the inside, it succeeded on resurfacing on the outside.[78]

Further:

> As Israel continues to take its place among sophisticated world economies, and as state-sponsored anti-Semitism (despite its periodic outbursts) continues to decline, there is ample reason to believe that both the *shtadlanic* and the philanthropic functions, which have long dominated this period, will be forced to undergo significant change. As J.J. Goldberg noted, contemporary Jewish political leadership: '... is in trouble ... These troubles are partly the aftermath of success: in a world where embattled Israel is signing peace treaties, where oppressed Jewish communities from Moscow to Damascus are stepping into the light of freedom, what battles remain? Without threats, what will rally Jews to the flag?'[79]

Nick Lambert, in his interview-based study of European Jewish thinkers, comes to similar conclusions. He uses a concept of branding to understand it.

> To maximise the marketability of the 'adversity and anti-Semitism' theme, communal leaders are said [by the interviewees] to link these twinned aspects to their constituents' fear of a declining diasporic population through the buzzwords of 'assimilation' ..., 'out-marriage' ... and 'secularisation'.[80]

As one of his interviewees, the writer Clive Sinclair, told him about Anglo Jewry in this period:

> The outside world must be portrayed as essentially hostile – or *bloodthirsty*… I think Anglo-Jewish communal leaders *need* these bogey men – whether Arab terrorists or 'assimilation' and so forth. They *do* exist, but the real question is the nature and severity of the threat. And if they didn't exist – the powers-that-be would certainly invent them.[81]

A new relationship with Israel?

By the early 1990s, Zionism was no longer proving as effective a source of communal mobilization as it used to be. The reason was not that Anglo Jewry had become any less Zionistic, but that Israel itself had changed from the fragile state born in 1948. Militarily, the Jewish state had showed itself post-1967 to be able to capture, hold and settle large expanses of territory with hostile populations. Beginning with the First Lebanon War, Israel had proved itself to be a regional superpower able to conduct wars outside its borders. Even if such actions were the subject of strong opposition in Israel and more muted opposition in the Diaspora, for even Israel's strongest defenders they meant that the image of Israel as weak and embattled was no longer sustainable. Indeed, the First Intifada underlined how far Israel's main security issues arose not from an inherent weakness but from the difficulties of how and whether to wield its considerable power over the Palestinians and its neighbours.

The year 1991 proved to be something of a turning point for Israel: the year of the first Gulf War, in which the country was attacked by Iraqi Scud missiles, and of the mass immigration of Jews from the former Soviet Union. The Soviet Jewish influx not only increased the population by several hundred thousand, it also largely completed a process through which most of those who wished to come to the country had now been enabled to do so. The aftermath of the Gulf War saw the commencement of public negotiations with the Palestinians at the Madrid peace conference in October 1991. The signing of the Oslo accords in September 1993 opened the possibility of an end to Israel's military struggles and a solution to the Israeli–Palestinian conflict. The 1980s and early 1990s were also a period in which Israel's economy was liberalized and connected to the global economy.

The increasing maturity of the Jewish state meant that Jewish thinkers in Israel and elsewhere increasingly came to re-evaluate what Zionism would mean in the future. The culmination of this process was the publication at the thirty-third Zionist Congress in 1997 of the document *Brit Am: Covenant of the People* written by the then chair of the Jewish Agency, Avraham Burg.[82] The document proposed a 'New Zionism', predicated on the recognition that the Diaspora would not disappear in the foreseeable future. This new Zionism would be based on a concern for Jewish continuity and the preservation of Jewish peoplehood, with Zionism becoming the unifying force to sustain this project. The document recognized not just that the threats to Jewish continuity in the Diaspora were primarily internal rather than external, but that in Israel itself there was a decline in feelings of attachment to the Jewish people. What was therefore required was a partnership between Israel and the Diaspora in developing 'Jewish-Zionist education' through a global educational infrastructure centred around Zionist, Israel-based institutions, the Jewish Agency in particular.

The optimism of the *Brit Am* document belonged to a specific moment in time. The hopes of peace were to be dashed in the collapse of the peace process from 2000. However, the document encapsulated changes that had been happening and continued to happen before and after 1997 in the field of Zionist education. The education department of the Jewish Agency and other Zionist educational organizations such as Melitz, had come to take on greater roles in Jewish education worldwide. Post-1948, organized educational trips to Israel had become an important part of Diaspora Jewish life, particularly for young people. While promoting *aliyah* remained an aim of these trips, increasingly Israel became *de facto* a resource for Diaspora Jewish education. Israel and Zionism provided a motivating tool and a unifying symbol that was intended to inspire greater Jewish engagement amongst Diaspora Jews. This engagement did not require *aliyah*, although for many Zionists emigration to Israel still symbolized the highest expression of Jewish commitment.[83]

This realigned relationship between Israel and the Diaspora refocused some of the energy that Zionism directed out of the British Jewish community. By the 1990s, to be a Zionist in the British Jewish community did not necessarily imply a lack of commitment to Jewish life in Britain. Rather, supporting Jewish life in Britain and in Israel became part of a single project.

A new generation of leaders

All the communal developments we have traced in the latter part of this chapter were embodied in the personal development of a new generation of professional leaders that emerged in the 1980s and 1990s. Jonathan Woocher, the 'Chief Ideas Officer' of the Jewish Educational Service of North America, argues that in the US:

> another generation was coming of age. The baby boomers, certainly the first of the baby boomers were now entering into adulthood. A second generation was giving way to the third, in American immigrant terms. In terms of leadership in the Jewish community, I think that there was a greater awareness of the fact that the old ethnically based Jewish life of urban neighbourhoods had given way to a new suburbanised Jewish community that needed to work harder to sustain a sense of Jewish community.[84]

The same was true in the UK. The generation that grew into adulthood in the post-war period were largely the children or grandchildren of immigrants. They were able to take advantage of the massive expansion of university education in the 1950s and 1960s. They were much more confident in their place in Britain than their parents were. They reached maturity in a period in which the state of Israel was a reality and in which Zionism became orthodoxy within the Jewish community. Israel's victory in the Six Day War allowed them to be secure about the continued existence of the Jewish state.

The generations of Jewish leaders that grew up in the post-war period also took advantage of new kinds of institution that had developed in the British and global Jewish communities. To take some of the key post-1990 communal leaders that we interviewed for this project: Rabbi Tony Bayfield, head of the Movement for Reform Judaism, received *semicha* from London's Leo Baeck College, the progressive Jewish seminary founded in 1956. Rabbi Saul Zneimer, chief executive of the United Synagogue from 2001 to 2007, became orthodox due to the efforts of Aish HaTorah, the Jewish outreach organization we will discuss later in this chapter; he received *semicha* from Yeshivat ha Mivtar, a bastion of resurgent post-1967 religious Zionism, located in Efrat on the West Bank. Jeremy Newmark, chief executive of the Jewish Leadership Council, was an activist in the Union of Jewish Students (UJS) which was founded in 1973.

The post-war period also saw the gradual accession of women to communal leadership positions. Jackie Tabick was ordained as Britain's first woman rabbi in 1975 and other women rabbis have become prominent in the Reform and Liberal movements, particularly Julia Neuberger (ordained soon after Tabick), who is now a Liberal Democrat peer with a high public profile. Although no woman has been president of the Board of Deputies or other representative organizations, Rosalind Preston and Jo Wagerman have both been vice-presidents and held other important leadership roles.

Particularly important in this generation was the development of an infrastructure for Zionist youth work and informal education. Although Zionist youth movements had existed since the early twentieth century, in the post-war period involvement in them became a standard feature of the British Jewish communal landscape. These movements were largely peer-led and provided a superb training in communal leadership. After the formation of the state of Israel in 1948, the youth movements made extended visits to Israel a central part of *hadracha* – leadership training. Although these visits were initially focused on preparation for emigration to Israel, they have increasingly become preparation for leadership positions in Diaspora communities.

Chief Rabbi Jonathan Sacks was part of this post-war generation of Jewish leaders. Born in 1948, he was not educated in Jewish schools but attended Christ's College in Finchley followed by a BA at Cambridge University and a PhD in philosophy at Oxford University. Unlike some of the younger communal figures discussed above, he did not reach a leadership position in the Jewish community by way of involvement in Jewish youth movements or UJS (indeed UJS did not exist when he was an undergraduate). Sacks has dated his journey towards becoming a rabbi to his reaction to the Six Day War:

My becoming a rabbi came from a seed planted during the Six-Day War [1967] when I was in my first year at university. For many of us that was a time when we suddenly realized that being Jewish was tied up with something called the state and people of Israel and that we were implicated in one another's fate.

...

After my second year at university I did a long tour of the U.S. and Canada, because I knew there were great rabbis there whom I wanted to meet. I took one of those $100 Greyhound bus tickets and spent two months on the road meeting as many as I could. I had the privilege of meeting Rabbi [Norman] Lamm, Rabbi [Emanuel]

Rackman, the great thinker Abraham J. Heschel. Most significantly, I had long conversations with Rav [Joseph B.] Soloveitchik and the Lubavitcher Rebbe [Menachem Mendel Schneerson], and this kindled in me a desire to learn more and study more. Once a rabbi, I was about to go back into secular academia, but the Rebbe's counsel guided me. It was he who told me I had to do two things: become a rabbi myself and then train other people to be rabbis.[85]

With the partial exception of Abraham Heschel, all these figures were associated with the resurgent post-war American orthodoxy (discussed in chapter 3). Throughout his career, Sacks has attempted to marry a commitment to intellectual achievement in the non-Jewish world with a deep respect both for historic Anglo Jewish orthodox institutions and for the self-confidence of post-war right-wing American and Israeli orthodoxy. He gained *semicha* both from Jews' College, the bastion of British mainstream orthodoxy, and from the more traditional London-based *yeshiva* Etz Chaim. In the 1970s and 1980s, he lectured at various British academic institutions and served as principal of Jews' College. He also developed a significant public profile as an intellectual, culminating in his delivery of the 1990 BBC Reith Lectures.

Conclusion

In the 1990s, as the following chapters will describe, the main threat that rallied Jews was the threat to Jewish continuity, born from assimilation, a result of the very success of the security strategy. In addressing this threat, the Jewish community was able finally to come to terms with multiculturalism. David Cesarani talks about a burgeoning multicultur-alism, which reached its 'apogee' in the 1990s, 'the growing pluralism of European societies, the emergence of protected space in which it was feasible to be Jewish in any number of ways'; the 'glorious moment' of this apogee coincided with the Israel/Palestine conflict going into 'remission'.[86] The Jewish continuity agenda, we will argue in the three next chapters, coinciding with this moment, led to something of a 'renaissance' of Jewish activity and culture, even though predicated on a new discourse around insecure Jewish belonging. However, as we will see in chapter 7, in the current century the discourse of insecurity took on a different note, with the emergence of what was seen as a 'new antisemitism'.

Chapter 2

Research and the 'Reflexive Turn' in Anglo Jewry

On 1 September1991, the new Chief Rabbi, Jonathan Sacks delivered an impassioned, televised induction address in front of a packed congregation at London's St John's Wood synagogue. The speech outlined the challenges he aimed to address over his first decade in office. While Sacks emphasized that Jews were 'one people', he argued that 'we are more deeply divided than at almost any time in our history' and that 'these are fundamental rifts which threaten the very integrity of Jewry as *am echad*, as a single people'.[1] He concluded that 'the Jewish people, *am Yisrael*, has lost its way'. The UK Jewish community, he said, faced other threats too:

> We are a declining and aging community, we are in the midst of a recession, we have to work with limited resources, there are in our community attitudes and divisions which will take a long time to change.

For Sacks, the paradox that Jews are faced with is that 'we survived slavery but can we handle freedom?'. The address closed with a call to action:

> Let us work together to plan and create a decade of renewal of Jewish leadership, of Jewish education, of Jewish spirituality.

Sacks's unflinching willingness to spell out the weaknesses of the Anglo Jewish community was an example of the new *strategy of insecurity* that emerged in the British Jewish community in the early 1990s. If the principal preoccupation of an earlier generation of Jewish communal leaders had been to ensure the security of Jews in the UK, by the early 1990s the principal preoccupation became to motivate action to make the long-term survival of Jewish identity and of Jewish community in the UK secure. To achieve this, Jewish leaders publicly stressed the weaknesses and insecurity of Anglo Jewry.

A crucial component of the strategy of insecurity as it developed in the 1990s was the use of social research on British Jews and Jewish institutions. Research was used to develop policy and also to nurture the insecurity that was deemed necessary to motivate action to ensure Jewish survival. As we shall see, the use of social research on Anglo Jewry could sometimes be tendentious. However, research carried out in the 1990s and 2000s marked a significant step forward in the self-knowledge of the British Jewish community.

Research and the reflexive turn in Anglo Jewry

Until well into the post-war period, Jewish communal institutions rarely sponsored research and were rarely informed by it in policy-making. By the 1990s, however, communal leaders came to pay much greater attention to social research than ever before and research came to play a much more central role in communal policy-making than ever before. Research was part of a broader process in which the communal leadership came to scrutinize Anglo Jewry and reflect on its practice with an unprecedented rigour and honesty. We call this post-1990 process the 'reflexive turn' in Anglo Jewry. Reflexivity is a sociological term for human beings' ability to be self-conscious about their actions and their consequences. Reflexivity is a potentially critical process that subjects practices, their causes and their effects to searching examination. Crucially for our purposes, reflexivity can be embedded in communities when they subject themselves to this process of self-examination.[2] Here we use the concept of 'reflexive turn' to emphasize the unprecedentedly searching nature of the self-criticism that has occurred in Anglo Jewry since 1990.

The reflexive turn was informed by a fear that the community was shrinking. As far back as 1955, Hannah Neustatter, reviewing statistical information that showed a declining birth rate in Anglo Jewry, concluded that:

As long as the trends in the vital statistics of the general population remain unchanged, the attitude of the majority group towards the Jewish minority is the same as at present, no other influences from outside make themselves felt, and, above all, the trends within the Jewish community are stable, the processes of absorption and assimilation are likely to continue unabated. The proportion of Jews in the general population will presumably fall steadily while those Jews who remain will be more and more integrated into the majority group. Thus, after the passage of some time, little may be left that is distinctively Jewish in this country.[3]

The Board of Deputies Community Research Unit was established in 1965 and for many years it has published statistics on births and deaths in the Jewish community. By 1977, when a conference was called to take stock of trends since the unit was formed, it was abundantly clear that the UK Jewish community was ageing, its births failing to keep up with deaths.[4] Periodic cumulative statistical reports have consistently tracked this decline.[5]

Despite these persistent warning signs, it took developments in the US Jewish community to place demography at the heart of the UK Jewish communal agenda. In 1990, the US Council of Jewish Federations sponsored the National Jewish Population Survey (NJPS), the largest and most methodologically sophisticated survey that had ever been carried out in the US.[6] The findings of the survey that attracted most attention concerned intermarriage:

> In recent years just over half of Born Jews who married, at any age, whether for the first time or not, chose a spouse who was born a Gentile and has remained so, while less than 5 percent of these marriages include a non-Jewish partner who became a Jew by Choice (JBC). As a result, since 1985 twice as many mixed couples ... have been created as Jewish couples.[7]

The 'headline' figure that was to be much quoted was that American Jewry had an 'intermarriage rate' of 52 per cent (i.e. over half of the Jews in America were married to non-Jews).[8] The NJPS further reported that fertility rates were getting lower with each generation of Jews and that intermarried Jews and their children had low rates of Jewish involvement.

The survey proved to be a milestone in the history of US Jewish public discourse. As the 1995 report of the North American Commission on Jewish Identity and Continuity proclaimed:

> North America has heard our *shofar* sound. The call to awaken came not from a ram's horn, but from a research study: the 1990 National

Jewish Population Survey, sponsored by the Council of Jewish Federations ... The statistics left no doubt: Unless we act in the next decade to reverse the trends of the past quarter century (or more), we can no longer take for granted a vibrant, vital Jewish future in North America.[9]

While the 1990 NJPS proved an invaluable tool in raising public awareness of threats to Jewish survival in the US, as we shall see in the next chapter, communal policy-makers had already begun to attend to these issues before the 1990s. In a sense, most post-Enlightenment Jewish initiatives were to some degree oriented towards the need to sustain Jewish life against the threat of assimilation, but in the post-World War II period this aspect of communal policy-making became more and more prominent. The findings of the 1990 NJPS were therefore disseminated on fertile ground.

In the early 1990s, the American Jewish community provided a substantial resource of expertise and knowledge that the UK community could draw upon. In the 1990 NJPS, the American community also provided a model for how a research-based strategy of insecurity could be wielded to stimulate Jewish communal action and funding.

The argument for Jewish continuity that Jonathan Sacks set out in his 1994 book *Will We Have Jewish Grandchildren?* was therefore grounded in research on Anglo Jewry:

> For the past few years the Board of Deputies Community Research Unit has been compiling yearly statistics on synagogue marriages within Anglo-Jewry. In 1991 the Unit completed a study which showed that the number of first marriages had fallen to significantly less than half of the figure at which it should stand if all Jews in Britain reaching marriageable age were marrying in a synagogue. The implication is simple. More than a half of young Jews are not marrying other Jews, or not marrying, or not celebrating their marriages under Jewish auspices ... Instead, the statistic spells disaffiliation and decline.[10]

Sacks went on to contrast the UK Jewish community's reaction to this research with that of the US Jewish community to the NJPS:

> The research that created the storm in America – the Council of Jewish Federation's 1990 National Jewish Population Survey – was conducted by an outstanding demographer, Dr Barry Kosmin ... The irony is that until a few years ago Dr Kosmin, himself an Anglo-

Jew, worked for the British Jewish community – for the Board of
Deputies Community Research Unit ... Eventually, he was driven to
leave by the sheer indifference to his work.[11]

Sacks was referring to a controversy that engulfed the Board of Deputies
in the mid 1980s. Building on his pioneering studies in the 1970s and
1980s,[12] Barry Kosmin had progressively refined the methodology used for
calculating the size of Anglo Jewry. Using these new methods, he argued
that the size of Anglo Jewry in the early 1980s was around 330,000.[13] This
new figure was a massive step down from the figure of 450,000–500,000
that had for a number of years been in common use by communal leaders,
and there was considerable debate in the Board of Deputies as to whether
this new figure should be circulated.[14] In an interview for this book, Barry
Kosmin recounted this controversy:[15]

Greville Janner[16] said 'we've got half a million Jews, politically I've
always said we have half a million Jews, I need to have half a million
Jews' and all the rest of it ... If you ever went back into the minutes
of all the Deputies, you'd see this personal attack on me for being
either a traitor or an incompetent at the Board of Deputies ... Anyway,
so that was the battle. He said that we can't have a declining Anglo
Jewry, and I said well how can you do it? You can't explain, you
know, that you have half the number of marriages now as in 1945.
And he said it doesn't really matter ... And that's when I decided it
wasn't possible to work at the Board.

The argument that, in order to be politically viable, Anglo Jewry needed
to show that it was not declining was part of the strategy of security. For
leaders such as Greville Janner, reflexivity was a lower priority than
ensuring effective Jewish communal representation. Kosmin is aware that
reflexivity may not an easy process:

We wanted to tell our people for very practical welfare, defence,
education and other purposes, for planning purposes, right, how
many children there are down the road, how many people, otherwise
you're looking for people who don't exist. It's a bit of a morale-
destroying activity.

The 1990s strategy of insecurity in the 1990s represented a willingness to
risk morale as a way of motivating action. By strategically opening the
community up to self-criticism, those such as Sacks who stressed communal

insecurity were calculating that public evidence of communal decline would create momentum for attempts to change the community.

Social research as self-criticism

Some of the research completed within the British Jewish community in the 1990s took the form of self-criticism by Jewish organizations. One of the most notable examples of this was *A Time for Change*, a wholesale review of the United Synagogue, conducted by Sir Stanley Kalms and released in 1992.[17] It included a review of the organization's finances, a complete audit of its activities and a report on a social survey of United Synagogue members.[18] The report pulled no punches:

> The United Synagogue is losing members, far more rapidly than any other synagogue organisation. Twenty-five years ago it represented three-quarters of affiliated Jews, today little more than half. The high age profile of its members indicates that it is failing to attract the young. Our market research has uncovered widespread dissatisfaction with what is seen as a remote and profligate head office, cold and unwelcoming communities and a drift away from the United Synagogue's tolerant religious ethos.[19]

The report excoriated the United Synagogue institution for its multiple failings – above all, its alienation from its members. This concern about the gap between institutions and their members was also found in *Beyond the Synagogue*, published in 1995 by the Reform Synagogue of Great Britain's 'Missing Generation' working group.[20] The project was set up in 1993 'in recognition of the conspicuous absence of young adults from all aspects of synagogue life'.[21] The report was based on a survey of young adults (from across the community) and of Reform synagogues together with young adult focus groups. It argued that:

> There is now a growing sense of urgency across the Jewish community. The bonds which have in the past held the community together seem to be weakening. The increases in 'out'-marriage, and in people opting out of Jewish life, are testament to this problem. Synagogue membership is declining and its average age increasing. There is increasing concern about the future dynamism and leadership of the Reform Movement.[22]

For *Beyond the Synagogue*, responding to the needs of young adults (defined as 18–35-year-olds) was critical in ensuring Jewish continuity. The report provided a voice for a previously invisible group within Anglo Jewry and the document was liberally sprinkled with quotes from young adults expressing their alienation from communal institutions.[23]

The 1994 *Women in the Community* report,[24] also based in part on social survey research,[25] allowed women's experience to be heard in Jewish communal deliberations for the first time. The research found considerable alienation among Jewish women from communal institutions and it brought to light neglected issues such as *agunah* and domestic violence. *Women in the Community* was initiated by the Chief Rabbi but dealt with the experience of women throughout the UK Jewish community, and members of non-orthodox movements were present on the various working groups for the project.

Another overview of the community was provided by the 1992 report, *Securing Our Future: An Inquiry into Jewish Education in the United Kingdom*,[26] known as 'The Worms Report' after its chair, Fred Worms. This was commissioned by the Jewish Educational Development Trust, an orthodox-run body that had nonetheless attempted to work cross-communally, building progressive as well as orthodox day schools. The report attempted to provide an overview of the educational situation in the entire community and included leaders of non-orthodox movements on its steering committee. *Securing Our Future* modelled itself on the 1990 report of the Commission on Jewish Education in North America and claimed that education was the 'solution' to the problem of Jewish continuity:

> The key to Anglo-Jewry's survival lies in education. Inter-marriage is rife. A large proportion of Jews have lost interest in their heritage. The number of one parent families is increasing and there are more children with problematical halachic provenance. The community is shrinking at the rate of 4,300 per annum. From a post-war 460,000, we are now less than 300,000 and if the rate of decline cannot be arrested, we shall be less than 250,000 in some twenty years time.[27]

The report was as unflinching as the Kalms report in its criticisms of the weaknesses of Jewish education in the UK. Worms pointed to a lack of coordination between bodies involved in Jewish education, a lack of innovation, a crisis in funding, a massive drop of young people in Jewish education post-Barmitzvah, weak growth in Jewish day school attendance, a chronic shortage of good staff in Jewish schools, and low status and pay for Jewish teachers in the UK.

Social research as strategic planning

In 1996, the Institute for Jewish Affairs, originally set up in 1941 as the research arm of the World Jewish Congress, was relaunched as the Institute for Jewish Policy Research. The relaunch coincided with the publication of the most methodologically sophisticated survey that had ever been conducted in Anglo Jewry, on the social and political attitudes of British Jews.[28] The summary report for the survey criticized the failures of communal organizations in strategic planning and research:

> British Jewry is not good at strategic planning or the formation of policy. In part this is due to the organizational structure of the community, to the arbitrary way in which communal agencies take decisions and interact with one another. These problems are increasingly recognized by communal leaders and have led to some initiatives to develop more rational and better co-ordinated planning structures. But there remains a second critical factor which inhibits constructive change: the paucity of research data about the community and the consequential lack of understanding of its social, political and religious dynamics.[29]

Just as the NJPS produced a 'headline rate' of intermarriage, the survey concluded that 'the rate at which Jewish men are marrying non-Jewish women' was 44 per cent,[30] suggesting intermarriage rates not far off those of the US. At the same time, the survey also found that a majority of those married to non-Jews were involved in Jewish life and identified as Jews. Moreover, 'that data clearly disprove the common assumption that intermarried, or uninvolved, or Secular Jews display negative attitudes towards Jewishness and the Jewish community'. While the majority of British Jews strongly identified as Jews, 'for most Jews, religious observance is a means of identifying with the Jewish community, rather than an expression of religious faith'. Above all 'the data show a growing sector of British Jews who feel firmly and securely rooted in British society'.

The 1995 JPR survey, together with the other reports that came out in the early 1990s, helped to establish the value of systematic, research-based strategic planning. The importance that research had come to take on in Anglo Jewry was highlighted by the return of Barry Kosmin in 1997 to work as director of research for the JPR to work on the 'Long-Term Planning for British Jewry Project', carried out between 1997 and 2003. Kosmin ran the majority of the project, taking over as director of the JPR in 1999 until he returned to America in 2005. Funded to the tune of around £750,000 by a variety of private trusts and Jewish communal charities, the programme produced twelve separate reports.[31] The programme focused in particular on the 'Jewish voluntary sector', introducing this unifying concept to a fragmented community. The final report argued that:

> In a climate of rapid transformations in which there are scarce resources but ever-increasing demands, it has become essential for individual Jewish voluntary organizations, and indeed the sector as a whole, to change. For the [Jewish voluntary sector] to remain viable and vibrant in the twenty-first century, organizations need to be more responsive to the needs of their clients and to plan their activities using research-based evidence rather than (as has tended to be the case) instinct and supposition.[32]

The programme provided the first serious research carried out in a number of areas of the Jewish community. Four of the studies looked at the Jewish voluntary sector, its resources, funding and governance. There were studies of the provision of long-term care for older people and of Jewish schooling. Four studies looked at the attitudes and practices of Jews themselves in London, Manchester and Leeds. In addition to a number of other pieces of social research carried out in the 1990s and 2000s,[33] the Long-Term Planning project added significantly to the knowledge that the Jewish community had of itself.

Perhaps the most significant resource for strategic planning in the Jewish community was the 2001 census. The census was the first to include a voluntary question asking for respondents' religions as well as another (compulsory) one asking for respondents' ethnic backgrounds. In the run-up to the 2001 census the Office for National Statistics consulted closely with the Jewish community as well as other religious and ethnic communities. The Board of Deputies and other communal organizations (including some from within the ultra-orthodox community) encouraged all Jews to complete the religion question – there was no longer any reticence to reveal publicly the size of Anglo Jewry.

The census data on British Jews was subject to a sophisticated analysis by David Graham and Stanley Waterman of the JPR and Marlena Schmool of the Board of Deputies.[34] The analysis found that 266,740 people identified themselves as Jewish in answer to the religion question. Including those who identified themselves as Jews in answer to the ethnicity question but not the religion question brought the total up to

270,499. Given the complexities of identity and the voluntary nature of the religion question, the authors of the report considered the number to be an undercount:

> whether this undercount was in the region of 10 or 15 per cent is far less significant than the fact that, thanks to the Census, there is now a dataset unparalleled in its detail and complexity, on Europe's second largest Jewish population.[35]

The 2001 census (and future censuses assuming the questions are retained) provides a valuable grounding for social research within the Jewish community. It allowed the Manchester Jewish community to undertake a sophisticated strategic planning exercise in 2004.[36]

By the time of the 2007 census report, the British Jewish community had, in research terms, come a very long way. In contrast to the situation in the 1980s – when research on Anglo Jewry was a marginal activity, viewed suspiciously by some – communal organizations had begun to use research to develop a sophisticated understanding of the community and its needs. This embracing of research extended even to the ultra-orthodox community.[37] Research had subjected Jewish communal practices to unprecedented scrutiny and allowed the concerns of Jews of a variety of kinds to be shared in communal debates. The community had become a much more reflexive community.

The limits of reflexivity

While the reflexivity of Anglo Jewry was greatly enhanced in the 1990s and beyond, like all forms of reflexivity it was limited in certain respects. Research on Anglo Jewry was based on assumptions that were rarely questioned. One of these assumptions was of the fundamental importance of demography and statistics. As Mitchell Hart[38] has argued (in regard to the US but applying equally to the UK):

> regardless of which side of the debate over Jewish decline one stands on, those involved in the debate appear united in their faith in the power of numbers and of social science to grasp the reality of the situation, to provide the tools with which to understand the questions of contemporary Jewish collective life, identify problems and challenges, and even help solve them.[39]

This faith in statistics has a long history in the Jewish world, dating back to the nineteenth century. Hart has shown how statistical surveys of Jews at that time drew on discourses that owed much to eugenics and ideas of racial 'purity':

> Lower birth rates served Jewish social scientists as a 'master pathology', the main indicator of a host of other social pathologies believed to be plaguing the Jewish community ... Qualitatively, the significance of intermarriage and conversion lay in their purported effects upon the purity and strength of the Jewish race.[40]

Early Zionism drew heavily on racial ideas that Diaspora Jews were at risk of bodily and racial enfeeblement, pathologies that only a Jewish state could cure.[41] Although ideas of Diaspora Jewry as literally physically feeble are no longer popular, the statistical diagnosis of communal pathologies is still very much alive. The contemporary pathology is 'disappearance', the literal vanishing of Jews (at least non-ultra-orthodox Jews) from the Diaspora.[42]

Sociology and social research have sometimes been used as ways of justifying normative standards of Jewish behaviour. Lila Corwen Berman has argued that sociology has often been used by US Jewish leaders to promote inmarriage among Jewish communal leaders.[43] This 'sociological Jewishness' attempted to demonstrate that inmarried households were more stable than intermarried ones and that inmarried communities were essential to the harmony and integration of American society. The problem with sociological Jewishness is that it could not in and of itself provide justification for Jewish continuity and, as intermarriage increased in the postwar period, it became clear that intermarriage was not in and of itself harmful to the individuals involved or to American society.

Even if social research was embraced by Anglo Jewish communal leaders in the 1990s, a certain kind of ambivalence about research has remained. At times, some Jewish leaders have appeared to assume that social research risks condoning the actions of its subjects. In *Will We Have Jewish Grandchildren?* Jonathan Sacks argues:

> Fortunately ... the Jewish people has never been led by behavioural scientists. We are a kingdom of priests, not an assembly of sociologists. We have never taken facts as inevitable, nor have we mistaken facts for commandments.[44]

This suspicion of research was demonstrated in some of the British reactions to Steven Cohen and Arnold Eisen's landmark study of US

Jewry *The Jew Within*.[45] Cohen and Eisen argued that American Jews viewed Judaism predominantly through the lens of the 'sovereign self' as part of an individualist search for meaning in Judaism. In his speech at a conference organized by the United Jewish Israel Appeal in 2002, Jonathan Sacks criticized the sovereign self, arguing:

> This is not something Judaism can endorse. To this cultural shift we have to be *am kshei oref* [a stiff-necked people]. We have obstinately to resist it. We believe in the primacy of community. That is not because we do not value the self, but because only in community can the self find identity.[46]

In his introduction to the collection of papers from the conference, Jonathan Boyd posited a distinction between the sovereign self which 'describes the state of identity in much of the western world, certainly in the decade leading up to 11 September 2001' and a 'situated self' which 'prescribes how identity in the western and perhaps wider world should be'.[47] Boyd went on to argue that 'the debate between the sovereign and situated self is essentially a debate between sociology and philosophy'.[48] Boyd's characterization of sociology demonstrates a concern that social research might, in its apparently naked descriptiveness, undermine motivation in the fight for Jewish continuity. Here we see echoes of the anxieties that led Greville Janner to demand half a million Jews in the UK.[49]

It is this ambivalence that has led research on Anglo Jewry to be highly focused and restricted in its methodology and aims. The primary concern with research has been to produce actionable conclusions to facilitate top-down strategic planning. Although there has been qualitative research on Anglo Jewry, the airing of the stories of individual Jews is a means to an end rather than an end in and of itself. Within the academy, most research on Anglo Jewry has focused on Anglo Jewish history, and Jewish studies departments in UK universities tend not to have social scientists on their faculty. By and large, the academics who have studied Anglo Jewry have done so through policy-oriented projects funded by Jewish communal bodies.[50]

At times, the urgent desire to ensure Jewish continuity leads to ambivalence regarding research on the lives of individual Jews. This ambivalence is one reason for the most remarkable limitation of the reflexivity of the UK Jewish community: no British Jewish organization has ever sponsored research on outmarried or non-identifying British Jews.[51] As long ago as 1989, Stephen Miller argued that in the face of the decline in communal numbers:

> We need urgently to discover exactly how this shortfall is made up, what is happening to the two-thirds of the younger community who are missing from the marriage statistics and, most importantly, we need to understand why this shift in marriage patterns has taken place.[52]

No research of this kind has ever been commissioned. Throughout much of the research that was commissioned to inform the Jewish communal policy-making there was an assumption that those who 'left' the Jewish community were lost forever. The possibility that an outmarried or non-identifying Jew or their spouse might retain an existing or potential connection to and identification with Judaism was a priori ruled out. To be sure, the Reform and particularly the Liberal movements have made increased steps towards the inclusion of non-Jewish partners, but this has not translated into any kind of research agenda.[53]

The only substantial work that discussed intermarried Jews was Emma Klein's journalistic study *Lost Jews* published in 1996.[54] Klein's book looked at Jews on the margins of the British and other Jewish communities, whether marginalized through intermarriage, being the child of intermarried parents, through lapsed practice or through lack of attachment to the organized Jewish community. She found that many of these 'lost' Jews were seeking a greater connection with Judaism but were alienated by a Jewish community from which they felt excluded. These perceptions of exclusion were often warranted, as Klein shows that much of the orthodox establishment felt unwilling or unable to reach out to those who were not Jewish according to *halacha*.

Jewish identity in a multicultural context

Policy-oriented research on the UK Jewish community has also proceeded with little reference to research conducted on other British ethnic and religious groups. Zvi Bekerman and Ezra Kopelowitz have discussed their frustration with the insularity of research on Jewish education:

> The frustration comes from our perception that research on Jewish education is a field that lives an almost solipsistic life, compartmentalized both from general research in education and from research done by other ethnic and minority groups struggling to sustain a sense of cultural integrity and belonging in contemporary society.[55]

Bekerman and Kopelowiz argue that this solipsism is shared by other minority groups searching for 'cultural sustainability' in 'Western' societies:

> The universality to which liberal Western cultural hegemony strives in general and to which postmodern sensitivities preach in particular lead those inside and outside of academia who are attempting to promote cultural sustainability to look inwards, each to their own ethnic experience, accepting the liberal claim that they are 'particular' or 'unique' and it is the public sphere of liberal society that is 'universal'.[56]

According to this view, the struggle for minority cultural sustainability in Western societies is beset by a failure to learn from or make common cause with other minority groups.

Comparative research on British Jews and other minorities could have offered some important insights into identity. Contemporary scholars of ethnic and racial identity have often taken a much more positive view of ambivalent and ambiguous identities. Much critical, phenomenological and postmodernist work on identity has criticized 'essentialist' models that view identity as unchanging, coherent, homogeneous and non-contradictory. Such essentialist identities cannot exist since the self is always in flux and identity is stitched together contingently through a patchwork or 'bricolage' of often contradictory discourses and fragments.[57] From this perspective, the desire to 'fix' Jewish or other identities is both futile and dangerous, leading to oppression and even violence. Those who reject essentialist models of identity focus on the creativity displayed in the ceaseless movement of identity. Paul Gilroy's work, for example, destabilizes essentialist conceptions of 'black' and 'white' identity in favour of an appreciation of movement, translation and encounter between different kinds of people at different times.[58] For such scholars, hybrid 'miscegenated' identities may be the subject of celebration.[59] This body of scholarship undermines concepts of assimilation that assume an undifferentiated majority identity under which one can be subsumed. Instead, for these scholars, the contemporary multicultural landscape is one in which new kinds of identities are constantly being created, rendering problematic any notion of a fixed identity.

Studies that are informed by this perspective have produced much more positive accounts of contemporary Jewish identity. Caryn Aviv and David Shneer's book *New Jews* demonstrates the diversity of Jewish identities and the panoply of possibilities for previously marginalized groups such as gay Jews.[60] The authors see the fluidity of Jewish identities

in the modern world as a positive development: 'it is the very slipperiness
of Jewish identity that provides so much fertile potential for creativity,
innovation, and adaptation in all of the places Jews call home'.[61]

Other authors have similarly called for an end to simplistic, essentialist
versions of Jewish identity in favour of a conception of Jewish identity that
is creative, reflexive and open to difference.[62] For such writers, intermarriage is not an end to Jewish life but an opening up of the possibilities for
new kinds of Jewish identity and practice.

Some scholars of Jewish identity have criticized such perspectives.
Charles Liebman, one of the most celebrated Jewish sociologists, argued
in one of the last articles he wrote:

> It is not only a concern for Jewish survival that directs us to look for
> the essentialist elements of Jewish culture; the question of which
> cultural elements are shared and which are not shared by all or
> most Jews and which cultural elements are or are not rooted in the
> Jewish tradition, is what defines the research program for the social
> scientific analysis of Jewish identity. I cannot imagine our scholarly
> agenda to be dictated by a postmodernist mood.[63]

Liebman conflates postmodernist approaches to the study of identity and
postmodern identity itself. Eschewing postmodern approaches to identity
research means eschewing the identities of most Jews: if an essentialist,
coherent identity is the norm that is aspired to, any other kind of Jewish
identity is necessarily a degraded one.

A desire to promote Jewish continuity may pathologize those Jews who
are seen as being 'to blame' for assimilation and communal erosion. For
instance, scholars in the US have shown that women in particular have at
times been blamed for failures to resist assimilation.[64] At the same time,
however, a rejection of essentialist models of Jewish identity does not imply
that all Jewish identities should be the uncritical object of celebration. One
of the weaknesses of some anti-essentialist accounts of Jewish identity is a
tendency to focus on the critical 'vanguard' rather than the 'rank and file'.
We have ample evidence that artists and intellectuals can produce creative
and challenging work that questions and plays with traditional Jewish
identities,[65] but it is much less clear whether the identities of the vast
majority of Jews should be similarly celebrated.

Research on other ethnic and religious groups has demonstrated that
mixed families produce complex identities and even encourage a greater
reflexivity in the development of individual identities.[66] There is some
evidence that intermarried and marginal Jews can remain strongly Jewishly

identifying. Emma Klein's work showed the persistence of feelings of attachment to and interest in Judaism among marginal Jews. Research in the US has shown that whilst outmarried Jews and their children are less engaged in Jewish communal life than those who are inmarried, they often retain a strong sense of abstract connection to Jewish peoplehood.[67] Further, in some cases 'mixed-marrying Americans often construct a more pointed definition of their own ethnoreligious identity'.[68] At the same time, though, there is considerable debate over how far intermarried families in the US are likely to raise Jewish children and to be involved in communal institutions, with some scholars seeing a significant rise in the numbers of such involved intermarried Jewish families, and others maintaining that intermarriage is *the* most significant indicator of communal non-involvement.[69] Steven M. Cohen has gone so far as to argue that we need to talk now of 'two Jewries' in the US – one of communally affiliated inmarried Jews and another of ambiguously or non-affiliated intermarrieds.[70] What does seem clear is that family background provides the most significant indicator of what kind of Jew a young person becomes. As Erik Cohen has argued, 'In the absence of family pressure, community involvement alone provides no guarantees that a young person will decide to marry a Jew.'[71]

Even if Jewish concerns about intermarriage have often been voiced in crudely essentialist terms, intermarriage does indeed raise difficult questions about the long-term continuity of Jewish identity. Even if feelings of Jewishness may persist over a number of generations of intermarriage and non-involvement in communal practice, Jewishness is not just reducible to feeling or identifying as Jewish. It is unclear whether Jewish identification decoupled from Jewish practice can persist longer than a few generations. It may well be the case then that intermarriage threatens the continuity of Judaism, at least for the children of intermarried parents, without some kind of enduring level of Jewish practice. If the first, second and even third generations of mixed married families may produce children with complex hybrid identities, what will the fourth, fifth and sixth generation produce? Intermarriage and intermixing in contemporary multicultural society has not produced a bland, homogeneous society – quite the opposite – but perhaps after several generations multicultural society may become much more monocultural. The result might be that the only sources of non-superficial difference that remain may be those groups – such as Haredi Jews – who practise fundamentalist forms of self-ghettoization.

Intermarriage may not always leads to total assimilation and inmarried Jewish families are not the only ones that can nurture Jewishness. Yet intermarriage and non-communal involvement makes Jewish continuity much more challenging to achieve. In a multicultural society there can never be any guarantees that any Jewish practice or identity will survive in the long term (assuming that a multicultural society survives of course), but some communal structures and practices, such as inmarriage, can make long-term survival more likely.

The impact of research on Anglo Jewry

For all their limitations, the research reports that were produced within the British Jewish community since the early 1990s illuminated that community with an unprecedented degree of detail. The increasingly complex picture that the various pieces of research painted was accompanied by a gradual de-emphasizing of the raw size of the community. Despite the 2001 census finding that the community had dropped well below 300,000, the publication of the data in 2007 did not trigger the kind of soul-searching that had been seen in the early 1990s. Part of the reason for the decreased concern about numbers was that evidence had emerged that the community's numerical decline might have been arrested. In 2008, the Board of Deputies released a report demonstrating that the Haredi Jewish population of the UK had been growing at a rate of 4 per cent per year for the previous two decades.[72] The report estimated that even though only 10 per cent of British Jews were Haredi, one-third of British Jewish under-eighteens were; evidence of a young age structure with massive growth potential. Yaacov Wise, a Haredi affiliated academic at Manchester University went further and claimed that, thanks to the Haredi birth rate, Anglo Jewry was now growing in size for the first time since World War II, although the Board was more cautious, claiming only that the population had stabilized.[73]

By the mid to late 2000s, research had become less of a priority within the community. After the completion of the JPR's Long-Term Planning project in 2003, the organization gradually wound down much of its research activity and in 2005 Barry Kosmin returned to America. The previous director, Tony Lerman, returned. In October 2006, he announced that the organization would now be concerned with developing policy on Europe. Lerman's controversial views on Israel and antisemitism meant that some other Jewish communal organizations refused to work with the JPR, and he retired in December 2008. Having appointed a new director, Jonathan Boyd, in January 2010, the JPR is, at the time of writing, beginning to build up its research capacity again in preparation for the 2011 census. The mid to late 2000s also saw the Board of Deputies wind down its Community Research Unit, following the retirement of key staff, although it continued to collect communal statistics and produce policy and research papers on an ad hoc basis. Research still continues within the British Jewish community, but the research 'cycle' begun in the early 1990s was largely concluded by the early to mid 2000s. Recent research in the Jewish community has proved modest in scope and less rigorous methodologically than in the 1990s. For example, the updated 'Women's Review' survey,[74] conducted in 2008 and the JPR survey on attitudes to Israel, conducted in 2010, both relied on 'opt-in' internet questionnaires without effective controls on sampling.

One of the weaknesses of many of the research reports produced in Anglo Jewry since the early 1990s was that the processes through which they would be translated into policy were never clear. The connection to policy-making tended to be strongest when reports were commissioned for the use of particular organizations. For example, as we shall see in chapter 5, the processes of 'renewal' that the United Synagogue and the Reform Movement underwent were guided by research reports on their organizations in the early 1990s. The various reports produced by the JPR were respected but the sheer volume of data and recommendations produced by the Long-Term Planning project made it unwieldy to translate into policy. The JPR's fierce independence and Barry Kosmin's sometimes abrasive personality made it a somewhat 'unclubbable' organization among the communal grandees whose support is crucial in any kind of Jewish communal transformation.

Yet the practical consequences of the research that was carried out from the early 1990s is perhaps of less importance than the fact that research was carried out at all. While research can and does have real consequences for Jewish communal practice, its value is not purely instrumental. The reflexive turn in Anglo Jewry represented the community turning to look at its strengths and weaknesses rather than suppressing this self-knowledge in favour of presenting a particular image to the non-Jewish world. Whatever the consequences of this reflexivity in terms of specific policies, the reflexive turn in Anglo Jewry strengthened a critical mood within the communal leadership. Moreover, this critical mood stimulated an appetite for change. Whatever specific research findings might have been ignored, the need for change was not. By the mid to late 2000s, the process of change was well under way and new orthodoxies and directions in policy-making had emerged within Anglo Jewry. The function of research in the Jewish community switched from provoking a desire for change, to servicing pre-existing policy agendas. In the next chapter we will examine how these policy agendas emerged.

Chapter 3

The Continuity Consensus

The strategy of insecurity, embedded in the reflexive turn in the Jewish community, was ultimately concerned with ensuring Jewish communal survival. Over its long history, the Jewish people have been intensely preoccupied with their own survival. As the sociologist Zygmunt Bauman has noted: '"Is there a future for the Jewish people?" – who else, but the Jews, would ask such a question? Who else would feel the need to ask it?'[1] Famously, Simon Rawidowicz called Jews the 'ever-dying people'[2] who, generation after generation, fear that they will be the last Jews. Rawidowicz shows how these fears have been expressed again and again in different settings back to antiquity. To be concerned with Jewish survival is in fact to continue a great and productive tradition:

> If we are the last – let us be the last as our fathers and forefathers were. Let us prepare the ground for the last Jews who will come after us, and for the last Jews who will rise after them, and so on until the end of days.
> If it has been decreed for Israel that it go on being a dying nation – let it be a nation that is constantly dying, which is to say: incessantly living and creating.[3]

Of course modernity also presents unique challenges to Jewish survival. The holocaust demonstrated the capacity for genocide in the modern nation-state. Post-emancipation, for the first time in history individual Jews had what appeared to be a choice whether to remain Jewish or not, even if the Holocaust demonstrated that 'assimilation' might not guarantee freedom from persecution.

In an argument that owes something to Jewish historian Jacob Katz, Zygmunt Bauman locates the emancipation and assimilation processes as part of the unfolding of *modernity* – as 'a typically modern phenomenon'.[4] Specifically, he looks at it as part of the modern state's crusade against the alternative sources of authority that stood in its path. Bauman quotes Hannah Arendt, who described the Jews as a 'non-national element in a world of growing or existing nations'. He adds

> By the very fact of their territorial dispersion and ubiquity, the Jews were an inter-national nation ... The boundaries of the nation were too narrow to define them; the horizons of national tradition were too short to see through their identity ... *The world tightly packed with nations and nation-states abhorred the non-national void.*[5]

The nation-state was a bid for 'legal, linguistic, cultural and ideological unification': 'the project of homogeneity [was] inherent in the idea of the nation', and it led to a 'cultural crusade against difference'.[6] Bauman shows assimilation was framed in terms of a linear, teleological model of progress:

> [Jews] were 'progressive' if they strove to imitate the dominant patterns and to erase all signs of the original ones. They were labeled 'backward' as long as they retained loyalty to the traditional patterns, or were not apt or fast enough in ridding themselves of their residual traces.
>   What made the standing invitation particularly alluring and morally disarming was the fact that it came in the disguise of benevolence and tolerance; indeed the assimilatory project went down in history as part of the *liberal* political programme, of the tolerant and enlightened stance that exemplified the most endearing traits of a 'civilized state'.[7]

By designating assimilation as progress, the nation-state project was able to represent its own values as universal and everyone else's values as particularistic: the entry ticket into the universal was acceptance of the cultural norms of the white Europeans.

Jews have therefore been, in David Roskies's phrase, the 'guinea pigs of modernity', bearing the brunt of the assimilation experiment.[8] But as modernity has moved on, and the monocultural settlement of the classic nation-state has shifted, assimilation has shifted too. Assimilation is today a much less urgent requirement in states such as the UK where multiculturalism has become the official ideology. Nonetheless, it remains a concern for the Jewish community.

In recent decades, the venerable concern for survival came to be embodied in the concept of 'Jewish continuity'. As the 1990s developed, a 'continuity agenda' developed in the UK Jewish community. The agenda drew on ideas and policies drawn from across the Jewish world, principally the US and Israel. The rest of this chapter explores the emergence of the continuity agenda and how it crystallized into a 'continuity consensus' in the UK. Crucial in this process was the work of Jonathan Sacks. Sacks, a widely published author both before and during his term as Chief Rabbi, is an adept synthesizer of ideas from Jewish and non-Jewish sources. Many of the ideas and developments discussed in this chapter found their way into his work.

The emergence of the continuity agenda in American Jewry

In the post-war period American Jewry, like British Jewry, was transformed from an immigrant-dominated community to a settled, upwardly mobile and rapidly assimilating community. In an incremental process, forward-thinking communal leaders sought to adapt the community's institutions and practices to this new reality. Although the 1990 National Jewish Population Survey (NJPS) was to spur increased efforts in the US, the process of communal transformation was already well under way by that stage. In this sense what was to become the Jewish continuity agenda had much deeper roots in the US than it did in the UK.

The American Jewish community has always been much more receptive to innovation in Jewish thought and practice than its counterpart in the UK. Whereas in the UK the largest synagogue movement has always been the orthodox United Synagogue, in the US the Conservative[9] and Reform movements long ago became predominant, with its institutions, such as the Conservative Jewish Theological Seminary and the Reform Hebrew Union College pre-eminent in the global development of twentieth-century non-orthodox religious thought. American orthodox Judaism has proved dynamic in the creation of centres of modern orthodox innovation such as Yeshiva University. The US Jewish community also has a dynamic anti-establishment tendency, embodied, for example, in the *chavurah* movement of small, informal prayer groups.

All these developments were instituted before the emergence of what we now understand as the Jewish continuity agenda. They were not motivated by an explicit desire to ensure Jewish continuity, but they all shared a conviction that the new circumstances in which the Jews found themselves required a rethinking of the institutions within which Judaism should be practised. This openness to innovation was in stark contrast to the UK Jewish community whose institutions were developed in the nineteenth century and remained largely unreformed for much of the twentieth.

The primary drivers of the American continuity agenda came out of the field of Jewish education. In 1976, the Coalition for Alternatives in Jewish Education (later renamed Coalition for the Advancement of Jewish Education) held the first of what was to be an annual conference. Bringing together Jewish educators from across the community, the conference was to become an important forum for new developments in Jewish education.[10] In 1981, the Jewish Educational Service of North America (JESNA) was founded, providing a clearing house for support and innovation in Jewish education. In 1990, the Commission on Jewish Education in North America published a widely publicized report that brought in most of the major institutional stakeholders in the US Jewish community to raise the profile of Jewish education.[11] The report placed Jewish education at the centre of efforts to ensure Jewish continuity: 'The responsibility for developing Jewish identity and installing a commitment to Judaism for this population now rests primarily with education.'[12]

By 1990, the term 'Jewish continuity' had come into use as a way of defining the goal of these Jewish education-based initiatives. Jewish Federations in a number of cities had begun to set up 'continuity commissions' to research and improve Jewish education in their cities. The publication of the 1995 report of the North American Commission on Jewish Identity and Continuity consolidated a process that was well under way.[13]

Unlike in the UK Jewish community, where the paucity of communally engaged intellectuals and the inertia of the community meant that the Chief Rabbi would play a pivotal role in defining and propounding the continuity agenda, in the US no single public figure was central to the articulation of the continuity agenda. Rather, the continuity agenda emerged organically through a gradually snowballing process of change. The key individuals in this process of change influenced its trajectory less through publications or speeches than through more subtle processes of influence. In this respect, no figure was more important in the development of the US continuity agenda than Seymour Fox.

Seymour Fox

Outside the realm of Jewish communal leadership, the name Seymour Fox would mean little to most Jews in the US and elsewhere. At the time of this book's writing he does not have a Wikipedia page devoted to him, nor does an internet search for his name give much of a clue to his importance.[14] This is perhaps appropriate as Fox was a leader who influenced through individual, private conversations and contacts. Fox, who died in 2006, was ordained by the Conservative movement in the US but spent much of his life as an academic engaged in the development of Jewish educational practice in the US and in Israel (to where he moved in the late 1960s).

Fox was heavily influenced by the American pragmatist tradition, particularly as articulated in the educational and social theory of John Dewey[15] and the curriculum specialist Joseph Schwab, his mentor during his doctoral studies at the University of Chicago.[16] This tradition emphasized the 'deliberative' approach to social problems, in which solutions developed out of a process of reflection and innovation, tied into 'real world' practice (the realm of what Schwab calls 'the practical') rather than the application of a set theory to a situation. In applying this approach to Jewish education, Fox was influenced by the work of Mordecai Kaplan, the founder of the Reconstructionist movement, who drew on the pragmatist tradition to develop a concept of 'Judaism as civilization' in which the Jewish tradition is reworked to be responsive to the practical realities of life in the modern era.[17] Fox's pragmatism made him eminently suitable for cross-communal work as it never ruled out a particular kind of Judaism a priori, but rather emphasized that particular 'visions'[18] of Jewish life had to be tested through intense, context-specific practices of deliberation.

Fox was involved in the building and running of a number of key educational institutions in the development of the continuity agenda. He made his name through transforming the Conservative-affiliated Camp Ramah summer camp system in the 1950s and 1960s. Under Fox's tutelage, Camp Ramah took on a heavy emphasis on developing intellectual excellence and Hebrew learning. The organization was unashamedly elitist and challenging – in Fox's words 'Ramah was not a laid back place'[19] – and grew a committed leadership cadre for the Conservative movement and the wider Jewish community. Throughout his subsequent work, the nurturing of leaders, grounded in intellectually rigorous Jewish education, would be a priority. The institutions he helped to found in the US, including the Melton Research Center for

Jewish Education, the Teachers' Institute at the Jewish Theological Seminary and the Council for Initiatives in Jewish Education, were all elitist institutions guided by a constantly evolving vision of what a Jewish leader could and should be.

Fox was based in Israel for much of his career. In addition to being involved in a number of initiatives within the Israeli education system, he founded what was to become a highly significant institution within Jewish education globally. The Jerusalem Fellows programme was founded in 1983, initially under the tutelage of the Jewish Agency and then as part of the Jerusalem-based Mandel Leadership Institute. The programme, which still exists, takes a cohort of mid-career Jewish educators from around the world for an intensive programme (first three years, then two years and, since 2008, one year) of group and private study in educational philosophy, social policy, leadership, psychology and Jewish studies.[20] The usual condition for acceptance onto the programme is that fellows will return to the Diaspora and work in a leadership position within the Jewish community for a number of years. The programme's location in Israel was a part of the increasing tendency since 1948 to use Israel as a resource in the training and education of Diaspora Jews. Until 2008, the programme was conducted exclusively in Hebrew and many former fellows have subsequently returned to Israel after their required period of 'service' in the Diaspora.

Fox was heavily involved in the teaching and administration of the Jerusalem Fellows programme. Although his sometimes aggressive personal style was not to everybody's taste, he left his mark on the careers of dozens of Jewish communal leaders around the world. His influence was wielded through mentoring and conversation, with his conceptual vocabulary of 'vision', 'the practical' and other elements finding its way into the everyday work of the leadership of the Jewish community worldwide. Although he was particularly concerned with practices and institutions of formal and informal Jewish education, education was defined widely enough by Fox to become a kind of all-encompassing practice of self and communal transformation, embodied and accessed through the work of leadership. Through Fox's wide influence and the work of over two decades of Jerusalem Fellows graduates, the educational paradigm became an increasingly important part of the discourse of Jewish communal leadership worldwide.

The significance of Seymour Fox to the development of the continuity agenda was through his 'seeding' across the Jewish world of highly trained practitioners who were prepared and willing to lead processes of communal transformation. Fox's pragmatist agenda saw the work of transformation as constant and self-renewing through the process of deliberation. As such, Jewish continuity is a permanent agenda rather than one specific moment in Jewish history. The discipline of education within which Fox was situated provided a highly effective base for training leaders. The self-image of the leader as educator helps to inculcate an awareness of the necessity of persuasion and consciousness-raising in the practice of Jewish communal leadership. Pragmatism also engendered sympathy for the validity of different streams of Jewishness, producing leaders who were able to work across communal boundaries.

Fox's project may have been egalitarian in its openness to different streams of Judaism, but the emphasis on elites inevitably entangled the project in complex power relations. Fox's own deliberations tended to be confined to tight-knit networks of people with whom he found it congenial to work. Deliberation in Fox's sense had little to do with a democratic process of communal transformation. The contrast between Fox's ubiquity in Jewish leadership circles and his lack of profile to grassroots Jews created a problematic imbalance. Fox's teachings may have emphasized the importance of learning from practice, but his elitism brought with it a constant danger of the disconnection of Jewish educational leadership from the realities and concerns of grassroots Jews.

The emphasis within the institutions that Fox set up on personal development and transformation continues to produce exceptionally knowledgeable and skilful educators who go on to work in a highly diverse range of settings. Thanks in part to Fox's efforts, the communal status of Jewish education and its attractiveness as a career have been greatly raised, particularly in the US. Yet, however talented and educated, an elite is still an elite; authority grounded in deliberation and knowledge is still authority. Even if elites are a near-inevitable part of any community, the power that they reproduce must be closely monitored if it is not to produce disconnection from and marginalization of those who lack authority. The lack of attention in Fox's work and that of his disciplines to questions of power is therefore problematic. The *sotto voce* criticisms of Fox's personal style as often bullying and abusive – hardly ever made on record, but commonly voiced privately – are revealing.

In the US, Fox was highly influential but he was just one leader in a large community with a concomitantly large and diverse leadership and education sector. In the UK, where Jewish education had been accorded a relatively low communal priority for decades and where few of the most powerful communal figures were educators (or even in many cases had much Jewish education themselves), the impact that a small group of highly trained individuals could make was considerable. As we shall see in the next chapter, a number of the key figures in Jewish communal transformations in the 1990s and beyond were Jerusalem Fellows, and Fox himself played a role in advising some of these developments. When the United Jewish Israel Appeal (UJIA) launched the Ashdown Fellows programme for lay leaders in 2000, faculty from the Mandel School in Jerusalem taught and helped design elements of the programme. The sophistication and skill with which Fox-trained and influenced leaders helped to transform Anglo Jewry was, as we shall see, considerable. At the same time, the lack of attention to issues of power was also to raise problematic questions in this transformation.

The Fox model of communal transformation fitted well into the British Jewish communal hierarchy. Although not straightforwardly 'conservative' – indeed, the emphasis on upgrading the status of Jewish education and Jewish educational leadership represented a marked change to existing British Jewish communal priorities – it was ultimately a hierarchical model of communal leadership. The Fox model may have required the training of a new generation of technocratic leaders for British Jewry, but there was no change to the emphasis on centralized, disciplined decision-making.

During Jonathan Sacks's year in Israel in 1990–91, Fox was one of the people he discussed his ideas with. Through Fox he came to know a number of the people he would work with in his time in office, particularly Jonathan Kestenbaum who was to become the director of his office. Yet Sacks also had his differences with Fox and his acolytes:

> there was no way that we could do something as simple as what they eventually came up with. Which was something called *A Time to Act*. You know, it was not couched in terms of a drama that would speak to people who had hitherto had no interest in Jewish education, Jewish knowledge, Jewish culture – we had to do something much more dramatic.[21]

While Sacks was conversant with Fox's work and with theorists of Jewish education, he was not himself a technocrat like many of Fox's disciples. Rather, his model was a rabbinic one, in which a suitably popularized Jewish theology would inspire the British Jewish community. He is also an orthodox rabbi, with a proscriptive vision of what being Jewish should mean, even if he has aimed to be 'inclusivist' to individuals from different Jewish denominations. This is in contrast to Fox who worked pluralistically across denominational boundaries.

Orthodox outreach

In developing this more normative approach to Jewish continuity, Sacks could not fail to have been influenced by the development of orthodox 'outreach' by the ultra-orthodox Chabad-Lubavitch[22] sect in the post-war period. Whereas much of the ultra-orthodox world sets its face against the modern world and has little to do with other kinds of Jews, Chabad has made a determined effort to work with non-orthodox Jews.[23] Like other ultra-orthodox sects, Chabad was decimated by the Holocaust and its base was relocated to New York. The high post-war birth rate of Chabad members allowed it to rejuvenate itself under its seventh leader, Rabbi Menachem Mendel Schneerson, known as 'The Rebbe', who served from 1950 to his death in 1994 and is still considered as the leader of the movement.[24] Chabad grew to take on an important position within the Jewish world. The Rebbe was adept at communicating with those outside his own sect and he managed to garner considerable support for Chabad's activities from the non-orthodox and modern orthodox.

Following the Rebbe's example, thousands of *shlichim* ('emissaries') have been sent out to even the smallest and most remote Jewish communities worldwide. Shlichim are often based at centres known as Chabad Houses, of which there are over 2,500 worldwide and which in small communities may be the only focus for Jewish activity. The shlichim, who often take up their posts in their early twenties, are happy to work with practically anyone. They emphasize joy in observance and the intrinsic value of performing each individual *mitzvah* (religious obligation). The ultimate ideal might be to 'convert' Jews to greater levels of observance – and ultimately to become part of the Chabad world – but they recognize that this is not a likely outcome for most Jews. Although the Chabad community itself has a normative standard of what a Jew should be and should do, Chabad's approach to Jewish continuity is one of making Jewish practice easy and attractive enough so individual Jews are inspired to 'do more'. While some Jews are inspired to make a 'conversion' to Chabad-style orthodoxy, the numbers who do this are unclear and it is certainly not the 'usual' outcome of participation in Chabad activity.

Chabad has had a formal presence in the UK since 1948. There are forty-two Chabad Lubavitch Centres in England. Some Chabad institutions work within the Chabad community but most are focused on outreach. Chabad-trained rabbis also have a presence within the United Synagogue rabbinate and within student chaplaincy. Individual Chabad rabbis have made a big impact on the UK Jewish community. Rabbi Shmuley Boteach came to the UK from the US as a newly ordained, twenty-two-year-old rabbi in 1988. He set up the L'Chaim Society in Oxford University in the same year, which quickly grew into a popular institution that welcomed non-Jews as well as Jews, attracted by high-profile guest speakers including Mikhail Gorbachev and O.J. Simpson. Boteach quickly established a high profile within the Jewish and non-Jewish media, particularly following the publication of his book *Kosher Sex* in 1999, the year that he returned to the US.

The strategy of inclusivity, dynamism and well-funded, eye-catching events is not confined to Chabad. Other outreach organizations in the UK such as Seed, the Jewish Learning Exchange and Aish HaTorah are all dedicated to providing attractive opportunities for non-orthodox Jews to engage further in Jewish life. Seed and the Jewish Learning Exchange focus on providing adult study opportunities, and in 2008 the strength of their financial support was demonstrated as they both announced schemes to pay participants to study with them.[25] Aish HaTorah is an international organization whose ultimate aim is to produce *Baalei Teshuvah* – newly observant – Jews. Like Chabad, it is well funded and runs subsidized tours for young adults to Israel and other countries, with a *yeshiva* that overlooks the Western Wall in Jerusalem.

Unlike Chabad, Aish rabbis are less obviously identifiable as ultra-orthodox (most do not have long beards, for example). Aish HaTorah has been described as a New Religious Movement, similar to the Unification Church or Scientology, in its techniques to attract members and in its authoritarian and fundamentalist ways of retaining them.[26] At its various centres in the UK, it runs well-attended social events for young adults such as speed-dating and casino nights, and they take great care to ensure that Jewish issues are raised with subtlety. Aish HaTorah and similar organizations place Jewish continuity at the centre of their ideology. Indeed, Aish has claimed that research demonstrates that 97 per cent of the alumni of their 'Aish Fellowships' programme go on to marry someone Jewish.[27]

The various orthodox outreach organizations are located on the right wing of orthodoxy, and in the case of Chabad within ultra-orthodoxy. This can lead to tensions when these organizations work within mainstream communal structures. Some members of United Synagogue-affiliated communities have been unhappy with Chabad rabbis changing the 'middle of the road' ethos. In 2005, for example, Bournemouth Hebrew Congregation was divided over the appointment of a Chabad rabbi as acting minister of the community; he later resigned.[28] Chabad has also been accused of duplicating or competing with existing communal institutions, as with controversies over rival plans by Chabad and the local community to build a new *mikvah* in Cambridge[29] and plans to increase numbers of student chaplains outside the framework of the University Jewish Chaplaincy.[30] Jewish outreach organizations, particularly Aish HaTorah, are sometimes accused of being duplicitous in hiding their 'real' agendas. In 2007, for example, some parents at the Jewish Free School complained that outreach groups were covertly instituting an ultra-orthodox, rather than modern orthodox, Jewish ethos in the school.[31] In contrast to Chabad, whose ideology is publicly accessible, it is sometimes argued that Aish HaTorah has a covert right-wing agenda linked to the Israeli settler movement.[32]

Whether decried or admired, there is no doubt that Jewish outreach organizations have had an important influence on contemporary British Jewry. The global growth in size and confidence of right-wing orthodoxy in the post-war period has led to a situation in which it is increasingly focused on outreach to the non-orthodox, whereas centrist modern orthodoxy has retrenched into focusing on the needs of its own constituency.[33] In the UK, Miri Freud-Kandel argues that the moderate orthodoxy of the United Synagogue was eroded under the Chief Rabbinates of Sacks's predecessors Israel Brodie (1948–65) and Immanuel Jakobovits (1966–91).[34] Meir Persoff argues that the reputation of the United Synagogue for moderation was never deserved and demonstrates how the Chief Rabbinate frequently tacked to the right even in the nineteenth century.[35]

In the post-war period, the United Synagogue found it more and more difficult to retain its position as a centrist, relatively heterogeneous movement. The 'Jacobs affair', which ran from 1961 under Israel Brodie's Chief Rabbinate, demonstrated the United Synagogue's increasing inability to tolerate a more critical approach to orthodox theology. The rapid post-war growth and increasing self-confidence of ultra-orthodoxy provided a constant challenge to the United Synagogue's ideological compromises. As Freud-Kandel shows, the United Synagogue Beth Din under Jakobovits and Brodie became dominated by rabbis who were allied with right-wing orthodoxy. United Synagogue rabbis have, in recent decades, generally been trained by Israeli-based right-wing orthodox *yeshivot*, with Jews' College London having stopped its *semicha* programme in the 1990s.

By the early 1990s, right-wing orthodoxy had come to exert a powerful influence on Anglo Jewish mainstream orthodoxy. Jonathan Sacks, however, principal of Jews' College, with an impeccable academic pedigree, and presenter of the 1990 Reith lectures, was seen as a proponent of a confident modern orthodoxy. However, as we shall see in the next chapter, the influence of Jewish outreach organizations on Jewish Continuity, the organization he would set up, was considerable. In the 1990s and 2000s he has on a number of occasions cleaved to right-wing orthodox opinion on controversial issues. Sacks himself met the Lubavitcher Rebbe in his early twenties and has been highly complimentary about him and Chabad.[36] In 1996, Sacks adapted a collection of discourses by the Lubavitcher Rebbe, published by a Chabad publishing house. Compared to the financial chaos, poor leadership and insular attitude of the United Synagogue that was described in the Kalms report, it is no wonder that the Jewish outreach movements provided a beacon of hope: here was proof that Jewish continuity *was* possible.[37]

Jonathan Sacks's vision of Jewish continuity

At the start of his period in his office, Sacks set out his version of the continuity agenda in a series of papers entitled 'Studies in Renewal' which subsequently became the basis of *Will We Have Jewish Grandchildren?*.[38] He outlined his argument as follows:

> We are entering a new era in modern Jewish history. The past two hundred years have been dominated, for Jews, by two concerns: integration into the societies of Europe and America, and survival against the onslaughts of antisemitism and the Holocaust. The 1990s will be seen in retrospect as the beginning of a new phase, one in which the predominant concern became the continuity of Jewish identity against the background of assimilation and inter-marriage in the diaspora and secularization in the State of Israel.[39]

Sacks argued that Anglo Jewry was in crisis and was not paying sufficient attention to this crisis: 'American Jewry knows it faces a crisis of continuity. We do not, and that is the crisis.'[40] For Sacks, the crisis of continuity is to a large extent a problem of intermarriage in which 'more than half of young Jews are not marrying other Jews'.[41] This has resulted in a situation in which 'we are losing the collective will to live as Jews'.[42]

Will We Have Jewish Grandchildren? also sought to develop policies to tackle the crisis through Jewish education. Sacks attacked the low priority that the Anglo Jewish community affords to education, noting that the community raises a fraction of the money for education that it does for welfare and for Israel. In an appendix he outlined the structure of a new organization called Jewish Continuity that seeks 'to secure the future of Anglo Jewry by creating a vibrant community of proud, knowledgeable and committed Jews'.[43] In the next chapter we will examine how this organization worked in practice.

Conclusion: the continuity consensus

The willingness of Jewish communal leaders such as Jonathan Sacks in the 1990s to emphasize the insecurity of Anglo Jewry was not a strategy of despair, but a strategy intended to bring results. Drawing on research on Anglo Jewry and the work of Jewish leaders from around the world, the strategy of insecurity brought about a consensus within the mainstream British Jewish communal leadership on the importance of Jewish continuity and the ways of achieving it. Here we set out this consensus in summary form:

The Jewish community needs to survive outside the ultra-orthodox
The consensus assumes that the long-term continuity of ultra-orthodox Jewry is assured. By definition then, Jewish continuity is concerned with the survival of non-ultra-orthodox Jewry. The reasons why Jewry should survive are sometimes spelled out, sometimes not. For religious thinkers such as Jonathan Sacks, Jewish continuity may be justified in religious or theological terms. For others, Jewish continuity has more to do with Emil Fackenheim's '614th commandment' to 'not grant Hitler a posthumous victory'.[44]

Jewish continuity cannot be guaranteed
Since Jewish emancipation began in the eighteenth century, it has become increasingly possible for Jews to choose whether or not to stay Jewish. The post-war experience of Jews in the English-speaking world demonstrated – to those who bought in to the continuity consensus – that Jews could assimilate completely.

Neither does the state of Israel necessarily provide an answer, as many secular Jews in the country define themselves as Israeli rather than Jewish.

Jewish continuity requires continuity of Jewish community

History demonstrates that the idea that civilizations can die or disappear is misleading. Elements of Roman culture persisted long after the end of the Roman empire. Similarly, elements of Jewish culture can become part of the wider culture despite the assimilation of Jews – as in the mainstreaming of Jewish humour in the United States.[45] However, the continuity consensus considers that this form of continuity is insufficient. The continuity that is required is not simply that of particular elements of Jewish culture; nor is it the continuity of nebulous feelings of being Jewish on the part of individual Jews. The continuity consensus attempts to ensure the continuity of *Jewish community*, embodied in institutions and practices.

Jewish continuity requires Jewish families

The basic building block of Jewish continuity is seen to be the Jewish family, the site where Jewishness is reproduced. Intermarriage threatens the Jewish family and hence threatens Jewish continuity. There are differences within the continuity consensus as to how to respond to this issue. Some try to work with intermarried families to ensure children are raised Jewishly, some encourage conversion of non-Jewish partners, some would exclude intermarried families from the Jewish community (while perhaps accepting individual Jewish family members). There remains a consensus that it is desirable to encourage Jews to marry other Jews. The continuity consensus tends not to be proscriptive as to the preferred size of the Jewish family. The strikingly successful ultra-orthodox solution to Jewish continuity – to have large families – is generally not emulated and not seen as realistic for most Jews.[46] Although the continuity consensus may well be embodied in normative constructions of gender and sexuality, this is not always the case. Women may be seen as the 'guardians' of continuity or they may not. Modern sexual freedom may be decried or it may not. While the emphasis on marriage may be heteronormative, there are also gay and lesbian proponents of Jewish continuity.

Jewish continuity requires Jewish identities
Jewish continuity requires the development of particular kinds of
Jewish identities that are robust enough to survive within modern
society. For some this means an essentialized Jewish identity
whereas others are more flexible. The consensus lies in the importance of identity as a concept and as a focus for policy-making
and research.

The continuity consensus was an important adjunct to the communal
strategy of insecurity, whereby the demographic fears described in the
last chapter were brought to bear to legitimate the activities of the
communal leadership. As we shall see, however, putting the continuity
consensus into action was no simple matter and it revealed fundamental differences over what the British Jewish community is and
should be.

Chapter 4

From Jewish continuity to Jewish Continuity

On 17 December 1993, readers of the *Jewish Chronicle* were confronted with a striking double-page advertisement for a new Jewish organization.[1] The left-hand page depicted a queue of people lining up passively to walk over a precipice into a dark void. The right hand page was headed 'Today we'll lose another ten Jews' and began by outlining a set of shocking statistics:

> Every day for the last forty years, we have been losing ten Jews a day. From a community of around 450,000 in the 1950s, we now stand at less than 300,000.
>
> And it's getting worse, much worse. Today, more than half of young Jews are not marrying, are marrying out, or are leaving the community in some other way. Jews are not dying but Judaism and Jewish identity are.

The advert did not simply diagnose the crisis, it also proposed a solution:

> Young Jews are marrying out because they don't have enough good reasons not to.
>
> Which is where Jewish Continuity comes in. 'Continuity' is not just a synonym for education. Anything that enlivens and enriches Jewish life contributes to Jewish continuity. Formal Jewish education is part of that. But we also have to reach those at the very margins of our community and give them a way back to Judaism and Jewish life.
>
> Jewish Continuity will be an enabling body. We will not own schools or programmes but aim to resource them. We will provide

a communal vision and strategy that encompasses and goes beyond the many excellent programmes already in existence. We will commission research and monitor programmes to ensure effectiveness and accountability. We will have a bias toward outreach and innovation. We will operate on the basis that in most cases it isn't new, exciting buildings that we need but new, exciting people and ideas.

The advert made a bold claim for the importance of the new organization among communal priorities:

Jewish Continuity cannot succeed unless we as a community put it first, recognising its vital overwhelming urgency. It's not a matter of competing with other causes. For if we have no future we have no other causes.

The advert closed with a call to arms:

This is the moment of truth. Do we simply stand by and watch the gradual disintegration of the community? Or do we join battle to do more than just survive, but to thrive? We do have a future. Believe that. Let's fight for it.

Like the Chief Rabbi's 1991 induction speech, the advert announcing the formation of Jewish Continuity was intended to create a stir. Jewish Continuity was set up to do nothing less than change Anglo Jewry from a community that was close to moribund to one that would be active, dynamic and growing. As an aspiration for the British Jewish community as a whole this was far-sighted and idealistic, but as an ambition for a one particular organization it risked hubris. From the start, Jewish Continuity set itself up as a hostage to fortune, creating expectations that would be extremely difficult to fulfil.

The establishment of Jewish Continuity

The 1992 *Securing Our Future* report ('the 'Worms report') discussed in chapter 2 envisaged an umbrella body for Jewish education that would work to encourage collaboration and planning within the UK Jewish education field. Following his accession Jonathan Sacks was closely involved in taking the report's recommendations further. Through a series of discussions and consultations in 1992–3, he developed the nucleus of Jewish Continuity. Although it was the Chief Rabbi whose vision initiated the new organization, and the organization grew in embryo within his office guided by Sacks's chief executive Jonathan Kestenbaum, Jewish Continuity was to be organizationally separate from the Chief Rabbi's office. The Chief Rabbi's powers within Jewish Continuity were, notionally at least, substantial, with the ability to appoint trustees and change the constitution laid out in the articles of association.

Jewish Continuity's chair, Michael Sinclair, was a doctor and successful businessman in the private health industry who had become orthodox as an adult. He had little track record in Jewish community leadership and was approached by the Chief Rabbi following a chance encounter at an event at a nursing home for which Sinclair was helping to raise funds.[2] Jewish Continuity's founding chief executive was Clive Lawton. Lawton's ponytail and sandals, his charisma and reputation as an inspirational, sometimes iconoclastic educator marked him out as something of a maverick. At the same time, he had a track record of working in the Jewish community as education officer for the Board of Deputies and head teacher of King David School in Liverpool. Lawton had also worked as deputy director of the Liverpool Education Authority, giving him proven experience as a manager within a complex organization. Much of the board and trustees of Jewish Continuity were made up of well-known Jewish philanthropists and lay leaders, but the appointment of Lawton and Sinclair was intended to give a fresh approach to the work of ensuring Jewish continuity.

In 1994, it was announced that the Joint Israel Appeal (JIA) had agreed to fund the new organization. A joint statement by Sinclair and JIA President Sir Trevor Chinn explained that:

> The issues of Israel and Jewish Continuity are inextricably entwined: the Diaspora needs a strong Israel and Israel needs a vibrant Diaspora. This move confirms that link, removes the duplication of separate fund-raising efforts and further enhances both organisations.[3]

The JIA had been one of Anglo Jewry's main fundraising vehicles for Israel. For many years it had also funded British Zionist youth movements and their educational visits to Israel. By the early 1990s, some of the JIA's leadership had taken on board the views of prominent Zionists that funding for Israel could not come at the expense of support for Diaspora

Jewish continuity. One of JIA's most senior lay leaders in the early 1990s explains (speaking anonymously):

> When I saw the famous handshake on the White House lawn in, was it '93 or '94, I realized the Jewish world had changed. I thought it had changed and I turned out to be wrong because I thought our war against the Arabs had finished and it was now a war against assimilation that mattered ... I was convinced that JIA has got to get into that Jewish education in varied forms.[4]

While this leader paints JIA's desire to support Jewish Continuity as a positive, forward-thinking act, both Michael Sinclair and Clive Lawton saw an element of fear in JIA's approach. Sinclair explains:

> The JIA approached Jewish Continuity because they were concerned that the emphasis of funding within the community would switch from funding for Israel to funding for Jewish education ... So there was a real concern, as articulated to us, that the JIA was going to wither on the vine of UK Jewish philanthropy. So they wanted to do a deal with us, and the deal that they did with us was that they guaranteed our funding.[5]

Clive Lawton puts it even more directly:

> The JIA was clearly afraid of what we were doing. Afraid of us as an organisation and the size of it and the danger that Continuity would seize some of its territory and some of its donors and so on.[6]

The money given to Jewish Continuity was to be substantial – from £3 million in 1995 rising to £5 million in 1997. The JIA funding gave Jewish Continuity freedom to concentrate on fulfilling its mission rather than fundraising. However, this freedom was much more apparent than real, as the JIA would inevitably retain an interest in Jewish Continuity's activities; Jewish Continuity would to some extent remain accountable to the JIA even if their ability to influence it was limited.

Much of Jewish Continuity's time was spent attempting to clarify its goals and priorities. The organization brought over key figures in the development of Jewish continuity worldwide to assist in its deliberations, including Seymour Fox (discussed in the previous chapter), Jonathan Woocher of the Jewish Education Service of North America (quoted in the previous chapter) and Steve Greenberg of the US-based National Jewish Center for Learning and Leadership (CLAL).

In December 1994, Jewish Continuity published its 'Strategic direction, 5 year goals and 1995 programme'.[7] Jewish Continuity's mission was explained as 'to secure the future of British Jewry by creating a vibrant community of proud, knowledgeable and committed Jews'. It set out an agenda of targeting key personnel in the heart of the community and working in collaboration with exciting communal frameworks, but also reaching out to younger age groups and women in the community and enabling 'initiatives in fields that other pre-existing organisations cannot or have not pursued ... that might enhance the prospects of Jewish continuity'.

Jewish Continuity's organizational structure was complicated. The Chief Rabbi served as president, there was a board of trustees and an executive board. A small professional staff serviced Jewish Continuity's activities which were structured through the work of eleven lay 'task groups', each covering priority areas as various as 'Arts, Media and Culture', 'Formal Education' and 'Leadership Development'. Great emphasis was placed on recruiting lay people onto the task groups who had not previously had much experience in Jewish community activities, many of whom were in their twenties. Although this infused the organization with enthusiasm and new ideas, the sheer number of task groups, the ambition and lack of clarity as to their aims and the lack of experience of many of their members in Jewish community politics also created confusion. Further, there was an imbalance between the membership of the board of trustees and executive board, which were overwhelmingly made up of senior lay and professional leaders, and the task groups, which had a much younger profile.

Even if much of Jewish Continuity's time, at least in its first years, was spent in trying to set priorities and establish itself as an organization, during its short existence it did have a number of notable achievements. It ran a popular Hebrew Reading Crash Course. It developed a series of eye-catching resources for use in Jewish assemblies in non-Jewish schools. It commissioned and disseminated research on Jewish single young adults.[8] It was instrumental in beginning the process that would lead to the establishment of Pikuach, a cross-communal body that inspected the Jewish studies component in Jewish schools. It gave bursaries for the career development of Jewish educators and community professionals. The Jewish Community Allocations Board gave money to a huge range of initiatives and institutions across the community (in 1994/5 £1,002,606 in eighty-two grants).

The problem of pluralism

Jewish Continuity was an ambiguous organization – an organization set up by an orthodox Chief Rabbi that aspired to work with the whole community. Its mission 'to secure the future of British Jewry by creating a vibrant community of proud, knowledgeable and committed Jews' covered the entire community. It was funded by the JIA, a body that received funds from members across the communal spectrum. All this clearly implied that Jewish Continuity would work with all streams of Judaism. Yet how could the Chief Rabbi be the head of an organization that would fund non-orthodox Judaism? There were in fact precedents for this. The Jewish Educational Development Trust (JEDT), set up by Chief Rabbi Immanuel Jakobovits in 1972, received funding from the JIA, had some progressive trustees and assisted in the development of non-orthodox Jewish day schools, although it refrained from funding their Jewish studies activities. But Jewish Continuity was a much more ambitious organization than the JEDT, and the recruitment of non-orthodox trustees and board members created an expectation that the organization would not be under exclusive orthodox control.

Jewish Continuity decided not to fund activities that involved participants breaking *Shabbat* or *kashrut* as defined by orthodox *halacha*. This decision was maintained in the programmes that Jewish Continuity ran, and indeed the organization sometimes went further in distancing itself from non-orthodox Judaism. For example, the Hebrew Reading Crash Course was not run in non-orthodox synagogue premises. At the same time, however, the Jewish Community Allocations Board was set up specifically to provide an independent 'arms-length' body that would respond to funding requests from across the community with no *halachic* preconditions.

Many of the problems that Jewish Continuity faced stemmed from the Chief Rabbi's own complicated relationship with pluralism. The idea that a chief rabbi could be representative of all of Anglo Jewry was only tenable when the community was relatively homogeneous and there was some sort of consensus that it was advantageous to have a prominent representative to the majority non-Jewish population of the UK. As Miri Freud-Kandel has argued,[9] the success of the post has depended on the post holder having sufficient strength of personality to build bridges across the community while being staunch in his own orthodoxy. The last time this was even remotely possible was during the time of Chief Rabbi Hertz (1913–46), who was a strong advocate for modern orthodoxy while still validating non-orthodox marriages and attending non-orthodox events. The aspiration of the Chief

Rabbinate to lead all of Anglo Jewry has become increasingly fictional in the post-war years.

As Geoffrey Alderman[10] points out, by the time of the accession of Jonathan Sacks, at least a third of British Jews did not recognize the authority of the Chief Rabbi. Even within orthodoxy, whilst the Chief Rabbi is titular head of the United Synagogue, the United Synagogue is administered separately through a different office, with a separate chief executive. Religious authority within the United Synagogue is maintained through the Beth Din – again administered through a separate office – whose members tend towards ultra-orthodoxy.

Sacks tackled the problem of what he saw as the fragmentation of the Jewish people in his 1993 book *One People?*.[11] He argued that whilst there had always been considerable variation in Jewish practice, the ideological division of Jewry is a post-Enlightenment phenomenon. This fragmentation conflicts with the traditional value accorded to Jewish peoplehood:

> Ideologically, Judaism recognizes neither denominations nor sects. Sociologically it is currently organized into just those forms ... The fragmentation of peoplehood, brought about by modernity, cannot simply be acceded to without deep conflict with inescapable Jewish values.[12]

For Sacks, Jewish peoplehood is a fundamentally religious category:

> The idea of 'one people' is a religious commitment that cannot be given coherence in any other frame of discourse ... That idea belongs not to nature, race, or politics, but to covenant.[13]

Sacks used *One People?* to develop a theological and philosophical defence of Jewish peoplehood. He was implacable that orthodoxy could not be pluralist, that it could not recognize the validity of other Judaisms. At the same time he also rejected 'exclusivist' attitudes to non-orthodox Jews that would treat them as non-Jews. Instead he posed 'inclusivism' as an alternative to both pluralism and exclusivism, which he defined as 'the belief that the covenant was made with a people, not with righteous individuals alone'.[14] Sacks's inclusivism would include all Jews within it, whilst not recognizing the denominations of which they might be part.

True to his inclusivist ideology, he included individual Jews from all denominations as lay and professional members of Jewish Continuity without recognizing the denominations to which they belonged. Yet Sacks's conception of inclusivism was not always understood, and he raised expectations that were impossible to fulfil. This misunderstanding helps to explain the shock and anger that followed a number of incidents in his first few years in office in which he was accused of acting in a narrowly orthodox manner.

In 1995, Sacks did nothing to challenge the United Synagogue Beth Din ruling that orthodox rabbis should not attend the cross-communal Limmud conference. Despite attending Limmud before assuming office, he has never attended since then, though a small number of United Synagogue rabbis have. In the same year he attacked the Masorti movement in an article in the *Jewish Tribune* (which primarily serves the ultra-orthodox community), stating that Jewish Continuity programmes would be 'based on Torah' and that he would prevent money from Jewish Continuity reaching the Masorti community.[15] As a result of the article, Sacks was heavily criticized by non-orthodox leaders and Stanley Kalms, Sacks's mentor and supporter at Jews' College, publicly distanced himself from him.[16]

The most damaging controversy in which Sacks was implicated occurred in August 1996 after the death of Rabbi Hugo Gryn, UK Reform Judaism's most respected rabbi, a Holocaust survivor and an important media figure. Sacks refused to attend the funeral, causing offence to the non-orthodox community, but under pressure he did subsequently speak at a memorial service for Rabbi Gryn (focusing only on his contribution to interfaith relations) and visited his widow privately. These actions attracted public and private criticism from Union of Orthodox Hebrew Congregations (UOHC) and Federation rabbis. Sacks responded to this criticism in a private letter to Dayan Padwa, head of the Beth Din of the ultra-orthodox UOHC, which was subsequently leaked[17] to the *Jewish Chronicle* and published on 14 March 1997. The letter, written in rabbinic Hebrew, spoke of Sacks's 'pain' in being obliged to praise 'one of those that destroy the faith', but argued that it was necessary for him to speak at the memorial in order for the Reform movement not to be granted a propaganda victory and to forestall the possibility of a rival Reform Chief Rabbinate. The publication of the letter caused enormous controversy and deep offence to the non-orthodox community and undermined Sacks's credibility in working cross-communally.[18]

While Sacks's day-to-day role in Jewish Continuity had begun to diminish almost from its founding, his personal association with the organization was such that when his reputation was damaged Jewish Continuity's was too. Jewish Continuity was formed in his image and Jewish Continuity shared the ambiguities of his position on pluralism. The difference between inclusivism as Sacks understood it and pluralism as it was understood by non-orthodox and other sections of the community was not widely recognized. Further, the difference between the Allocations Board – which did work cross-communally – and the main organization – which was much more restricted – was not clear to everyone. In any case, even in its own terms, one could argue that Sacks's inclusivism was imperfectly practised. He repeatedly proved anxious to placate the exclusivist ultra-orthodox even though he had notionally rejected exclusivism in *One People?*. Geoffrey Alderman has argued that 'The fate of Jewish Continuity proved to be the most spectacular example of Dr Sacks's inability to reconcile his own inclusivist agenda with the exclusivist agendas of his orthodox opponents.'[19] It is certainly true that his very public attempts to keep the ultra-orthodox onside alienated the non-orthodox and that the resulting distrust extended to and damaged Jewish Continuity.

It is hard to imagine how anyone could have expected that an organization that was funded by cross-communal money via the JIA, that involved non-orthodox leaders and that saw itself as responsible for the overall fate of Anglo Jewry could ever have excluded non-orthodox organizations without creating uproar. Here it is worth examining a substantial excerpt of Keith Kahn-Harris's interview with Michael Sinclair.[20]

> Keith Kahn-Harris: And in the initial phase, when it was still being set up and thought about, what was the vision for how cross-communal issues would be dealt with?
>
> Michael Sinclair: This was an initiative of the Chief Rabbi, and it was an Orthodox organization. It was going to, all of its programmes and activities were going to be available to everybody. So, in that sense, it was cross-communal in that it was, I mean it was for everybody, and so it was available equally to all Jews, but it was an Orthodox organization that would be run in accordance with the Normative Judaism; like principles of Normative Judaism.
>
> KK: Now that sounds very clear that ….
>
> MS: He was absolutely crystal clear.
>
> KK: So how then did it happen that it became a source of such confusion, from going from being an orthodox organization to one that also gave to progressive …?
>
> MS: All I can tell you is, and I can quote what the leading Reform rabbi said to me, and that was that they had picked this to be a background to which to have a fight with orthodoxy.

Michael Sinclair's version of the Jewish Continuity story then is that of an orthodox organization compromised by political pressure. Had Jewish Continuity been set up as a clearly orthodox organization that attempted to involve the entire community then it may have looked something like Aish HaTorah or other existing outreach organizations. Such organizations do attract non-orthodox criticism but they are sustainable in their own terms. Yet it is hard to imagine that Jewish Continuity could ever have ended up conforming to this model. From the very outset it aspired towards engaging in strategic planning and such activities go far beyond the outreach model and necessitate the ability to work cross-communally if they are to be effective.

In contrast, Clive Lawton emphasizes the cross-communal nature of Jewish Continuity:[21]

> What I found very attractive about Jewish Continuity was in all its public articulation it was cross-communal. It was divergent, it was interested in different ways of doing things, it was not insistent on a definition of how one ought to be Jewish or any of those things, it was just interested.

Over a decade since the events in question, two of the leading figures in Jewish Continuity continue to reproduce the ambiguities inherent in the organization. Jewish Continuity was too orthodox to be fully acceptable to non-orthodox denominations; it was too inclusive to be fully acceptable to the right-wing orthodox. The Chief Rabbi's involvement eventually undermined Jewish Continuity's cross-communal credibility. As a former member of Jewish Continuity's board (speaking anonymously) put it:[22]

> Unfortunately, the role of the Chief Rabbi, who was a big part of the inspiration of it, just didn't work politically and such an organization ... has got to be able to work with all elements of the community. And because the Chief Rabbi was the President of Jewish Continuity, it had difficulty with the other elements in the community.

One of the paradoxes – perhaps even the tragedy – of Jewish Continuity was that it would not have existed but for Jonathan Sacks, but that Sacks's own position effectively made it impossible for the organization to work effectively.

Between communal conservatism and communal innovation

As its opening advert demonstrated, Jewish Continuity sought to challenge and even shock the community into doing things differently. At the same time, it also sought to work with existing institutions, and in its deal with the JIA its fate was inextricably tied into a large, conservative communal bureaucracy. To manage these tensions would require exceptionally deft leadership skills.

Even if the trustees and board members of Jewish Continuity incorporated many of the key figures that would need to be brought onside, inevitably much depended on Michael Sinclair and Clive Lawton. While both had experience of management, they were also recruited because they stood somewhat outside the existing communal hierarchy. Sinclair was a particularly unknown quality for many in the Jewish community and according to him this led to some suspicion:

> [The president of a major Jewish charity] said to me, I don't know who you are, I've never met you at a dinner party, you're not on the Jewish social networking circuit, you know, who are you to come along and run an organization … in this way? I've never met you before. He actually said, who are your friends? So I mentioned my ten friends, my ten closest friends, well actually I probably only got to seven, and he said, well, I don't know any of them either.

Continuity's efforts to bring in new volunteers also led to concerns from the communal hierarchy. As Sinclair puts it:

> I remember the Chairman and Chief Executive of JIA and Jewish Care and JNF all saying, you've got all these people making decisions about how money's spent, we don't know who they are, who are they?

Sinclair further emphasizes the importance of empowering people in Jewish Continuity:

> It was an organization that we deliberately ran, established, to operate in a way that was not the standard way. We didn't pay lip service to young people; we empowered young people. We didn't pay lip service to giving people the opportunity to suggest and run with projects; we actually made that happen.

Similarly, Clive Lawton talks about Jewish Continuity using the language of 'liberation':

> I think that in something as unknown, as un-understood, like the Jewish Continuity agenda, the right thing to do was try lots of things and see what worked. All of my instincts are about liberating people's capacities and letting a thousand flowers bloom and all of that now is talk.

The organization, and in particular the Allocations Board's commitment to 'try lots of things and see what worked', led to grants being given to some highly unconventional projects. One example that was frequently mentioned by Jewish Continuity's detractors was a modest grant that was given to a resident of Argyll in Scotland to create a community network for the few other Jewish residents there. Another was a grant given to a Jewish puppet theatre.

Among Jewish Continuity's employees were a number of young and enthusiastic workers who were given considerable initiative and responsibility.[23] In Jewish Continuity's open-plan office there was a strong sense of cohesion and vitality among its small staff and its larger cohort of volunteers. Every day the staff ate lunch together, usually accompanied by vigorous debates and discussions. The tight-knit nature of the professionals and key lay people could create the impression of a secretive and arrogant clique. Accusations of bad management dogged the organization from the beginning. Clive Lawton accepts that he and Jewish Continuity did make a distinctive impression, but rejects accusations of bad management:

> Jenny Fraser wrote in the *Jewish Chronicle* in the last few months of Continuity, where she made a contrast between visiting the smart, snappy, be-suited offices of the JIA to the happy, clappy, easy-going, relaxed offices of Jewish Continuity. And there's no doubt about it that my own personal appearance had a huge impact on people's understanding of what Jewish Continuity was about, and whether that was a political error or not, who cares really? But it angered me as an article because in actual fact Jewish Continuity was infinitely more tightly organized than the JIA.
>
> Jewish Continuity could tell you where every penny was spent; the JIA certainly couldn't. Jewish Continuity could show you the job contracts and the appraisal processes of its staff; the JIA definitely couldn't. There are all kinds of ways in which we could demonstrate that we in fact are [sic] much more professionally run, much more organized organization than the JIA.

The problem of management within Jewish Continuity was similar in some ways to that of pluralism. Just as there was considerable naivety about the possibility of maintaining an inclusivist ethos using pluralist funding, so there was considerable naïveté about creating an anti-establishment organization using establishment funding.

The end of Jewish Continuity

The decision to accept funding from the JIA for Jewish Continuity was a fateful one. The lack of financial independence meant that Jewish Continuity was accountable to people who did not necessarily share its vision or buy into its distinctive way of doing things. The size of Jewish Continuity's executive board and board of trustees, together with the JIA's similarly large and complex management structure, put the organization under a constant spotlight from a diverse set of critics. More generally, the high expectations that Jewish Continuity encouraged across the community meant that much of the community felt that the organization should be accountable to them. The only kind of leader that could possibly meet these demands would have been a careful one, committed to achieving consensus, yet Lawton and Sinclair were not consensus-formers of this kind.

It was not long before the JIA began to claim that it was having trouble raising funds for the organization and would not be able to meet its financial commitments. Clive Lawton argues that the JIA acted cynically against Jewish Continuity's interests:

> Well, within a year [of the JIA-Continuity deal], they were saying we can't raise this money, it's just not possible. We've tried and Jewish Continuity has got such a bad reputation and nobody wants to give and there's nothing we can do, so I'll tell you what we'll do, we'll give you half a million pounds or we'll give you three-quarters of a million pounds. I'll tell you, we'll pay just for these things and those things but not those other things. And this, for the last eighteen months of the three years of Jewish Continuity's life, was a continuing and obsessive issue at the Board. Should we go public, should we expose this cynicism?

Michael Sinclair also blames the JIA for the funding crisis:

> The deal that they did with us was that they guaranteed our funding. It was not conditional on funding on non-normative Judaism projects. It was not conditional on that; that was never raised. It was only after that that happened. And that happened, I believe, as a defensive move on the part of the JIA to maintain their position within the hierarchy of Jewish philanthropy in the UK.

The crisis in funding led Jewish Continuity to carry out a protracted review process, commissioning market research and consultancy from

Jonathan Woocher and from the Mandel School, culminating in Professor Leslie Wagner being commissioned in October 1995 to 'review the functions, structure, governance, religious complexion and funding of Jewish Continuity; and to recommend a range of options for its restructuring and operations to enable it to continue to improve its service to the community'. Wagner's report, *Change in Continuity* was completed in March 1996. The review identified (politely) many of the criticisms that Jewish Continuity faced in its early years. Wagner reported that Sacks's criticism of the Masorti movement in early 1995 was seen by many as precipitating the current crisis.[24] Sacks's article:

> was claimed to be a significant factor in the reluctance of some donors to the JIA to agree to donations to Jewish Continuity. That in turn resulted in an actual 1995 out-turn of JIA allocations to the organisation substantially less than had been anticipated when the two organisations had planned the funding arrangements for the first three-year period.[25]

Even before the article, Jewish Continuity's work in 1994 had been criticized. The Jewish Continuity Strategy Document of December 1994 was censured by many 'on the grounds ... that it did not define goals, priorities or the means of achieving them' nor set out accountability or monitoring procedures.[26]

There were competing views as to what sort of organization Jewish Continuity should be, but none thought that the current structure was acceptable. There was criticism from competing groups across the religious spectrum that it was not responsive to their respective needs and concerns. The religious complexion of Jewish Continuity, and in particular the role of the Chief Rabbi, was a particularly vexed question, with disquiet from both orthodox and progressive voices. The organization was seen as aggressive, aloof and as having taken on too many tasks at once. It was accused of having spent money too freely on too many disparate groups, with too little focus. The decision-making processes 'were felt to be "opaque"'[27] and 'a number of criticisms were directed at what was claimed to be a lack of communal experience and understanding of the community by some individuals in the top echelons of the organisation'.[28] Decision-making was seen to be carried out by a small group, without due consultation with either of the boards or the wider community. Wagner reported that 'the emphasis on marginal Jews has led to criticism that it is ignoring the mainstream'.[29] There was, in short, 'a unanimous view that there had to be changes to the present organisation and its decision-making process'.[30]

Jewish Continuity in the end transformed into a cross-community strategic planning and development agency, the option favoured by the report's advisory group, which included Sinclair, but the process which led to this happening was a messy one. In 1996 and the first months of 1997, complicated political manoeuvres took place behind the scenes, while Jewish Continuity continued to function. In 1997, Jewish Continuity merged with the JIA, creating an organization called the United Jewish Israel Appeal (UJIA). The details of the negotiations that led to the merger remain obscure, but it is clear that there was a consensus that neither the Chief Rabbi nor Clive Lawton would have a role in the new organization. Lawton was one of the few immediate casualties of the merger. Michael Sinclair (as vice-chair), many of the lay volunteers and board members and most of the paid staff[31] survived the transition. Initially, most of the JIA staff also remained, with the notable exception of the Chief Executive Alan Fox.

Lawton himself blames Seymour Fox, amongst others, for his redundancy. Lawton recalls meeting Fox towards the end of 1996 prior to his visit to consult with Jewish Continuity:

> I went to Israel to meet Seymour Fox. The first thing he said to me was, 'Clive, I do want to be absolutely clear about this, I'm not coming over to be your executioner.' Well at that point I knew I was doomed. This completely surprised me. But what became clear was that Seymour Fox ... had been incandescent that Jewish Continuity had not appointed a Jerusalem Fellow as its chief executive.

Whether or not Lawton's account exaggerates Fox's importance, Jonathan Ariel who was eventually chosen to replace him and manage the transition to the new organization *was* a Jerusalem Fellow and so was Jonathan Kestenbaum, the new chief executive of UJIA. Ariel had in fact been courted for several months by a number of key figures in Jewish Continuity (including Lawton) before finally agreeing on a job description.[32] Ariel had been involved in the Habonim youth movement and worked in Jewish education in the UK before emigrating to Israel. Prior to joining Jewish Continuity/UJIA he was working for Melitz, an organization that works on informal education for Diaspora and Israeli youth. Jonathan Kestenbaum had also grown up in the UK and was head of Bnei Akiva, the orthodox Jewish youth movement, before emigrating to Israel. In 1991, he was head-hunted by Jonathan Sacks to be the chief executive of his office and as such was involved in the early days of Jewish Continuity.

The dramatic difference between Jewish Continuity and UJIA was in how they were perceived politically. Whereas Jewish Continuity was embroiled in endless political struggles from its inception, UJIA has rarely been involved in public controversies. The team of Ariel as head of renewal and Kestenbaum as chief executive lasted until Ariel's return to Israel in 2001 (to take up a post at the Mandel School) and proved highly successful in creating and stabilizing the new organization. Clive Lawton gives due credit to them for doing so:

> It's very clear to me when Jonny became the first head of Continuity, of the renewal side of things, I've said very publicly that he managed the politics of it far better than I did; he was a Mandel man, he knew the politics, I didn't. And they finessed the denominational thing far better than I did, but that's not least because the Chief Rabbi stepped back, which I had always wanted to happen and it didn't. And I admire what the UJIA has done with the Continuity agenda since.

Since leaving Jewish Continuity, Clive Lawton has pursued a portfolio career, but has never again managed a Jewish organization. He was the part-time head of Limmud for a number of years but, as we shall see later in this chapter, Limmud was not run by a large professional staff and his role was mostly to mentor and act as a figurehead to promote the organization. He remains a popular and inspirational educator in the Jewish community.

The legacy and significance of Jewish Continuity

The Jewish Continuity episode raised strong emotions in its protagonists, but readers might be forgiven for dismissing it as a matter of arcane micropolitics. Certainly the significance of who had responsibility for which decision is now limited, but the organization raised crucial questions that go beyond the parochial interests of a small group of communally involved British Jews. Most importantly, if the goal of Jewish continuity, as described in the previous chapter, is to stimulate a complex and far-reaching change in the attitudes and behaviours of thousands of people, is this goal amenable to being institutionalized within a particular organization? Can Jewish continuity be 'led' by an organization? If so, who should lead the organization that leads this process? And what vision of Jewish continuity should be promoted?

Jewish Continuity's answers to these questions were never entirely clear and, given the short period in which it functioned and the resource constraints it faced, there were limits to what it could achieve in terms of quantifiable outcomes. When those involved in Jewish Continuity are asked to identify its achievements, the answers tend to emphasize less measurable outcomes and stress the less tangible changes that were central to the Jewish Continuity view of Jewish continuity. In his interview, the anonymous board member stressed Jewish Continuity's stimulation of 'innovation': 'I think to a great extent, the Jewish community got fossilized and I think it needed something like Continuity with innovative ideas ... and I think Jewish Continuity encouraging innovative thinking.'

Michael Sinclair argues that Jewish Continuity was:

> wake-up call, catalyst, cold shower ... it's very difficult to change the attitudes of a whole community. Change the agenda, get people thinking. Look, you know, if I can caricature it, there was a time when the most important thing, as far as the Jewish community was concerned, was which dinner parties you got invited to and how close to the top table you sat at a communal event, or whether you were on the board of management of your local synagogue, even if you didn't go to the synagogue more than a few times a year. That had to be changed ... It couldn't be changed slowly; it had to be changed dramatically. It had to be changed quickly ... there had to be really shock tactics to get people to sort of pay attention and realize that hey this is really serious, we have to do something about it.

For Clive Lawton:

> I think Continuity taught the community to be a bit more irreverent ... it was a time when the irreverent were able to take over a bit and push a bit and encourage the possibilities of people trying things.

Lawton also stresses Jewish Continuity's empowerment and career development of a cohort of people that have come to assume leadership positions in the Jewish community:

> a huge number of the people who were brought forward in Continuity days ... and given a sense of how things could be done, a different understanding of the way things could be, and I think those people are having an impact too. And I think, despite the politics of it, I think empowerment was not given a bad name.

The birth of UJIA: from continuity to renewal

UJIA at a stroke got rid of the cross-communal issues that had dogged
Jewish Continuity. Like the JIA, UJIA was a cross-communal organization that raised and donated money from and to all sections of the
community. UJIA had a far broader agenda than the JIA, however, treating
Anglo Jewry as important, fundable and not as an afterthought. UJIA
remained strongly Zionist, but it was very much a 1990s Zionism,
committed to the mutual survival of Diaspora and Israeli Jewry. The new
organization embodied this twin commitment in the concept of 'rescue and
renewal' – the traditional Zionist mission of 'rescuing' vulnerable Jewish
populations and resettling them in Israel, twinned with the renewal of
Jewish life in both the UK and Israel.

The use of the term 'renewal' helped to distance UJIA from Jewish
Continuity. As Jonathan Ariel, UJIA's first Director of Renewal, explains:

> Jewish continuity with a small c: I couldn't figure out for the life of
> me why anyone would think that would be a good idea, because my
> own experience in Jewish life would lead me to say it's an entirely
> intelligent thing on the whole to want to leave the portals of the
> Jewish community because it's bloody boring, you know, and it
> seems to be filled with guilt and nothing else. So why anyone would
> wish to continue such a thing, I couldn't figure out.

'Renewal' therefore encapsulated what Jewish Continuity stood for while
freeing UJIA from the associations that had weighed down Jewish
Continuity.

In contrast to the considerable publicity and big plans with which
Jewish Continuity announced itself, UJIA's first years were characterized
by a cautious approach, ensuring that all the key funders and stakeholders
were kept on board. It took until 2000 for the UJIA fully to outline its
mission in a document called 'The Next Horizon'[33] which set out UJIA's
three-year plan. The document argued that: 'The renewal of British Jewry
is dependent upon all British Jews constantly striving to build a meaningful
Jewish life for themselves, their families and their community.'[34] This
statement, while fairly anodyne, implies that Jewish renewal is a process
of empowerment in which individual Jews work towards a fuller Jewish
life. As such, the statement was perfectly in keeping with the style of
Jewish Continuity. The mechanism through which this empowerment
was to happen was principally educational: 'We believe that by improving
the quality of Jewish educational opportunities throughout the community,

British Jews will generate and promote effective Jewish communal renewal.'[35]

While Jewish Continuity had treated Jewish education as a major part of its work, the centrality of education in UJIA's vision was a significant departure from the Continuity approach. But what was most significant in 'The Next Horizon' was the clarity with which UJIA's role in the community was defined. The organization was to be a catalyst for renewal, driven by a threefold 'vision of change', produced by:

1 Nurturing visionary frameworks.
2 Mobilising effective leadership.
3 Cultivating upbeat culture.[36]

The emphasis on vision and leadership clearly owed a lot to the Mandel School and the work of Seymour Fox discussed in chapter 3. Again, 'cultivating upbeat culture' was something on which Jewish Continuity had laid great stress, even if UJIA was much more explicit and clear about it.

In some ways UJIA was to resemble a think tank, a source of expertise and advice. While it would provide financial support to projects across the community, UJIA would not be a service provider. Whereas Jewish Continuity never ruled out any area of intervention a priori, UJIA was much more focused on accomplishing a more limited agenda effectively. It sought out areas and modes of intervention – educational leadership, educational tours of Israel, informal education, research and development – in which the resources of the organization could produce the most far-reaching changes in the wider Jewish community.

UJIA's work was facilitated by its strong connections to international networks of Jewish policy-making, particularly to Fox and the Mandel School. Like Ariel and Kestenbaum, Ariel's successors Shalom Orzach (2000–2002) and Michael Wegier (2002–2007) had been Jerusalem Fellows. Jonathan Boyd, UJIA's director of research and development from 2000 and 2003, also went on to become a Jerusalem Fellow. From the outset UJIA stressed research and strategic planning. The organization commissioned Keith Kahn-Harris and Steven M. Cohen to conduct research on 'moderately engaged' British Jews which was intended to guide UJIA's planning process.[37] In 2002, UJIA organized a major conference that brought together some of the leading figures in British, Israeli and American Jewish education in order to expose the communal leadership to the latest trends in Jewish educational thinking.[38]

Much of UJIA's work was accomplished through nurturing Jewish leadership. It initiated or hosted considerable activity in this field, such as a bursary programme to fund the studies of Jewish communal professionals, the Adam Science training programme for young lay leaders, the Ashdown Fellows programme for communal professionals (which in its early years included heavy input into its curriculum from the Mandel School), and the Florence Melton adult education programme in the UK. The organization was also highly supportive of the Limmud conference (see chapter 6), funding subsidies for young adults to attend. All these programmes were considered effective in developing an educated and motivated Jewish leadership and laity.

As a self-described 'critical friend', the UJIA also worked quietly to implement changes within other Jewish organizations, particularly those concerned with Jewish education. Most notably, it worked to assist the process through which the venerable but ailing Jews' College, previously a higher-education institute and orthodox rabbinic seminary, was restructured into the adult education institute the London School of Jewish Studies in the early 2000s.

UJIA became expert in using relatively modest amounts of money, together with the considerable expertise it had at policy-making and community transformation, to place itself at the centre of British Jewish life. By funding leadership development and becoming a stakeholder in most Jewish organizations that had some educational element, UJIA built up a position of influence within the community. This was particularly the case in the field of 'informal education'. In the 1990s, the term 'informal education' was increasingly commonly used to describe the work of Jewish youth organizations.[39] While the JIA had long been involved in funding Jewish youth work due to the Zionist orientation of most Jewish youth movements, UJIA made a systematic effort to intervene in the *content* of Jewish youth work. UJIA's subsidizing and coordination of Israel tours, and its development of the Jewish Life Education Centre as a hub of expertise in Jewish youth work, gave it considerable influence on practices that touched the lives of thousands of Jewish young people every year.

In theory, British Jewish youth movements represent a cross-section of Zionist views, from the secular socialism of Habonim to the orthodox religious Zionism of Bnei Akiva. Most of the youth movements have connections to global movements with roots in Israeli Zionist factions. Despite these different ideological stances, in recent decades the movements have come to be increasingly interconnected. From independent, even antagonistic organizations whose primary purpose was to prepare their members for immigration to Israel, in the post-1948 period the youth movements came to be increasingly integrated into a consolidated infrastructure whose emphasis was as much on developing the Jewish identities of their members as it was on *aliyah*. Important in this process was the Jerusalem-based Machon L'Madrichei Chutz La'Aretz (Institute for Youth Leaders from Abroad), the Jewish Agency-run institute that runs post-eighteen year-long training programmes for the movements.

While the programmes differed according to the youth movement, the Machon ensured a core youth movement identity and effectively reduced the autonomy of the movements. The Jewish Agency came to take a more central role in the youth movements and in the UK, UJIA/JIA worked to place youth work within an overarching framework. This system certainly increased the quality of leadership within the movements and ensured economies of scale. However, it also potentially threatened some of their autonomy and ideological distinctiveness. For instance, in 2004, UJIA announced that it was withdrawing funding from Beitar, the right-wing Zionist youth movement, due to its focus on 'political' activities such as street demonstrations.[40]

Whereas Jewish Continuity funded a great variety of initiatives, UJIA was much more suspicious of funding anything that could cause controversy. The aggressively political approach of Beitar could not only have threatened UJIA's charitable status (charities are barred from funding 'political activities'), but could also have attracted the kind of controversy that bedevilled Jewish Continuity. In the same way, UJIA has been very wary of funding arts and cultural activities. Such activities could attract the criticism that Jewish Continuity's funding puppet theatre had. Arts and culture – like the political activities of Beitar – is also hard to monitor and often ambiguous in its 'effectiveness'.

UJIA's lack of enthusiasm for funding Jewish arts and cultural activities ties in with its move away from Jewish Continuity's approach to funding. Jewish Continuity's Allocations Board acted as an innovations fund to consider applications for projects and institutions whose 'outcomes' were often unclear and which would inevitably have a high failure rate. The Allocations Board was wound down following the merger and no UJIA innovations fund took its place. Indeed, a proposal to establish one made by a senior UJIA professional in the mid-2000s was turned down by the board.[41] Similarly, UJIA did not inherit Jewish Continuity's focus on Jews on the margins of the community. Instead, the emphasis was on the 'moderately engaged' and on improving the quality of existing communal institutions and projects. In short, UJIA's approach was cautious, emphasizing value for money, and effectiveness.

To a large degree, this caution was necessary as, following the deal with Jewish Continuity, it was hard to keep some of the funders on board.

Jonathan Ariel emphasizes the work that UJIA needed to do to ensure that donors trusted it:

> Going round talking to donors in the first few months, it was clear as daylight that they just didn't trust it. And so ... it was necessary to have a level of discipline about what was happening and how it was going to happen.

The long years of work to create an organization whose funders would support a renewal agenda paid dividends. UJIA has never been implicated in the kinds of controversy that embroiled Jewish Continuity. The most dramatic example of the care which UJIA has taken to ensure this can be seen in a decision of 2008 to support projects in Israel intended to benefit non-Jewish Israelis. This decision *could* have been controversial, but it passed with virtually no comment.

From charisma to bureaucracy

In many ways, the contrast between the Jewish Continuity and UJIA approaches can be understood using Max Weber's classic distinction between charisma and bureaucracy as modes of authority.[42] Jewish Continuity emphasized flexibility and innovation, and was reliant on Clive Lawton and Michael Sinclair's abilities to motivate and inspire. UJIA emphasizes effectiveness, strategic planning and careful adherence to bureaucratic procedures. That is not to say that Jewish Continuity had no bureaucracy and UJIA has no charismatic leaders, but the emphasis in both organizations is highly distinctive. The flexibility of Jewish Continuity allowed those who were close to the leadership considerable freedom to innovate – but those outside this circle felt excluded. UJIA's carefully structured bureaucracy allowed for much more clarity and equality in approaching the organization – but this could be disempowering, especially when reproduced in partner organizations. UJIA had clearer lines of accountability internally, but these were opaque from the outside. To give one example, UJIA did not develop a website until the end of 2002. When the website was set up, it was clearly tailored to encourage donation and publicize UJIA activities. It gave very little information as to who worked for the organization and how it worked. It publicized its bursary scheme for Jewish educators but gave no information as to how to apply for one.

To sum up, Jewish Continuity sought – sometimes successfully and sometimes unsuccessfully – to transform the community through stimulating grassroots creativity and innovation; UJIA sought to transform the community through improving its leadership and organizational management. The UJIA's attention to the needs of donors, at times, particularly in its early years, may have meant that its freedom to take risks was compromised, but it ensured that the organization remained viable. The continuity agenda pursued by Jewish Continuity was transformed into a cautious, but far-reaching process of Jewish renewal. UJIA proved that it was possible to enshrine the transformation of Anglo Jewry within the activities of a Jewish organization. As such, it proved to be the vanguard of what we shall call a *renewal agenda* that transformed the community in the 1990s and 2000s. In the next chapter, we will examine the renewal agenda, arguing that the top-down, bureaucratic, leadership-oriented approach of UJIA has typified the agenda more broadly, in contrast to the bottom-up cultural innovation we will explore in chapter 6. We will also show that the insecurity strategy became muted but was nonetheless present in the renewal agenda – a presence which, as we will see in chapter 7, was more explicit in a parallel development, the fight against 'the new antisemitism'.

Chapter 5

The Renewal Agenda

The continuity consensus in the early 1990s was deeply enmeshed in the strategy of insecurity. The first attempts to develop policies to ensure Jewish continuity were frequently marked by urgency – even in some cases panic – to do *something* to address communal decline. The story of Jewish Continuity demonstrates that this urgency could generate exceptional creative accomplishments, but also chaotic debacles. As the 1990s progressed, unfocused responses to the continuity consensus came to be replaced by a more measured and bureaucratic approach pioneered by the United Jewish Israel Appeal (UJIA). As policies to ensure Jewish continuity began to be put into practice, the strategy of insecurity as a motivator for change became less important as the drive to change the community took on a momentum of its own.

By the late 1990s, a great variety of initiatives were under way across the community that shared the approach of UJIA, whether through the organization's direct influence or parallel to it. Although the continuity consensus provided the ideological bedrock for these initiatives, they reflected the establishment of a more practical, policy-oriented agenda. This is what we call the *renewal agenda*. The renewal agenda reflected a consensus that had developed among mainstream Jewish communal institutions as to how continuity could be achieved practically. As with the continuity consensus, the principles behind the renewal agenda were rarely directly articulated. In this section we summarize these before going on to demonstrate how they were operationalized.

Jewish renewal requires Jewish education.
The principal means of ensuring the renewal of the Jewish community was Jewish education. There is no consensus as to what Jewish education is and what its goals should be. There is a consensus that education is broader than simply schooling, although Jewish schooling is an important area to develop.

Jewish institutions need to be transformed.
Jewish institutions need to be comprehensively transformed and reinvigorated to ensure they are up to the challenge of renewing the Jewish community. Most Jewish institutions, while they may have served the Jewish community well in the past, have not managed to stem the tide of assimilation.

Jewish renewal requires outreach.
Jewish renewal cannot be guaranteed simply through the renewal of Jewish communal institutions, but needs to reach out to individual Jews. Individual Jewish identities are also in need of renewal and education. There is no consensus as to the target of outreach. For some, those on the periphery of the community are most 'at risk' and should be targeted, whereas others would confine outreach work to those who are already engaged with the community.[1]

Jewish renewal requires effective leadership.
Effective Jewish education and effective outreach require leaders who are knowledgeable and capable of enthusing other Jews. The development of such a leadership necessitates effective training and support to ensure that careers in Jewish leadership become prestigious and lucrative enough to attract the brightest and the best.

Jewish renewal requires planning.
Changes will not 'just happen'; they require careful planning. Where possible resources should be pooled, knowledge shared and efforts consolidated. Even where communal divisions exist, cross-communal bodies should ensure that strategic planning takes place on a communal basis.

In the next sections, we will show how this renewal consensus played out on the ground, in two key sites of Jewish community: synagogues and Jewish schools.

Renewal in action: synagogue movements

Synagogues are clearly vital in any strategy to ensure Jewish renewal. However, aside from the theological differences between synagogues, synagogues differ widely in size, location and management structure. Even within an individual synagogue, organizational politics are complicated, with rabbi, lay board members, volunteers and 'rank and file' members often having conflicting priorities.[2] The various synagogue umbrella movements provide both an added complication in synagogue life and a powerful means of instituting a process of renewal through their constituent synagogues. Individual synagogues relate to the different umbrella movements with varying degrees of autonomy. The United Synagogue has traditionally exerted a large amount of centralized control over its constituent synagogues, whereas Reform Judaism, Liberal Judaism and the Assembly of Masorti Synagogues are much looser organizations.

As we saw in the previous chapter, Stanley Kalms's, 1992 report on the United Synagogue was devastating in its indictment of the organization's outdated and inefficient practices and its financial incompetence. The organization clearly needed to be 'renewed' in multiple ways. Writing from the viewpoint of the late 2000s, what is striking is what was *not* renewed. The United Synagogue's ambiguous leadership structure, in which authority is shared between the Chief Rabbi, a lay president, a professional chief executive and the Beth Din, remains unreformed. The United Synagogue's religious affiliation also remains ambiguous: an organization leaning towards modern orthodoxy has a Beth Din that leans towards ultra-orthodoxy with a membership (and much of its lay leadership) that tends not to be orthodox in practice. The United Synagogue's attitude to women's participation was only partially reformed – women are still unable to act as chairs of United Synagogue congregations and are unable to lead services. Jewish renewal within the United Synagogue did not involve an attempt to reform what kind of organization it was, but to make the organization as it was work.

For much of the 1990s, the United Synagogue's principal task was addressing the precarious financial position that the Kalms report had highlighted. This necessitated a process of drastic cuts that weakened the United Synagogue's ability to develop new programmes but saved the organization financially. The process of renewal within the United Synagogue was, in the first instance, a quiet and unglamorous one to ensure the organization's financial and professional viability, embedding procedures and methods of governance that would provide a basis for the future. The bloated organizational structure was reformed, slimming down the number of lay leaders. Some of the Kalms recommendations were followed, others not, but the United Synagogue gradually became a less centralized and more professional institution that was better able to address the challenge of the renewal and continuity of Jewish life in Britain.

The United Synagogue benefited from broader processes of renewal within the orthodox community. Chabad rabbis became a common presence in United Synagogue pulpits as did rabbis who had spent time in other outreach-oriented *yeshivot*. As Jews' College declined as an institution design to train modern orthodox British rabbis, United Synagogue rabbis were increasingly likely to have received *semicha* or at least to have studied in the booming and self-confident Israeli *yeshivot*. These tended to be more right wing ideologically than the United Synagogue had traditionally been. The rightward drift of the United Synagogue rabbinate has often been criticized and the disjuncture between the organization's rank and file and its leadership became more acute, but synagogues clearly benefited from the drive of this new, outreach-attuned rabbinate.

The increasing self-confidence of Anglo Jewish orthodoxy was also manifested in the development of the North London *eruv* in the 1990s.[3] An *eruv* is a symbolic boundary allowing orthodox Jews to carry out certain activities on the Sabbath and festivals within it that would otherwise be prohibited, such as pushing pushchairs and carrying certain kinds of objects. Building the *eruv* required only the erection of a number of poles linked by wires but it occasioned fierce hostility from some of the existing Jewish population of the area. The objections, principally that the area would become dominated by orthodox families, demonstrated a deep anxiety about public and visible signs of Jewishness. The determination to build the *eruv* and to undertake highly public lobbying for it demonstrated the self-confidence of right-wing orthodoxy in Britain. After years of planning disputes, the *eruv* was opened in the early 2000s, and other *eruvim* have been built and planned in other areas.

New ideas and new energy entered the United Synagogue from a number of sources. Through much of the 1990s, the Encounter conference saw hundreds of people attending lectures by prominent orthodox figures. The ailing Jews' College withdrew from *semicha* programmes and academic degrees and was reborn in the early 2000s as the London School of Jewish Studies, becoming a successful centre for adult education. In the 1990s, the Chief Rabbi's office became a source of new ideas and renewed practice. During a period in which the United Synagogue struggled to ensure its financial future, the autonomy of the Chief Rabbi helped to sustain the organization. The office pioneered experimental programmes in adult education in synagogues and developed what would become the United Synagogue's community development department. Whereas the Chief Rabbi's ability to institute new programmes across the community died with Jewish Continuity, he was much more successful in encouraging renewal and innovation within the organizsation of which he was the religious leader.

Part of the Chief Rabbi's work was to try to install self-confidence in the United Synagogue. His 1995 book *Community of Faith*,[4] published to mark the United Synagogue's 125th anniversary, provided a robust defence of the organization. Sacks's argument was that United Synagogue was an inclusive organization and that its largely non-orthodox membership was actually a sign of its strength. Whereas in most parts of the Jewish world, orthodoxy has either become a minority or an exclusive, isolationist movement, in the UK the United Synagogue has never been so explicitly ideological and this has allowed it to be an inclusive organization. The United Synagogue's current vision statement reflects this ideological coyness: 'The United Synagogue strives to be a modern and united family of communities with members connected to vibrant Jewish life and Torah values.'[5]

Many would argue that in the post-war period, for all its notionally inclusive ethos, the United Synagogue has effectively been hijacked by right-wing orthodoxy as embodied by its Beth Din.[6] Nonetheless, even when the standards by which *halachic* decisions are made have become more and more stringent, the United Synagogue remains the largest synagogue movement and still manages to include a membership of which only a small minority are right-wing orthodox.

The United Synagogue has placed great emphasis on community. The organization's community development department was during the 1990s and 2000s one of its most active sections. In 2001, for example, it held a community conference at Wembley Conference Centre involving over a thousand members. The emphasis on community was also demonstrated in the most ambitious project of the United Synagogue in the 2000s, Tribe, which began in 2003. Tribe attempts to tie the United Synagogue's young people into the community, with activities for persons from birth until the age of thirty. These activities are not necessarily religious or educational, including summer schemes and holidays with the emphasis on fun, sport and adventure. Tribe is specifically designed for the needs of United Synagogue members who are not orthodox in practice and would be suspicious of activities designed to ensure conversion to an orthodox lifestyle. As with its community development department, the United Synagogue has come to recognize that creating a sense of ownership and membership in relation both to itself and the wider community is at least as essential as ensuring orthodox practice.

The paradoxical quality of the United Synagogue remains unaddressed and the decisions of its Beth Din are often bitterly contested, particularly regarding conversion and Jewish status issues. Despite this, Saul Zneimer, chief executive of the United Synagogue between 2001 and 2007, argues that the organization has renewed itself since the dark days of the early 1990s:

> The most noteworthy change I think is a change in attitude and outlook towards the brightness or the bleakness of the future of the United Synagogue. And one of the things I wanted to try and do was just as the UJIA had transformed itself and was perceived and became perceived as being absolutely essential to the future of the United Kingdom's Jewish community and that there was some credibility of that, we wanted to do the same for the United Synagogue.[7]

Non-orthodox synagogue movements also attempted to renew themselves. This process was inextricably linked to their fight for status within UK Jewry. As Meir Persoff has demonstrated,[8] the Chief Rabbinate and the organs of orthodox Judaism in the UK have, since the formation of the first reform synagogue in 1841, fought a continual rearguard action to prevent the spread of non-orthodox Judaism. By the early 1990s, the Liberal, Reform and Masorti movements, while still representing a minority of British Jews, were strong enough to make a concerted effort to assert their desire for recognition both within and without the community. Much of this work involved political struggles, as over the funding of non-orthodox projects by Jewish Continuity.

For Rabbi Tony Bayfield, head[9] of the Movement for Reform Judaism, the ethos of Reform Judaism is closer to that of the majority of British Jews than that of the United Synagogue. Bayfield believes that the Reform movement, long a minority, should be the mainstream Jewish movement:

> what you've seen over the last decade is the Reform Movement coming in from the margins, presenting itself as a major component at the heart of the mainstream of British Jewry and latterly working ever more closely with the Liberal and Masorti Movements to establish the fact that for the 80 per cent of the community that is not fundamentalist that is non-orthodox or secular, and the recognition of the secular component is very important, we can reach and facilitate reaching the majority of the community, the 80 per cent.

Part of the attempt to mainstream the movement involved the 2005 'rebranding' of the Reform Synagogues of Great Britain as the Movement for Reform Judaism:

> the move in 2005 to becoming the movement for reformed Judaism was not just a cosmetic change but a profound change in our aspirations to move from being a trade association for synagogue *machers* to being a movement for synagogues, schools, other institutions, to which, with which rank and file membership could identify and feel inspired by because of its values, its ideology, its theology.

The process of renewal within Reform Judaism has been turbulent. The movement is much less centralized than the United Synagogue with much less influence over what happens in its member synagogues. As late as the early 2000s, a few Reform synagogues in the UK still did not allow women to hold the Torah scroll at services, even though gender equality had become an important commitment in most other Reform synagogues. Following the 1995 *Missing Generation* report, discussed in chapter 2, a major focus of its work has been on developing provision for students and young adults. By the early 2000s, the movement had raised funds for a number of student chaplains and field workers, together with a dedicated young adults worker. Yet by the mid 2000s funding had dried up for all these positions as the movement tackled a serious funding crisis.

The crisis was in part due to overly rapid expansion of student and young adult work, together with the initiation of the highly ambitious Living Judaism programme in 2000. Living Judaism was modelled on an

American programme, Synagogue 2000, that sought to transform Reform and Conservative synagogues into more attractive, welcoming and stimulating environments for 'baby boomers' and 'generation Xers'. The process of synagogue transformation was piloted in two Reform synagogues but, despite some achievements within those synagogues, the programme never had enough funding or support to be rolled out to the rest of the Reform movement.

The process of transformation within Reform Judaism took another turn in the mid 2000s. Along with the rebranding came a new set of commitments encapsulated in what became known from 2005 as the '20 20 Vision'. Tony Bayfield describes the transformation as:

> our new philosophy of shifting the focus from organizations and the primacy of the needs of the organization ... and understanding that what we are about is trying to meet the deepest needs, lacks, wants of people out there ... So that led into a much more rigorous insistence on being demand-led and trying to understand what is the demand out there.

This focus on being 'demand led' was stimulated by a new piece of research published in 2006 on eighteen-to-thirty-five-year-olds who had previously been Bar/Bat Mitzvahed in a Reform synagogue.[10] The report emphasized that Jewish young adults were positively inclined towards Judaism but that they lived within 'shifting networks of friends and family' that were resistant to institutionalization. Rather than treat young adults as a 'problem' to be dealt with by developing programmes that would 'draw them in', the report suggested that community should be thought of as 'made up of emerging and shifting connections which arise to meet the needs, concerns and aspirations of the people involved'.[11]

Unlike the 1995 'Missing Generation' report, the 2006 report was light on policy recommendations and instead suggested an approach to young adults that would be based on listening and responding to their needs, offering choice, encouraging connections and networking between Jewish individuals. This approach was followed by Jeneration, the relaunched students and young adults section of the movement. Jeneration plays down its connection to the Reform Movement in its publicity material and actively publicizes events run by other organizations as well as putting on events that encourage networking and connection between Jews of whatever denomination.

There are, however, some possible contradictions in the transformation that Bayfield, Jeneration and those in the upper echelons of the

Reform Movement are attempting to stimulate. The implication of Jeneration is that membership of the Reform Movement is less important than the broader 'Jewish journey' that individuals undertake. However, the rebranding of the Reform Movement and the attempt by Bayfield and others to develop a cohesive message involves an attempt to facilitate its becoming a leading Jewish religious institution in the UK. Bayfield argues:

> I think we are moving towards the possibility of joint Reform, Liberal and Masorti leadership of the 80 per cent of the community who are non-orthodox. It'll take a generation ... I think that we will have the majority of synagogue affiliations by 2020.

This desire for institutional growth is potentially contradictory to the post-denominational, post-institutional vision, embodied in Jeneration, of being responsive and flexible to individual needs. It is based on the observation that the majority of members of the United Synagogue are not themselves orthodox and that the progressive movements are closer ideologically to what most British Jews believe. The United Synagogue, however, has made great efforts to recover from its early 1990s moribundity and if the future is really a post-denominational one in which Jews 'pick and choose' from whichever institution suits their needs at a particular time, then there is no reason that the United Synagogue should not be one of those institutions.

Liberal Judaism (which also changed its name from the Union of Liberal and Progressive Synagogues in the mid 2000s) has undergone a less dramatic but still significant process of renewal. Its Tent programme for young adults is similar to Jeneration in developing a pluralistically minded informal community. The Masorti movement, while still small, has also become a significant force in Anglo Jewry since the early 1990s, expanding the number of Masorti synagogues and developing a niche as a home for the intellectual elite of the non-orthodox world. Its success in the latter regard is embodied in the fact that a number of senior professional leaders in Reform Judaism are members of New North London synagogue, which under Rabbi Jonathan Wittenberg has become a hub of educational innovation. The three non-orthodox movements issued a 'statement on communal collaboration' in September 2008, pledging to work closer together on matters of mutual interest and concern.[12]

Even while the main synagogue movements have undergone processes of renewal, the impact on individual synagogues and their members is much less clear. Synagogue life in the UK awaits a dedicated study. It is clear though that serious attention has been paid to transforming the resources that the movements offer to their members. This effort has been motivated by the discourse of insecurity that characterized the 1990s – the sense of a community losing members, of declining rates of observance and growing outmarriage – but it contributed to the increased vibrancy and self-assertion of the mainstream community, both orthodox and progressive.

Renewal in action: education

The second key site of Jewish renewal has been education. If in synagogues the discourse of insecurity has been a muted presence in the renewal agenda, in the field of education it has played a more pronounced role. The most noteworthy indication of the increased importance of education in the British Jewish communal agenda lies in the dramatic increase in the numbers of Jewish day schools and the pupils attending them. The 2008 document *The Future of Jewish Schools* by the Jewish Leadership Council's Commission on Jewish Schools[13] reported that more than 26,000 Jewish pupils attended Jewish day schools compared to fewer than 13,000 thirty years before. Although a considerable proportion of this increase came from the Haredi population, the commission reported that non-Haredi enrolments had also increased 30 per cent in the previous decade and that 60 per cent of Jewish school-age children attended Jewish day schools compared to 25 per cent thirty years before. This increase is even more significant given that it occurred during a period in which the numbers of school-age non-Haredi Jewish children has been declining. The number of Jewish day schools has also risen, including outside the Haredi sector, and existing schools have expanded. Thirty-two new primary and secondary schools were established between 1992 and 1999 alone, of which twenty-five were Haredi.[14] Most importantly, three large new Jewish secondary schools have been founded in the last two decades: Immanuel College in Bushey in 1990, Yavneh College in Borehamwood in 2006 and the Jewish Community Secondary School in Barnet in 2010. The latter is particularly significant as it provides the first Jewish secondary school in the UK not to be under the auspices of an orthodox religious authority and specifically designed to be cross-communal.

In some respects, the expansion of Jewish day schools is the form of Jewish renewal with the longest history. In 1971, Chief Rabbi Jakobovits launched the Jewish Educational Development Trust (JEDT) which raised funds for and itself established a number of new schools in the 1970s and 1980s. As noted in chapter 4, JEDT provided a foundation for Jewish Continuity in terms of personnel and priorities. JEDT's founding report and statement of intent, *Let My People Know*, argued that:

> Although much has been achieved in the sphere of Jewish Education ... Anglo-Jewry is still confronted with a grim prospect for the concluding decades of this century. The defection of our young people, a growing rate of intermarriage and the dropout rate of our uncommitted threaten an unprecedented crisis. Inadequate Jewish education clearly lies at the root of the problem and only a thorough and mature understanding of Judaism, through a greatly improved Jewish education, can provide a solution.[15]

By the 1990s, a firm consensus had been established among communal leaders that Jewish day schools were essential to Jewish continuity. Helena Miller has argued that:

> The major stimulus for the remarkable growth of the full-time school system is the conviction by Jewish communal and education leaders that the continuity of Jewish life is dependent on the perpetuation of intensive and rich patterns of Jewish education.[16]

This conviction has also been demonstrated in the US, where the number of Jewish day schools grew from thirty-nine schools in 1944 to over seven hundred in 2000.[17] Further, there has been a pronounced growth in day schools built by other religious minorities in the UK for very similar reasons.[18]

Miller argues that one of the main reasons why full-time schooling became the focus for development was that the system of part-time supplementary Jewish education, generally carried out within synagogues (*chedarim*) was seen by Jewish educators to be of generally poor quality. In contrast, full-time schooling allows for much more time to be spent on Jewish studies. However, the reason parents have sent their children to Jewish day schools in increasing numbers is not necessarily the Jewish education that their children may receive. Rather, given the largely middle-class nature of the Jewish community, Jewish day schools offer an educational environment that is consistent with their aspirations. As Miller puts it:

Not all parents send their children to Jewish full-time schools because they want a vibrant and strong Jewish education. By the end of the last century, an increasing number of families became dissatisfied with wider society, its values and mores. Jewish state-aided schools are perceived as populated with a more homogeneous pupil intake than the equivalent state-aided non-denominational schools. Traditional values and a religious ethos suggest security and protection from the harsher aspects of life in 21st-century Britain.[19]

The growth in Jewish day schools raises issues regarding the place of Jews in multicultural Britain. The growth of single-faith schools was actively supported by the Labour government and increasing numbers have been brought within the state school system.[20] This has led to concerns that children may become ghettoized and that multicultural Britain may fragment into mutually hostile camps. The Accord Coalition, formed in 2008, has campaigned against state-funded schools discriminating on the grounds of religious belief. Its chair, Rabbi Jonathan Romain, is a prominent Reform rabbi and at the time of Accord's formation he was chair of the Reform Assembly of Rabbis (although Romain received little support from the Reform movement for his stance). Whether or not state-funded faith schools have a negative impact on community cohesion in general, it is certainly true that outside the Haredi community, the strong aspirational rather than religious motivation of many Jewish parents who send their children to Jewish day schools suggests that there is little separatist religious fervour behind the increasing numbers who do so. That said, a 2002 Institute for Jewish Policy Research (JPR) report argued that the quality of multicultural and inter-faith religious education was poor or non-existent in Jewish secondary schools.[21] This situation may be to a limited extent mitigated by the Board of Deputies' Shared Futures project, launched in 2008, which creates links between Jewish and other faith schools.

The majority of Jewish schools, including all secondary schools with the exception of the Jewish Community Secondary School, take their religious guidance from orthodox authorities. Outside the Haredi sector and a few right-wing orthodox schools, there is usually a gap between the orthodox ethos of the schools and their largely non-orthodox practising pupils. Complaints are sometimes made that those in charge of Jewish education are at the right-wing end of orthodoxy and push their agenda aggressively.[22] In over-subscribed Jewish schools under orthodox auspices, entry is restricted to those whose Jewish status is beyond *halachic* reproach (under-subscribed orthodox Jewish schools have been obliged to admit children of non-orthodox converts for some time). Some of those whose children have been excluded on *halachic* grounds have complained bitterly about their treatment. One such complaint led, in 2009, to what may prove to be a significant change in how Jewish day schools work.

In 2007, an eleven-year-old boy whose mother was a progressive convert – making him non-Jewish in orthodox eyes – was refused entry to the Jews' Free School (JFS) in London. The father of the boy subsequently took JFS to court to try to prove that they had racially discriminated against his son (known as 'Boy M'). In 2008, the High Court ruled in favour of JFS, but an appeal court judgment in June 2009 found that JFS had discriminated against the boy, arguing that the admissions criteria were racially, rather than religiously, based. The Chief Rabbi attacked the ruling, arguing that it painted the UK Jewish community as 'racist'.[23] Tony Bayfield also condemned the ruling on the grounds that, while the Reform Movement deplored JFS's entry policies, it was for the Jewish community to decide the grounds on which pupils were admitted into Jewish schools.[24] Following the ruling, JFS appealed to the newly formed Supreme Court who heard the case at the end of October 2009. The Supreme Court announced their upholding of the appeal court judgment on 16 December 2009.[25] The court was split five to four in favour of the judgment, which stressed explicitly that JFS had not been found guilty of racism.

The JFS case demonstrated the inadequacies in the categorization of minorities in the UK. The case hinged on whether JFS's entry criteria were racially or religiously based. The original judgment claimed the criteria were the latter as *halachic* definitions of Jewish status were religious in character, whereas the appeal claimed they were the former in that *halachic* status was grounded in notions of racial/ethnic descent. The appeal court ruled that admissions criteria for Jewish schools could only be based on a 'faith test' (which was not defined). The ruling also prohibited Jewish schools from basing admissions on synagogue membership, as this was seen as indirect discrimination in that eligibility for synagogue membership is based on Jewish status. This element of the ruling affected non-orthodox schools as well as orthodox in that some of them gave priority to members of non-orthodox synagogues in admissions.

Ironically, the ruling has the potential to make Jewish schools much more exclusive than previously. In basing entry requirements solely on Jewish status, JFS, like many other orthodox-run Jewish schools, required no test of Jewish belief or practice, making for a diverse school population in terms of Jewish belief or practice, although homogeneous in *halachic* status. If Jewish belief becomes the main criteria for entry, this raises complex questions as to how to measure it and particularly what role Jewish practice might play. In preparing its response to the appeal court ruling, the United Synagogue, as the religious authority for JFS and other schools, reiterated its commitment to maintain the 'orthodox inclusivism' of their schools. As Simon Hochhauser, president of the United Synagogue, declared in an article in the *Jewish Chronicle*: 'We will therefore set the religious practice bar as low as possible, with the aim of excluding as few as possible.'[26]

At the start of September 2009, JFS announced its amended entry procedure for 2010. For a child to be treated as a 'priority applicant', a 'certificate of religious practice' would need to be completed. The certificate provided information on synagogue attendance, previous Jewish education and other previous Jewish communal activity, all of which had to be certified by the relevant communal bodies. Positive responses to these questions were totalled on a 'points' system with three points sufficient for priority applicant status. Significantly, it was not specified that religious practice had to occur in an orthodox context – attendance at non-orthodox synagogues met the criteria. Other Jewish schools, including non-orthodox ones, were obliged to institute similar points-based entry schemes. On 18 September 2009, the *Jewish Chronicle* reported that synagogues were struggling to cope with the extra administrative load that recording and certifying attendance had brought.[27]

In setting out these procedures JFS made it clear that they had had no choice and that they would change the procedures if future appeals were successful:

> The School very much hopes that the Supreme Court will allow its appeal, so enabling the School to revert to the admission policy which the School considers to be appropriate, proportionate and necessary for it as an Orthodox Jewish school: that is, to give priority to those children who are Jewish according to religious principles stated by the Chief Rabbi, irrespective of the extent to which the applicants and their families practise their Judaism.[28]

Further, it made clear that the certificate of religious practice was no guarantee of Jewish status: 'It should be noted that the certificate of religious practice does not confirm that the child is Jewish in accordance with Jewish law.'[29]

'Boy M' was in fact admitted to JFS in September 2009 and during the Supreme Court hearing the school undertook not to remove the child even if their appeal was unsuccessful. In reality, of course, neither the category of race/ethnicity nor that of religion is satisfactory to describe what Jewishness and Jewish identity are, as the religious and ethnic dimensions are intertwined. In some ways, the debate provides an ironic echo of Anglo Jewry's historic deferential anglicization in which the communal leadership insisted that Jewry was nothing but a 'community of faith'. In the JFS case, the school defended their definition of who is a Jew as a faith matter. In rejecting this defence, the appeal court forced JFS to embrace a definition of faith that they found uncongenial. The case revealed JFS, the United Synagogue and the Chief Rabbi to be simultaneously stubborn, principled and hopelessly naive. Had they quietly admitted the boy in question as a 'one-off', they could have avoided legal action without necessarily setting a precedent regarding entry requirements. Instead, by refusing to compromise one iota on admissions they incurred an expensive court case that they should have known had an uncertain outcome. Further, they were forced to admit 'Boy M' whatever the final outcome of the appeal, thereby losing the case whatever the final judgment. Many commentators and communal leaders were highly critical of the Chief Rabbinate and the United Synagogue for provoking far-reaching changes to schooling throughout the community and for creating a situation in which 'who is a Jew' judgements can be made outside the community.[30]

The case demonstrates that the ambiguities of faith, race and ethnicity raised by definitions of Jewishness cannot effectively be encompassed in the world of legal clarity. By forcing a legal ruling to be made, creative ambiguity was replaced by crude legalism that both orthodox and many non-orthodox dislike. The lack of sophistication in thinking about such issues is revealing of a section of Anglo Jewry that has never fully accepted that it is an 'ethnic' community in multicultural Britain – a failure that has resulted in the community being ill-protected from assimilation in an earlier moment, and ill-prepared for the debates arising from the JFS case today.

The December 2009 Supreme Court judgment was followed by attempts to broker a compromise way forward. The Board of Deputies attempted to put together a coalition of religious umbrella groups to push for an amendment in the law in response to the ruling. This putative coalition fell apart in early January 2010 when non-orthodox leaders refused to countenance a return to a situation in which orthodox schools could exclude the children of progressive converts. The Rabbinical Council of the United Synagogue issued a statement that reflected the acrimony generated by the JFS affair, arguing that: 'It is untenable that a movement that has been around little more than 100 years should seek to impose their standards on a community that has remained faithful to the tenets of

Jewish tradition for nearly 3500 years.'[31] Partially in response to this statement, two United Synagogue rabbis known for their moderation argued that it was time to 'accept reality' and work to change the law while accepting the necessity of admitting those who are not *halachically* Jewish according to orthodox definitions.[32] These rabbis were in turn criticized by others on the Rabbinical Council of the United Synagogue,[33] demonstrating the continuing controversy over pluralism in the orthodox world.

The Supreme Court judgment and its aftermath occurred while proofs were being prepared for this book. At the time of writing (February 2010), there have been no resignations or apologies within the United Synagogue or Chief Rabbinate. Jewish school admission remains based on religious practice, a situation unsatisfactory to many across the community. How and whether this situation might change in the future remains unclear. The wider impact on Jewish schooling is also unclear, although it seems likely that orthodox schools will become more pluralist with regard to *halachic* status and that synagogues will increasingly be 'used' by Jewish parents to establish credentials for school admissions.

Whatever the future holds for Jewish day school admissions, the frequent disjunction between school and parent ethos raises questions about the effectiveness of Jewish day schools in promoting Jewish continuity. A 1988 study of Jewish students in British Jewish and non-Jewish schools suggested that the Jewish schools had little impact on the students' degree of religious belief and attachment to Judaism, although they did increase measures of practical observance, and that the nature of students' households was a stronger predictor of Jewish feeling and behaviour than schooling.[34] In a 2005 article, Geoffrey Short argued that one of the central premises of Jonathan Sacks's approach to Jewish continuity, that Jewish education has over the course of history been the principal means through which Jewish continuity has been achieved, is mistaken and that the role of schools in Jewish continuity has been overestimated:

> In summary, there appears to be little evidence that Jewish secondary schools in contemporary Britain successfully promote positive outcomes in terms of their pupils' Jewish identity. While it does not follow that Jewish education in the past has been equally ineffectual, the research findings indicate that Sacks might have overestimated the historical contribution that education has made to Jewish continuity. At the same time, there is a danger that he has underestimated the important role to be played by a range of non-educational institutions in the future of Anglo-Jewry.[35]

Of course it does not follow that Jewish day schools cannot be effective in promoting continuity, nor that they may have other benefits than the narrowly continuity-based. It is certainly true though that in the rush to expand Jewish day school education, questions about what Jewish schools can achieve and how they should achieve it have often been inadequately addressed. Attempts to address the content of what is taught in Jewish schools have often followed the establishment and expansion of schools. As Helena Miller argues, 'the focus for the Jewish community has been on the establishment of institutions and not on curriculum development'.[36] It was not until the late 2000s that UJIA began a lengthy process of developing a curriculum for orthodox-run schools. UJIA has also, since the late 1990s, funded Jewish studies teacher training and recruitment, and the Board of Deputies has run the Pikuach inspectorate for Jewish studies teaching.

The most difficult question regarding the expansion of Jewish day schools is whether the community can support the number of schools that have been and will be built. A 2001 JPR report suggested that issues of over-supply of places and difficulties with financing and staffing were rapidly emerging.[37] The Commission on Jewish Schools was 'cautiously optimistic' about the sustainability of demand for Jewish primary schools, but was less optimistic about whether the secondary school 'market' would expand to keep pace with the expansion in places. The report estimated that by 2018–19, 89 per cent of the market for Jewish mainstream schools will have to take up places in Jewish secondary schools in order for them to remain 100 per cent Jewish, and argued that 'it is likely that more than one secondary school will be enrolling non-Jewish children in the near future'.[38] Some Jewish schools outside London admit non-Jews: the majority of pupils at King David secondary school in Liverpool are not Jewish, for example. This is by no means a 'doomsday' scenario as it would oblige Jewish schools to take a more multicultural approach to education and also attract Jews whose *halachic* status would otherwise prevent them from attending orthodox-run schools. Nevertheless, it would certainly question many of the assumptions underlying the renewal and continuity agendas.

Following the publication of *The Supply and Demand for Jewish Day School Places*, one of the constituent reports that paved the way for *The Future of Jewish Schools*, an editorial in the *Jewish Chronicle* commented:

> The report, produced by the newly formed Commission on Jewish Schools, with data produced by the Board of Deputies' research department, predicts a surplus of close to 50% in Jewish primary- and secondary-school places within a decade. This is not the first time such fears have been posited: the Institute for Jewish Policy Research also

predicted a massive surplus five years ago. The difference is that, since the JPR study, two new secondary schools – Yavneh College and the Jewish Community Secondary School – have appeared on the landscape, sending the number of places needing to be filled into orbit and raising the spectre of large numbers of non-Jewish children in Jewish schools.

[...]

Now, arguably the thorniest nettle to grasp: why has the community's leadership woken up to this only now? Why wasn't a Commission set up five years ago, after the JPR report, so that communal education could have progressed with some semblance of order? If the vast supply-and-demand gap does transpire as predicted, this generation's community leaders are going to have to give some tough answers to the next's.[39]

The desire to expand Jewish day schooling stemmed, at least in part, from a leap of faith, a desire to do *something* dramatic to change the Jewish communal landscape. The unspoken assumption was that sustainability issues would not arise as the expansion of Jewish day schools would ensure an expansion in the Jewish population, thereby ensuring the schools' futures in a virtuous cycle. This faith provided a striking limit to the growing reflexivity of the British Jewish community that was discussed in chapter 2. One of the most passionate funders of new Jewish schools in the UK, Benjamin Perl of the Huntingdon Foundation, exemplified this lack of reflexivity in an article in the *Jewish Chronicle* in April 2009.[40] For him there was no doubt that Jewish schools will ensure Jewish continuity: 'Assimilation is our biggest threat. We need more Jewish schools to counter it ... It is clear that, without Jewish education, our battle to eradicate the cancer in our midst – assimilation – will be lost.' Perl went on to denounce the research done on Jewish schools and contradicts their evidence:

Commissions, reports, and demographic surveys have consumed valuable resources to investigate the state of Jewish schools in Britain. Alarmingly, and contrary to all the evidence on the ground, the findings of more or less all of these warn us that we have too many schools ... Yet masses of young parents are clamouring to get places in a Jewish school. Prospective parents are demanding more schools. Can we afford to turn a deaf ear?

In treating research as a waste of time and in confusing the research data on the future sustainability of schools with the current demand for places,

Perl demonstrates how the impetus towards expanding Jewish day schools has often been driven by faith rather than strategic planning. He is correct to point out though that the expansion in Jewish day schools has been demand-led and that demand currently outstrips supply in many areas. However, there is a clear tension between the educational element of the renewal agenda and its strategic planning element.

Whether or not the rise in Jewish day school capacity is ultimately sustainable, whether or not Jewish day schools really are effective in ensuring Jewish continuity, the huge investment in Jewish day schools is one of the most significant expressions of the renewal of Anglo Jewry. Even if the decision to focus on Jewish day schools has to some extent been under-taken as a leap of faith, the desire to take that leap is evidence of a community that is determined to take every effort to secure its future. For good or for ill, the rise in Jewish day schools will have an impact on what kind of community Anglo Jewry is in the future.

The renewal and consolidation of Jewish leadership

The renewal agenda was explicitly intended to have real consequences for the Jews of Britain, most importantly to ensure its continuity. This book is less concerned with the 'success' or otherwise of the agenda than with noting the breadth and depth of the agenda itself. Whether or not the initiatives discussed above 'worked' as their protagonists wished or claimed, there is no question that the efforts of mainstream British Jewish organizations to renew Jewish life in Britain and ensure its continuity were the subject of considerable and serious effort and motivated by a desire to make a far-reaching impact. At least in their impact on the Anglo Jewish institutional archipelago, the community was transformed. Education came to take a much higher place on the communal agenda, synagogue umbrella bodies aimed to be sources of innovation rather than conservatism and long-held practices were subject to searching reflexive scrutiny.

Above all, the process of renewal was a renewal of leadership, an attempt to ensure that the Anglo Jewish leadership provided models of transfor-mation rather than stasis. The renewal of leadership in the community involved a slow but determined process of professionalization and stream-lining of communal leadership, what Israel Finestein has called 'the enhanced professionalism in high-profile specialized areas of communal life'.[41] Historically, the key leaders of Anglo Jewry were the Anglo Jewish 'gentry' laity. While the Chief Rabbi had considerable authority, there was a dearth of rabbis in Anglo Jewry until well into the twentieth century, with many United Synagogue communities until very recently led by 'reverends' whose religious training fell short of *semicha*.

In the post-war period, the 'cousinhood' gradually lost authority in favour of self-made businessmen. While it can be argued that one unelected clique simply supplanted the other, the dominance of businessmen in the last few decades brought with it a desire to inculcate 'businesslike' procedures within the Jewish community. Even if it may frequently be anachronistic to treat Jewish institutions as a business, the value of this approach was certainly demonstrated in the Kalms report which revealed the financial and organizational inefficiency of the United Synagogue.

In addition to the business-minded lay leadership of the community, a small but increasingly well-motivated and well-qualified cohort of professional Jewish leaders emerged. The Association of Jewish Communal Professionals worked in the 1980s and 1990s to improve the quality and status of Jewish professional leaders. The demand for Jewish studies' teachers in the day schools was addressed by UJIA and other bodies. The progressive Jewish community developed and expanded its leadership cadre through the founding of the Leo Baeck College rabbinic seminary in 1956, boosted by the arrival of a number of well-qualified German rabbis after the war.

Although Jews' College's *semicha* programme had almost stopped by the 1990s, the United Synagogue made use of *rabbanim* trained by right-wing orthodox *yeshivot* in the US and Israel who, even if they produced a marked turn to the right in the United Synagogue rabbinic leadership, also brought with them a marked degree of enthusiasm and confidence. Further, in 2006 the Montefiore London Semicha Programme was initiated and began the process of preparing a new generation of British modern orthodox rabbis.

The slow progress towards a more efficiently run Jewish community was also demonstrated in a move towards greater consolidation and centralization. An early demonstration of this move occurred in the welfare sphere. The large welfare charities the Jewish Welfare Board and the Jewish Blind Society merged into a single organization called Jewish Care in 1990, and Norwood and Ravenswood, which both dealt with disabilities and child welfare, were amalgamated in 1996. However, an attempt at developing a coordinating body for welfare, the Central Council for Jewish Community Services, formed in 1993 by Lord David Young, did not even last until the end of the decade.

Outside the welfare sector the drive to consolidation was more erratic and challenging. The Board of Deputies, which attempts to represent Anglo Jewry and to provide coordinating services to the community, has an exceedingly complex organizational structure that is ultimately accountable to an unwieldy group of several hundred 'deputies' from synagogues and a number of other communal organizations. A JPR report on the representation of Anglo Jewry pointed out that the Board of Deputies no longer had a monopoly on representation and that it did not represent substantial numbers of Jews (primarily non-synagogue members and most of the Haredi community).[42]

The most significant response to the perceived need for greater coordination was not reform of the Board but the formation of a new body, the Jewish Leadership Council (JLC) in 2003, based in part on the Conference of Presidents of Major American Jewish Organizations.[43] Whereas the Board's representational structure privileged leaders within synagogues, the JLC privileged senior leaders of major Jewish organizations. The JLC has throughout its existence been chaired by the president of the Board of Deputies and among JLC's members are the *ex officio* lay leaders of the main synagogue bodies and other major organizations such as Jewish Care and the Community Security Trust.

The JLC also includes a number of *ad personam* members, including philanthropists and grandees such as Gerald Ronson, Sir Trevor Chinn, Lord Janner and Baroness Deech (who in mid 2009 was one of only two female members). The JLC provides a formal structure to a system that is at least in part an oligarchy[44] and in this respect represents a flight away from a democratic approach to communal representation. Ironically enough, however, the JLC was set up in part as a response to the *lack* of oligarchy within the community – as chief executive Jeremy Newmark points out, previous generations of lay leaders all knew each other, were tightly intermarried and had no need for any formal coordinating body.[45]

The JLC is primarily a coordinating body rather than a service delivery organization. However, the JLC has inevitably replicated or supplanted the Board in some areas. Like the Board, it conducts representational activities and was instrumental in instituting a system in which the community could respond to international crises. This was in the light of the perceived inadequacies of the communal response to the Israel–Hezbollah war of summer 2006. The lack of accountability of such initiatives has not gone unchallenged. Less controversially, the JLC also ran (partially in conjunction with the Board) the Commission on the Future of Jewish Schools and has worked to encourage space sharing and bulk purchasing among Jewish organizations. The JLC thus demonstrates both the dangers and advantages of greater coordination within the community: it can enshrine the power of an unelected elite at the same time as it brings greater efficiency to Jewish communal organizations.

The move to consolidate and coordinate is not just a British one. For example, in 2002 the Jewish Agency founded the Jewish People Policy Planning Institute as a high-level think tank intended to stimulate and coordinate planning and policy-making for the Jewish people as a whole. Faced with contracting Jewish populations in many places, there is a strong tendency to create greater efficiency by consolidating resources. As Jonathan Sarna has argued:

> Where most of the world's great religions – Christianity, Islam and Eastern religions – are today expanding, Judaism is contracting. Where other people are preaching the gospel of globalism and spreading their diasporas north, south, east and west, Jews, who invented the very concept of diaspora, are reducing their exposure to the larger world and practicing consolidation.[46]

This consolidation occurred in the UK not simply through a contraction in numbers but through a precipitous decline in most Jewish communities outside London. A smaller but more concentrated Jewish community creates ample possibilities for consolidation. The drive to consolidation is intimately tied into the renewal and continuity agendas, motivated ultimately by the strategy of insecurity.

This approach to renewal also has serious drawbacks. Such an unabashedly top-down strategy may produce dynamic institutions, but the connection to grassroots renewal is by no means guaranteed. There are real issues of hierarchy and power in any approach to policy-making that emphasizes institutional transformation above all else. Making an institution efficient, strategically focused and creative in its thinking does not necessarily mean that that institution will not be unaccountable, secretive and hierarchical. As we argued in the case of UJIA, emphasis on making an organization work well can result in a lack of attention being paid to such elusive things as atmosphere and empowerment. The JLC may have improved on the Board's cumbersome structure but at the cost of democratic accountability.

Conclusion

In this chapter we have looked at how the renewal agenda was pursued by mainstream Jewish institutions as a largely top-down, bureaucratic process. The drive to renew Jewish life in Britain was not confined to these organizations, however. The continuity consensus and the renewal agenda were not only elite bureaucratic discourses but permeated, or at the very least influenced, changes that took place across the community. The changes we have discussed in this and the previous chapter took place alongside a whole host of other changes that were less 'disciplined', less hierarchical and less narrow in their understanding of what a renewed Jewish life in Britain should mean. In the next chapter we will examine these developments in the fields of arts, cultural, educational and grassroots Jewish activities.

Chapter 6

From Renewal to Renaissance

From the early 1990s, Jewish lay and professional leaders carried out a far-reaching process of institutional renewal that was ultimately intended to ensure Jewish continuity. The limitations of this process lay in the limitations of institutions themselves. Not all Jewish activity is amenable to institutionalization, and a committed Jewish life does not simply involve institutional activity. In a world whose trajectory is never fully under control, strategic planning cannot provide for every eventuality. The more inchoate signs of a healthy Jewish community – 'vibrancy', 'enthusiasm', 'creativity', 'excitement' – cannot easily be produced or contained.

In this chapter we will explain how alongside the processes of institutional renewal engendered by the continuity consensus, a whole series of other changes took place that were just as important in the transformation of the UK Jewish community. Some of these changes were complementary to the changes discussed in the previous chapter; others, such as the more radical elements in the Jewish cultural scene, departed from the continuity and renewal consensus to such a degree as to be antagonistic to them.

Arts and cultural activity

In this book's introduction, we quoted from a number of books that voiced scathing opinions on the cultural vitality of Anglo Jewry. Although British Jews have been highly active in the arts, until recently they have rarely done so *as Jews*. Although the continuity consensus did not of course 'proscribe' Jewish arts and cultural activities, neither were they seen as central to the process by which Jewish life in Britain might be renewed.

As we saw, the United Jewish Israel Appeal (UJIA) did not continue Jewish Continuity's (often controversial) attempts to support Jewish arts and cultural organizations. In an interview in 2008, the Chief Rabbi argued that Jewish culture was not essential to the process of Jewish Continuity:

> To suppose that Jewish culture has anything to do with Jewish conti-
> nuity is a category mistake. Non-Jews visit Auschwitz, remember the
> Holocaust, read the novels of Isaac Bashevis Singer and Philip Roth,
> love Woody Allen's humour and the rap music of Matisyahu. A
> vibrant Jewish culture is meaningful and valuable, and should be
> supported in every way. But it has nothing to do with whether our
> grandchildren will be Jewish. Culture does not command.[1]

Sacks's view of culture depends on a minimalist definition of the term as synonymous with art rather than seeing culture as a whole way of life. This view of culture has been widespread in the British Jewish community, both on the part of those such as Sacks, who see it as a worthy but ultimately peripheral part of Jewish life, and on the part of those who see it as more essential to the Jewish community. What is missing in this minimalist view of Jewish culture is an appreciation of Jewish culture as the everyday life of the Jewish people, as a 'thick' layer of practices, meanings and assumptions that reproduces the lives that Jews live. In this sense, the historic lack of attention paid to Jewish culture by British Jewish leaders has sometimes limited the effectiveness of policies intended to ensure Jewish continuity, insofar as they lacked an appreciation of the more intangible elements of Jewish community.

The presence or otherwise of arts activities in the British Jewish community does not in and of itself guarantee or doom the possibility of a vibrant British Jewish culture. It is extremely difficult to know how to institute a sophisticated, intellectually curious, creative and vibrant 'atmos-phere'. We would argue that the kinds of community for which *both* Jewish continuity proponents like Sacks *and* those who are concerned with Jewish culture and arts yearn are fairly similar. What a Jewish community that ensures both its own continuity and its artistic creativity requires is the embedding of that elusive creative, vibrant, intellectual atmosphere in everyday practices and institutions.

In the twentieth century, institutions that sought to develop Anglo Jewry's intellectual and cultural life developed slowly. The Ben Uri Gallery, for example, was founded in 1915 to provide a platform for Jewish immigrant artists excluded from the British art world through antisemitism; the Jewish Museum was founded in 1932; the *Jewish Quarterly*, the community's longest-standing literary magazine, in 1953; the Jewish Book Council in 1947. The community's longest-standing publication, the *Jewish Chronicle*, founded in 1841, has provided the main forum for intellectual, cultural and political debate, although its quality has varied considerably over the years.

British Jews have also formed a number of higher educational institutions. The Gateshead Yeshiva, formed in 1929, is highly regarded in the ultra-orthodox world. Jews' College, founded in 1855, for many years provided the principal institution for the training of orthodox British rabbis. The college was renamed the London School of Jewish Studies in 1999 and recreated itself as a centre for adult learning. Leo Baeck College was founded in 1956 and became the principal institution for training British non-orthodox rabbis, as well as a university-accredited institute of higher learning. Academic Jewish studies in Britain also grew in the post-war period with the University of London's Institute of Jewish Studies formed in 1953, the Oxford Centre for Hebrew and Jewish Studies founded in 1972 and the British Association for Jewish Studies founded in 1975. A pioneer in adult education was the Spiro Institute, founded in 1978, which became a centre for cultural and literary activities and talks, as well as modern Hebrew teaching.[2] Another organization, Yakar, founded in 1979, pioneered an independent orthodox approach to adult learning that explicitly resisted the rightward turn of the United Synagogue.

All these institutions provided an increasingly sturdy framework for intellectual and cultural life in Anglo Jewry. It was not until the 1990s that a more dramatic change in the 'atmosphere' of the community began to occur. This came about not simply through the building of institutions, but also through self-conscious attempts to challenge and confront the practices and assumptions of the established Jewish community. One of the most noteworthy of these attempts was the magazine *New Moon* which ran between 1990 and 1997.

New Moon was founded by Matthew Kalman, who had previously been an activist in the Union of Jewish Students and the World Union of Jewish Students, as well as working for Natan Sharansky's office in Israel. An unpublished document Kalman wrote on *New Moon* in 2009[3] demonstrates how his motivations were similar to those of others who shared in the continuity consensus:

In a talk entitled 'Death and the *Jewish Chronicle*' to students and groups in Jerusalem, I suggested that these two Anglo-Jewish institutions were the last items of Jewish identity to be shed even by assimilated Jews. The demographic statistics took as their basis the fact that even the most non-Jewish Jews preferred a Jewish burial and extrapolated the number of supposed living Jews from the number of certainly dead ones. Meanwhile, the circulation figures of the JC, each copy of which was read by 5 or 6 people, almost all in London, suggested a hinterland of invisible Jews whose only affiliation with the community was through reading the JC each week.

The *Jewish Chronicle* therefore provided a powerful tool for Jewish renewal, but it needed to be renewed itself:

It seemed to me that the JC had its priorities rooted firmly in the 1950s. It spoke for a generation of immigrants who were still happily surprised to find they had gained acceptance in the non-Jewish world, even if that meant abandoning Jewish values.

My generation, on the other hand, did not feel that same immigrant gratitude. On the contrary, just as we had demanded as equals that Jewish student rights be recognized like those of women, gays, blacks and other specific groups at the National Union of Students, so we were confident of claiming our place as equals – and Jews – in British society. The mainstream newspapers were full of the kind of writing about Jewish issues that I hoped and failed to find in the JC. Why couldn't a Jewish publication be as intelligent, cynical and basically modern about Judaism as the *Independent* or the *Guardian*?

Kalman's analysis of the *Jewish Chronicle* as out of sync with the times is also reflected in his analysis of his generation of Jewish young adults:

My friends were beginning to settle down and get married. More than half of my Jewish childhood friends were with non-Jewish partners but when they gathered round our dinner table on Shabbat lunchtime they were hungry for Jewish culture, theatre, books and news about Israel. They were critical, secular and disdainful of establishment Anglo-Jewish activities like charity fundraising or synagogue membership, but they wanted their Jewish identity to have some role in their lives.

New Moon aimed to be 'part *Time Out*, part *Private Eye*' and to include listings, journalism on unreported strands in the Jewish community' and 'to approach Jewish issues in a modern way'. Above all, it aimed 'to make it fun to be Jewish again', often through biting satire. The October 1990 launch issue included a page laid out like the cover of the *Jewish Chronicle*, titled 'The Jewish Chronic', with the headline 'Israel "can do no wrong" – official', trailing stories such as 'Man in dinner suit shaking hands. Picture special page 5'. *New Moon* attracted controversy on occasions, as in its inclusion of gay and lesbian listings which sparked furious letters in the August–October 1991 issues. It had a pronounced interest in sex, featuring interviews with Jewish prostitutes, articles on Jews and AIDS, and in March 1994, an article on 'How to ditch your non-Jewish partner' accompanied by a cartoon parodying the opening Jewish Continuity advert with Jews pushing non-Jews off a cliff.

Satires of Anglo Jewish social mores aside, *New Moon* also commissioned serious, investigative reporting, running feature-length stories that the *Jewish Chronicle* could rarely match, including highly critical articles about Jonathan Sacks and the Board of Deputies. *New Moon* highlighted the work of emerging Jewish writers such as Jay Rayner, Jonathan Freedland and Linda Grant, and encouraged the work of Jewish cultural producers such as the Besht Tellers theatre company. *New Moon* also featured hundreds of personal adverts, mainly from Jewish twenty and thirtysomethings, demonstrating a market for Jewish dating that was later to be filled by JDate.com.

New Moon never managed to become financially self-sustaining, and in its later years was increasingly dependent on the financial support of Michael Sinclair (chair of Jewish Continuity). Matthew Kalman left for Israel at the end of 1996, and in 1997 the magazine was relaunched as a less intellectual publication with a heavy emphasis on Jewish celebrities, fashion and lifestyle. This too was unsuccessful, and the magazine folded in 1998.

New Moon prefigured and in part helped to stimulate changes in the *Jewish Chronicle* in the 1990s. Shortly after the launch of *New Moon*, the *Chronicle* launched a free listings section and gradually improved its cultural coverage. Under the editorship of Ned Temko from 1990, it became more irreverent and willing to take a more investigative approach to Jewish institutions. In publishing extracts from Sacks's letter to Dayan Padwa in 1997 (discussed in chapter 4), it regained its position as a major player in communal politics, much as it had done under William Frankel's editorship when it was central to the unfolding of the Jacobs affair.

The popularity and diversity of Jewish arts and cultural activities expanded significantly in the 1990s and beyond. Jewish Book Week, which was founded by the Jewish Book Council in 1952, grew rapidly in the 1990s and 2000s to become an important part of London's literary calendar, inviting a great variety of Jewish and non-Jewish speakers. Jewish Book Week 2009 attracted 5,000 ticket sales to sixty-eight different events. The

Jewish Film Festival (founded in 1985) also grew to become an important part of the cultural landscape of both the Jewish and wider communities. The Jewish Music Institute, which was also founded in 1984, expanded in the 1990s and 2000s, organizing not only performances, but academic courses and an annual participatory 'KlezFest' celebrating klezmer music. In the mid 2000s, an Association of UK Jewish Culture Providers was formed with forty-eight member organizations with an interest in Jewish culture. It organized a festival of Jewish Culture to celebrate the 350th anniversary of the readmission of Jews to Britain in 2006 and two Jewish music festivals in Trafalgar Square called 'Simcha on the Square' in 2007 and 2008.

Even if Jewish arts and culture had traditionally been neglected by UK Jewish organizations, that does not mean that the activities promoted in this resurgence of interest in Jewish culture were necessarily 'anti-establishment'. Jewish Book Week has hosted the Chief Rabbi on a number of occasions, as well as figures such as Julia Kristeva. The Jewish Music Institute often puts on concerts of cantorial music, as well as (on one occasion in the mid 2000s) a DJing course. The increased interest in Jewish cultural activities helped to make what had once been marginal activities mainstream. An interest in klezmer music and in Yiddish were for a long time disparaged and even (in some Zionist circles) seen as positively retrograde, but they are now commonplace.

Another notable initiative was London's Jewish Community Centre (JCC). Jewish Community Centres emerged in the nineteenth century and there are over a thousand in the US and elsewhere. They offer a wide range of educational, cultural, sporting and social programming, as well as community resources such as nurseries. They are designed to be open to everyone within the Jewish community but non-Jews also participate in some activities. The UK had never had a Jewish Community Centre until, following an initiative of the Clore Duffield Foundation, work began to develop one in the mid 2000s. Recognizing that building the centre itself would require time and money, the JCC began putting on events prior to the existence of a physical building to house them. The model the London JCC followed was that of the Manhattan JCC, which has a reputation for innovative and creative programming. The JCC has emphasized its inclusive nature:

> The JCC [is] for anyone interested in Jewish life and our programme ... The JCC actively welcomes observant and secular Jews, mixed partnerships, and non-Jews. Indeed, an important part of our vision is to create better understanding between different faiths and cultures.[4]

The JCC has made particular efforts to engage young adults and those from non-conventional Jewish backgrounds. Its programming has a heavy emphasis on innovative arts and cultural activities, marketed in attractive ways and making full use of the internet and social networking. It has built partnerships with Jewish and non-Jewish arts and cultural organizations with a strong 'multicultural' bent. One example is the arts consultancy Yad Arts, whose slogan 'radical diaspora culture in the present tense' is exemplified in events that blur the boundaries of Jewish and non-Jewish culture such as their 'Radio Gagarin' club nights that feature musicians and DJs from Jewish and other Diasporic backgrounds.

An interest in Jewish arts and culture has often been anti-establishment, associated with radical and secular Jewish identities. The 2000s saw increasing efforts to create spaces within the Jewish community, such as the JCC, that would be open to the participation of secular Jews within Jewish communal institutions. Some UK Jewish cultural work also challenged the secular–religious distinction. The Moishe House for London was formed in 2007 by a US-based foundation that aims to:

> set up grassroots community centers that cater towards the twenty-something post-college Jewish population. By offering a rent subsidy and a monthly program budget to a group of young, responsible, and *social* Jews living in the same house, they in turn agree to host events that range from a simple Shabbat Dinner to a Purim mega-party ... Events are designed around the local Jewish population but are *always* inclusive of non-Jewish guests and are sometimes non-Jewish in nature.[5]

The Moishe House's activities include much that could be identified as radical, secular Jewish culture – 'open mic' nights, jam sessions, political discussions and so on – but they also include a *beit midrash* and religious celebrations.

A more radical initiative is Jewdas, which has organized events since 2006 with provocative titles such as 'Punk Purim' and 'Night of Ritual Slaughter' (a Chanukah celebration) which mix music, DJing, art, cinema and Jewish learning. Jewdas celebrates the Jewish radical tradition and events have featured guest speakers who would be beyond the pale at most other Jewish events, such as Jews advocating a boycott of Israel. Jewdas's website features polemics against the Jewish 'establishment' as well as satirical cartoons such as a United Synagogue logo reworked to read 'provoking moronic Judaism since 1870'.

Jewdas achieved some notoriety for two of its projects. In September 2006, four Jewdas organizers gave away flyers for its 'Protocols of the Elders of Hackney' event at the 'Simcha on the Square' and were arrested (but not charged) for distributing racially inflammatory material with intent to incite racial hatred. On 9 January 2009, Jewdas sent a hoax email to its mailing list, purporting to be from the Board of Deputies, announcing that the Sunday 11 January Israel Solidarity Rally had been cancelled. Once the hoax was discovered, one Jewdas member was briefly arrested on charges of racial hatred, but again no charges were brought. A few days later Jewdas admitted the hoax:[6]

> we wanted, in this action, to show another possible reality, to suggest that 'another Jewish community is possible.
>
> Those who believed it, even for a moment, were being given a gift, a vision of the Jewish leadership who stood up for peace and justice, rather than standing for mindless ethnic solidarity. These people should not be considered gullible, rather they showed the imagination to see an inspiring, alternative vision. We offered a Midrash on Anglo-Jewish life, a *dvar aher* (another path), an aggadah for the Talmud of the present. In this 'temporary imaginary zone' the Jewish Establishment opened up, listening to the voices it usually shuts out, thought outside the box, and took a brave decision on principle rather than in accordance with political expediency.

While Jewdas's approach was undoubtedly confrontational, its justification was couched in unmistakably Jewish terms. Rather than sniping from the outside at the Jewish community, Jewdas saw itself as offering a 'Midrash'. In this respect Jewdas seeks not simply to satirize the community, but also to change it, on terms that resist easy oppositions between alternative and mainstream and, indeed, religious and secular. Jewdas is linked in to the 'mainstream' community more firmly than might be imagined. It has received funding from the Rothschild Foundation, which also funds many other communal projects, for one of its events. Its organizers and many of those involved at its events are also involved in many other more conventional activities.

In the 1990s and 2000s, there was a gradual process of mainstreaming previously marginal Jewish activities. One example was the growing interest in social action projects, once a marker of leftist Jewish separatism, that spread into the mainstream, such as the United Synagogue's Project Chesed, which organizes projects such as blood drives, food parcels to the needy and ethically sourcing kosher food. Another example is alternative *minyanim*, once (and sometimes still) seen as threatening to the unity of synagogue communities, which have become more common in both orthodox and progressive congregations. A significant number of independent *minyanim* also exist, some of them, such as 'Wandering Jews', specifically designed for young adults

The irresistible rise of Limmud

One of the principle reasons why innovation in the Jewish community has resisted any simple bifurcation into alternative and mainstream camps is the Limmud conference. The first Limmud conference took place in 1980, with eighty participants.[7] For its first few years it was primarily a conference for Jewish educators, modelled on the US Conference on Alternatives in Jewish Education. Limmud was held over the Christmas break, often including Christmas day itself, on university and school campuses outside London. Over the 1980s, programming expanded to include cultural activities and a young peoples' programme, and guest speakers started to come from elsewhere in the Jewish world. In the 1990s, Limmud attracted significant funding first from Jewish Continuity and then UJIA. In the 2000s, the annual conference was attended by over two thousand people, with many other day Limmuds held elsewhere in the country, and a summer Limmud Fest established. The 2007 conference handbook reported that throughout its history 20,000 participants had attended a UK Limmud event.

From its inception, the distinctiveness of the Limmud approach has been its pluralism which seeks to transcend disabling communal divisions. According to Limmud's mission statement:[8] 'Limmud does not participate in legitimising or de-legitimising any religious or political position found in the worldwide Jewish community. Anyone who comes to Limmud events seeking opportunities for this will not find it.' It further states: 'We believe in the richness of our diverse community and create cross-communal and cross-generational experiences.' In order to facilitate participation of individuals from across the communal spectrum, religious observance is respected but not mandated:

> Shabbat and kashrut are observed in all public areas. We recognise that in private areas people will behave as they wish.
>
> Should participants wish to hold a prayer group, they may do so providing they supply all resources and are responsible for the session or prayer group in its entirety.

The structure of the conference is based around multiple sessions run in parallel, so no one is obliged to be exposed to opinions they may find objectionable. Anyone is entitled to lead a session and Limmud itself also subsidizes a number of speakers itself, enabling prominent Jewish leaders, educators and artists from across the world to attend. There is no special treatment given to speakers – as the mission statement says: 'Everyone can be a teacher and everyone should be a student' – and no details are given of individuals' titles on name badges. There are no official barriers to the participation of non-Jews, the intermarried or those with ambiguous *halachic* status.

Limmud includes orthodox, progressive and secular Jews. It is true that the participation of British orthodox rabbis dramatically declined after Dayan Ehrentreu, the effective head of the United Synagogue Beth Din, ruled in 1995 that orthodox leaders should not attend the conference (a prohibition that appears to have continued following Ehrentreu's retirement in 2007).[9] Before being installed as Chief Rabbi, Jonathan Sacks was a regular Limmud participant, but he has never attended since his installation (although his son-in-law has chaired Limmud and he himself has spoken warmly of the organization). While only a small number of United Synagogue rabbis now attend Limmud, other orthodox rabbis and leaders from across the world do attend the conference. The conference also includes those who are generally received as pariahs in much of the community, such as the journalist Robert Fisk, a prominent critic of Israel, who attended in 2002. Jews who are highly critical of Israel, such as Deborah Fink (co-founder of Jews for Boycotting Israeli Goods), are able to participate equally. Limmud has also become known as a space for inter-faith dialogue, with Muslim and Christian speakers attending most years.

The first words of Limmud's mission statement are: 'Wherever you are going, Limmud will take you one step further along your Jewish journey.' It does not specify the destination of this journey, rather it offers a resource for Jewish 'travellers' within a 'community of learning'. The communal aspect of Limmud is demonstrated in its remarkable volunteer culture. The organization only opened its own office in 1998 and has a tiny paid staff, with a full-time executive director only appointed in 2006. In 2009, Limmud had around seven hundred volunteers planning and running the conference and other activities. Limmud continues to grow in capacity with multiple regional day Limmuds (seven in 2009) and a summer Limmud Fest (which six hundred attended in 2008). There is great emphasis on young adult involvement and, since the early 1990s, bursaries have been offered to people in their twenties to attend Limmud for a nominal amount in return for volunteering at the conference.

The conference allows participants to experiment with new ways of being Jewish in a temporarily (nearly) all-Jewish environment. While the structure of the annual conference remains the same, the content of each conference is shaped by the priorities and interests of each year's volunteers. Over the years, theatre, film, art and musical performances have come to take on an increasingly important part of the conference. The summer Limmud Fest emphasizes outdoor activities. The annual conference has begun to offer volunteering opportunities for local Christmas charity projects. Limmud's flexibility and openness to innovation as an organization has stayed strong in part because the concentration of young adult volunteers ensures that it is constantly self-renewing. Even though Limmud has taken significant sums of money from Jewish philanthropic bodies, it remains largely immune from the careful strategic planning and bureaucratization discussed in the previous chapter.

Limmud's most important contribution to British Jewish life is that through its nurturance of young people, it has engendered a generation that is innovative and open to Jewish experience. As Jonathan Boyd points out: 'From its earliest days, Limmud was built by friends.'[10] Limmud's longest-serving leaders, such as Clive Lawton, have spent years networking and reaching out to individuals. Limmud both draws on and creates networks of friendship that endure beyond the conference:

> In the course of their work building the community of Limmud, the links between [the volunteers] have grown stronger and stronger, to the extent now that many of those individuals ... have bought homes in close proximity to one another. They even joke among themselves that there is a small area of London called 'Limmudistan'. They don't necessarily belong to the same synagogues or send their children to the same schools, but they are tied to one another in less formal, but in many respects much stronger and deeper ways.[11]

Where once there was often a gap in Jewish involvement between teenage and student years and parenthood, Limmud now fills that gap.

In building a community Limmud has helped to transform the expectations of the wider Jewish community. It has imbued significant numbers of people with an enthusiasm for and literacy in things Jewish that has had repercussions throughout Anglo Jewry. The emphasis on study of Jewish texts in its *Chevruta* project and by many of its teachers has helped to transform Jewish literacy and created greater expectation for Jewish education in Jewish organizations. Limmud leaders have gone on to lead other Jewish organizations. The growth of similarly pluralist, similarly innovative institutions such as the JCC is informed by the experiences and expectations of the Limmud generation. Limmud is therefore part of the story of many of the transformations we have discussed in this book.

Limmud has also exported itself globally. In the early 2000s, Limmud events – independent of the parent organization but sharing the same 'brand' and cross-communal model – began to spring up worldwide, facilitated by a new organization, Limmud International. In 2008, thirty-five thousand attended Limmud events across the world. There are forty different Limmud communities in seventeen countries, including the US and Israel but also countries with small Jewish populations such as Turkey, Poland and Bulgaria. This process is historically unique: never before has Anglo Jewry exported a new model of Jewish practice worldwide.

Limmud is not without its limitations. Its pluralism can be criticized as a form of relativism, and orthodox leaders[12] and right-wing Zionists[13] have critiqued the organization on these grounds. Limmud can also be criticized for not encouraging encounters between different streams of Jewish opinions, as its parallel sessions allow participants to go through the conference without being challenged. The frenetic atmosphere of the December conference can also work against reflection and analysis,[14] and the enormous choice available at the conference can encourage a kind of consumerist approach to Jewish learning. Even if over twenty thousand British Jews have attended Limmud, that still leaves over a quarter of a million who have not, and there is a danger that a gap may develop between an engaged, active and pluralist Limmud generation and a more staid majority. The celebratory rhetoric that often surrounds Limmud may hide some of these issues, and there is always the possibility that in the future celebration will become complacency and the organization's vitality will dissipate. At present though, Limmud remains a dynamic source of innovation within Anglo Jewry and the Jewish world more generally.

A Jewish renaissance?

In October 2001, a new Jewish cultural magazine was launched in the UK called *Jewish Renaissance*. The magazine aims 'to encourage and intensify the current renaissance in Jewish culture'.[15] 'Renaissance' is an extravagant, even hyperbolic term and the fact that it was seen as a credible title is testament to the dramatic change that has occurred in Anglo Jewry. The concept of a Jewish renaissance is not new, having been applied both posthumously and contemporaneously to various periods in Jewish history.[16] Historians and theologians have demonstrated that, even in the darkest times and in the wake of the worst of catastrophes, the Jewish people can be, has been and should be 'reborn' and renewed.[17] The revival of Jewish life in post-Holocaust Europe, particularly in Eastern Europe, is one current demonstration of the potential of Jewish renewal.[18]

Is it appropriate to apply the concept of renaissance to contemporary Anglo Jewry? Renaissance implies a previous 'golden age' when it is unclear whether Jewish life in Britain was ever more vibrant than it is now. It certainly seems that for many Jewish leaders there is much to celebrate in the British Jewish community today. Most of our interviewees agreed that the British Jewish community had changed dramatically, for the better, since the early 1990s. To take the most striking example, Jonathan Sacks ended our interview with him on a very upbeat note when asked how the community had changed since he took office:[19]

> Well, firstly, it is very, very much more creative, and in many ways more creative than any other Diaspora Jewish community. I mean no other Diaspora community created something like Limmud.[20] Now, Limmud had been going on long before I became Chief Rabbi, because I used to be there in all the early years, but it suddenly became very big. I don't think that was incidentally an effect of my Chief Rabbinate ... I think there are a whole series of things that I just watch from the sidelines in awe, like Jewish Book Week.

Sacks continued:

> We have built more schools faster pro rata than any other Diaspora Jewish community. Now, how good is that? The truth is we were lagging behind. We were lagging behind both Australia and South Africa, and we haven't fully caught up yet, but my goodness me we've put on a spurt in the last fifteen years.
> So I think Anglo-Jewry is so much more energetic and creative, and I don't know what a member of high Victorian Anglican Judaism would make about today's laid-back, thoroughly alternative, diverse and extremely creative community. Read what was said about it, you know, a couple of two or three decades ago.

Like most of our interviewees, Sacks points to both the renewal and growth of Jewish institutions that we discussed in the previous chapter, as well as the cultural and educational initiatives we discussed in this chapter, as evidence of the vitality of modern British Jewry.

Jewish renaissance, the renewal agenda and the continuity consensus

In part, the Jewish renaissance was an unintended consequence of the renewal process. Sacks has been critical of more 'ethnic' and 'cultural' definitions of Judaism and robust in his defence of the centrality of the United Synagogue.[21] Neither he nor Jewish Continuity, the organization he tried to create in his image, would be 'content' with this kind of Judaism and although they were happy to use unconventional means, their ends were the renewal of normative, institutionalized Judaism, with an inmarried, *halachically* acceptable Jewish population. The renewal agenda was generally predicated on a 'thick' essentialist notion of Jewish identity that was to be expressed through commitment to Jewish institutions. Yet the renewal agenda set in train processes that strengthened non-institutionalized, more critical, less essentialist versions of Jewishness as much as they strengthened more mainstream kinds.

The development of a more Jewishly educated population, and particularly more Jewishly educated young people, also endowed this population with the 'raw materials' that could be exploited in novel ways. The Zionist youth movements, which had been brought into the mainstream Jewish community by Jewish Immigrant Aid (JIA) and UJIA, provide an excellent training in leadership and innovation that can be used for a whole range of ends. In fact, pretty much *all* kinds of Jewish activity that were stimulated in the 1990s and beyond were 'good for each other' in helping to creating a nebulous, but clearly identifiable 'atmosphere' of Jewish creativity and expression. Even if Jewdas and the United Synagogue would seem to be mutually antagonistic and exclusive phenomena, their histories in the 1990s and 2000s are connected in complex, mutually reinforcing ways.

The Jewish renaissance demonstrates the limitations of strategic planning in the Jewish community. Far-reaching change can happen in a community even if it is unplanned, provided that well-motivated, well-trained leaders are present to stimulate it. This is the lesson that has long been learned by Chabad, whose *shlichim* have virtually no formal training and whose central direction is extremely weak, but who are able to be dynamic agents of change by virtue of their intense commitment to the *rebbe* and to Judaism, inculcated within the Chabad education system.[22] As Yoel Finkelman has noted, sociologically grounded attempts at Jewish 'reconstruction' have ultimately been less far-reaching in their effects than right-wing orthodoxy's unplanned, sociologically ignorant but nevertheless dramatic growth.[23]

At the same time, the UK Jewish renaissance also vindicates the strategic planning at the heart of the renewal agenda in that it provided the basis for unplanned creativity through producing well-trained, well-motivated individuals. The renewal agenda has, of course, begun to move on from the 1990s. Whereas UJIA has never developed an innovations fund, in the 2000s the UK Jewish community began to develop better resources for innovation. In 2007, the Clore Duffield Foundation, which had been instrumental in developing the JCC, launched 'Sparks', an innovation fund for projects outside Greater London. In 2008, the Pears Foundation launched 'JHub' to house and support innovative Jewish social action projects.

It is significant that these projects were funded by private foundations. The experience of Jewish Continuity demonstrated some of the difficulties in funding innovation within an organization dependent on a large number of donors. In the US, private foundations have been at the forefront of an upsurge in Jewish innovation in the 2000s, with organizations such as Bikkurim and Joshua Venture behind a large number of youth-led innovations. This explosion of 'social entrepreneurship', 'venture philanthropy', together with the decline in importance of the Federation system of fundraising has been dubbed 'The Second American Jewish Revolution'.[24] While in the UK the impact of venture philanthropy has been less pronounced, there is no doubt that the UK Jewish community has become much more open to social entrepreneurship.

The UK Jewish community, like other Jewish communities around the world has so far managed to balance centrifugal and centripetal forces. It has consolidated, streamlined and centralized its most important institutions just as its population has become more concentrated in a small number of areas.[25] It has also revitalized its fringes, with a broader range of opportunities for a broader range of Jews to express themselves Jewishly. So far, these twin developments have been complementary and interlinked but there is no necessary reason why this should always be the case. The continued vitality of Anglo Jewry requires that its fringes and its centre remain innovative and renewal-minded.

What didn't change

Despite the changes that have occurred in the British Jewish community since the early 1990s, there remain institutions that were more resistant to change and aspects of the community that remain relatively unreformed.

As we saw in chapter 2, the upsurge in social research began to peter out in the mid 2000s and the community has had difficulty in developing sustainable research capacity. Further, despite the research carried out in the community in the 1990s and first half of the noughties, the impact of this research was highly uneven. The extent to which the far-reaching conclusions of the JPR's long-term planning projects were turned into policy is unclear. Certainly, as we saw in the previous chapter, the JPR's research on schools was largely ignored and had to be repeated by the JLC's Commission on the Future of Jewish Schools.

The *Women in the Community* report, commissioned by the Chief Rabbi and published in 1994, did have an impact, for example, in the opening of a refuge for battered women run by the charity Jewish Women's Aid and in addressing (although not solving) the *agunah* problem through pre-nuptial agreements and pressure on recalcitrant husbands.[26] There remain few opportunities for women's participation in United Synagogue services and although women can now join United Synagogue boards, they remain prohibited from chairing them.[27] *Women in the Community* was revisited in a more modest report, published in 2009 not this time by the Chief Rabbi but by the Board of Deputies.[28] While it did acknowledge progress in some areas, it repeated concerns that the community was unresponsive to the needs of those who did not conform to the model of the nuclear family, such as singles and divorced and single parents. It criticized the limited opportunities for female leadership and participation in the orthodox community. The report suggested that there remained much to do in women's education, particularly in the orthodox community, suggesting that the expansion in Jewish education has its limits. It could also have noted how few women there are at the most senior levels of lay and professional leadership across the community. The UJIA, for example, has no female presidents, vice-presidents or chairs and has only one female trustee.[29]

In institutional structure, the community has hardly changed for decades. Despite some incremental reforms, the Board of Deputies retains the structure it had for much of the twentieth century and is regularly criticized for not representing all of the people it claims to represent. The Jewish Leadership Council has institutionalized the oligarchical influence of a small number of wealthy donors. The Chief Rabbinate is unrecognized by large sections of the community and the United Synagogue remains caught between an ever-more right-wing Beth Din and rabbinate and a moderate membership that is generally non-orthodox in practice. The JFS court case demonstrated much of the orthodox leadership's continuing obduracy concerning *halachic* status issues, its profound opposition to pluralism and its lack of understanding of the wider context of UK Jewry. Progressive modern orthodoxy of the kind that has begun to pioneer female rabbis and female participation in services in certain congregations in the US and Israel is virtually unknown in the UK. Inter-denominational divisions remain wide. Synagogues still struggle to respond to the needs of inter-married Jews and there is no inter-denominational consensus as to the *halachic* status of converts. Zionism has become so much an orthodoxy in the community that, as we shall see in the next chapter, there are great problems in including critics of Israel within the communal polity. In Jewish youth work, no new alternatives have emerged to the Zionist youth movements and previously non-Israel-focused movements, such as the Jewish Lads and Girls Brigade, have become increasingly Zionistic.

Against this backdrop there has been little response to one of the most striking changes in Anglo Jewry – the rapid growth of the Haredi community, who now constitute 17 per cent of the Anglo Jewish population and nearly 75 per cent of British Jewish births.[30] While the mainstream community is declining or static in numbers, the Haredi community is growing as a proportion of the Jewish community. The Haredi community is not part of the Board of Deputies and does not engage with most non-Haredi Jewish institutions. It is concentrated in certain areas such as London's Stamford Hill and suffers from acute housing and welfare needs. With the exception of the London Jewish Forum, which has tried to bring the *Haredi* community on board, there is no consensus in other Jewish institutions as to whether the mainstream community needs to engage with them or take on some responsibility for their needs. As the *Haredi* population becomes an ever-greater percentage of the total British Jewish population, there are real issues as to how existing Jewish mainstream institutions will be regarded by British national and local government.

Another difficult question regarding the changes discussed in this and the previous chapters is how far they have had an impact on the 'grass-roots'. Clearly, there have been many more educational and cultural opportunities available to those who have wished to take them and the quality of leadership has risen dramatically in many Jewish institutions. But has the renewal of Anglo Jewry simply met the needs of those who were already yearning for a more vibrant Jewish community or did it also create a new kind of British Jew? Research conducted by Steven M. Cohen and Keith Kahn-Harris in the early 2000s suggested that the British 'moderately engaged' Jewish population divided between a majority of 'dwellers', who were content to conduct 'middle of the road' Jewish lives with minimal spiritual or intellectual content, as they imagined their parents and grandparents had done, and a minority of 'seekers' who sought to find greater meaning in their Jewish lives.[31]

It is clear that seekers now have many more opportunities than they used to, but dwellers may simply find the JCC, Limmud and other revitalized forms of Jewish activity to be irrelevant to their lives. We can say, however, that the growth in Jewish day schools unquestionably has touched the lives of all kinds of Jews. The dwellers researched by Cohen and Kahn-Harris had generally not attended Jewish day schools, and even if they had, it was at a time when the quality of Jewish leadership and resources available for Jewish education were poorer. The schools offer an unparalleled opportunity for Jewish leaders to 'reach' people they have not reached previously. It seems highly likely that a new generation of Jews is emerging that at the very least has greater Jewish knowledge and more opportunities to make use of that knowledge in a diversity of ways.

Even if a 'renewed generation' might be emerging, that still leaves a substantial proportion of the Jewish community that was brought up in a very different kind of Jewish environment. For example, those secularly minded intellectuals who felt estranged from the community in the 1960s may be too disillusioned to take advantage of the more open contemporary Jewish atmosphere. Those who grew up to treat Jewish identity as a private, discrete matter may be unable or unwilling to adapt to the greater desire for public articulations of Jewishness.

Conclusion: the strategy of insecurity two decades on

The strategy of insecurity remains a popular tool to encourage support for and commitment to Jewish projects. As we saw in the previous chapter, philanthropist Benjamin Perl, who funds the development of new Jewish schools, placed much emphasis on the need to combat assimilation and intermarriage in his public pronouncement. Similarly, the introduction to the 2008 publicity brochure for the new Jewish Community Secondary School by the philanthropist Gerald Ronson argues:

> Over the past 50 years, the Jewish population of the UK has declined by 150,000. Many Jews have married out or simply lost interest. Mainstream British Jewry won't withstand another fifty years of decline at this rate.[32]

In other respects, however, the strategy of insecurity has become less prevalent. For one thing, most of our interviewees were keen to stress the many positive developments that had been achieved in the community. Warnings of impending disaster can only be made for a short time if their 'shock value' is not to dissipate. For those like Sacks who had been instrumental in establishing the strategy in the early 1990s, to remain attached to it would raise awkward questions about what exactly they had managed to achieve.

It is now common for Jewish leaders to emphasize the exciting things that are happening in Anglo Jewry. There has also been a move towards a much more sophisticated understanding of Jewish continuity in which policies judged by their ability to bring people further into the community are replaced by a paradigm in which creative projects are supported for their own sake. In the US, the cruder understandings of young adults as a 'problem' to be 'solved' that dominated the earlier phases of Jewish continuity are giving way to more complex understandings of the needs and potentials of the younger generation of Jews.[33]

No one would argue that the goal of Jewish continuity has been 'achieved', but that elusive thing, an 'atmosphere' of vibrancy and innovation, has been achieved. It is still unclear whether the numerical decline of Anglo Jewry has been arrested, but the continued vitality of Jewish life in the UK does not necessarily depend on sheer numbers and the question of how many British Jews are in-married or *halachically* Jewish as much as the earlier proponents of Jewish continuity might have believed. It is possible that the Jewish population (when defined rigidly) of the UK will continue to decline on paper, but the quality of Jewish existence in the UK will remain strong.

Even if the strategy of insecurity is losing some of its usefulness in motivating the UK Jewish community to renew itself, the strategy has increasingly come to be applied to the relationship of the Jewish community to wider society. While British Jewish communal leaders were becoming more upbeat about the internal life of the UK Jewish community, many were also becoming increasingly pessimistic about the position of the community in the UK, for reasons that had nothing to do with fears of intermarriage and assimilation. As the next chapter will show, since 2000, a new strategy of insecurity has emerged as a response to the perception of increased external threats to the community from the 'new antisemitism'.

Chapter 7

New Antisemitism, New Insecurity

In sharp counterpoint to the renaissance in Jewish culture described in the previous chapters, a number of commentators, both within and outside of the Jewish community, have claimed that a new wave of antisemitism, possibly of a qualitatively different form than earlier antisemitisms, has swept the world in recent years.[1] This wave has been defined by some as 'the new antisemitism'. Many believe that it poses a significant threat to Jewish people, that it is a major cause of insecurity.

There are a number of overlapping definitions given of this alleged 'new antisemitism': it is hatred of or discrimination against Jews as a *nation* (rather than as a *religion*, as in Christian antisemitism, or as a *race*, as in modern racial antisemitism), or hatred of Jews disguised behind a new non-racial language of anti-Zionism; or it is a globalized rather than a nationalist form of antisemitism; or it is an antisemitism that draws on leftist, anti-imperialist and indeed anti-racist, rather than reactionary themes.

The term 'the new antisemitism' is highly contentious. The usage of the term ranges from very precise definitions to invocations of a vague and nebulous phenomenon, from stark black and white pronouncements to extremely cautious and qualified claims, from accounts which stress fundamental breaks with previous antisemitisms and those which claim broad continuity and simply a change in outward appearance. Other commentators, especially on the left, argue that there is no such thing as a new antisemitism.[2]

It is not our purpose here to weigh in with a preferred definition, or to attempt to prove or disprove the existence of a 'new antisemitism'. It is clear, however, that violent attacks on Jews increased from the 1990s to the 2000s in most European countries, including the UK,[3] and that the majority of these are no longer perpetuated by traditional Nazi-style far-right groups. It is not clear, however, that the threat posed by 'the new antisemitism' is commensurate with some of the more extreme fears expressed in the Jewish community.

Rather than weighing in on one side or the other of an often vitriolic debate, our purpose in this chapter is to examine the talk about 'the new antisemitism' as a *discourse*: as a bundle of linked assumptions, embedded in language as particular themes, symbols and images, which do a certain sort of work when they are expressed and repeated. By using the concept of 'discourse', we want to get at the way in which language opens up possibilities in – and also creates limits to – what we can think and know about.[4] We will examine how this discourse emerged and how it has circulated within Anglo Jewry. And, in particular, we will examine how it has been *used* in the Jewish community, arguing that it has, along with concerns about Jewish continuity, been drawn into a communal strategy of insecurity: an approach from communal leaders to foster a greater sense of insecurity within the Anglo Jewish community.

Three features will be discussed in this chapter as particularly salient about this discourse and its circulation. First, the discourse circulates in widely differing contexts, including academia, the non-Jewish media, spaces of communal policy-making, and the wider 'Jewish public sphere'. Crucially, as we saw with the related discourse of Jewish continuity, the circulation has been transnational, with the Jewry of America and, to a lesser extent, Israel and continental Europe, playing a major role in defining terms which have tended to be uncritically accepted in the Anglo Jewish context. Second, the definitions of the 'new antisemitism' which circulate most widely tend to be the vaguest, the most simplistic and those that most emphasize continuity with older forms of antisemitism. Not surprisingly, therefore, and third, the language of the discourse has tended to be alarmist, and this has fed into the sense of insecurity which communal strategies have fostered in the same period. This alarmist language has generated a kind of 'gallery of others' threatening Jewry today and a discursive equivalence between each of them. We can see the depiction of this gallery of others as the elaboration of Anglo Jewry's 'constitutive outside' – the external dangers which threaten its survival, much as the panic around intermarriage and declining observance were posited as the internal dangers by the Jewish continuity discourse of the 1990s.

In the final section of this chapter, we will turn to the uses to which this discourse has been put in the community. We will more closely examine its role as part of a strategy of insecurity on the part of communal institutions such as the Chief Rabbi, the British Israel Communications and

Research Centre (BICOM), Stop the Boycott and the Jewish Leadership Council. We will look at the rejection of this discourse by critics of Israel within and outside the community but also, crucially, a dissenting stream within – or, rather, at the margins of – communal Anglo Jewry. This phenomenon is epitomized by Independent Jewish Voices (IJV), who have contested dominant communal conceptions of Jewish identity on very public platforms within and outside the communal public sphere (and this very public expression perhaps raises questions regarding their self-perception as marginalized voices).

Background

The phrase 'new antisemitism' is not exactly new. It was, for example, used by the Board of Deputies in 1921 in an attempt to describe the twin threat of Nazism in Germany and Mosley's fascism at home.[5] The 'new' then referred to the predominance of pseudo-scientific racial themes, qualitatively different from older social prejudices and religious themes. Similarly, the phrase, in quotation marks, was also used for racial theories by Cecil Roth in 1936.[6] In today's academic literature, the antisemitism defined as 'new' in those earlier texts has come to be thought of as the modern form of antisemitism, organized around hatred of Jews as a 'race', whose heyday is generally agreed to have lasted from the 1880s to the fall of Hitler in 1945, lingering on in neo-Nazi formations on the margins of Western political culture.

In the 1970s, a number of writers began to describe a 'new antisemitism' linked to anti-imperialist, anti-Zionist and Third Worldist themes, whose purchase was not on the political right but on the political left. The declining significance of biological 'race' as an organizing principle of antisemitism was noted, as was the shift in the left's sympathy from Israel to the Palestinians at the time of the Six Day War in 1967 and the elaboration of Nazi themes in Soviet 'anti-Zionist' propaganda, even in places where there were few if any Jews.

Robert Wistrich describes this post-1967 period:

The origins of this development go back to the rise of militant 'gauchisme' in most Western societies in the late 1960s, the emergence of a radical generation for whom the Palestinians were depicted as belonging to the wave of the future. [Since then, this current's fringe views have] contaminat[ed] the mainstream [of the left].[7]

`For Wistrich and for David Cesarani, the 1967 war was key. The Six Day War inspired a shift from a radical left view of Israel as the embattled and heroic land of kibbutz egalitarianism to an acceptance of Arab narratives of Israel as militarist oppressor state and occupier, part of the American hegemony, accompanied by the glorification of Palestine informed by what Wistrich calls the New Left's 'romantic cult of *guerilleros*'. This, Wistrich argues, has been supported by a shift to the right within Israel over the same period, and the rise in particular of religious nationalism, further turning the left away from Zionism, so that, as Cesarani puts it, anti-Zionism migrated from right to left.[8]

In the wake of 1967, Jewish writers began to identify a shift towards a left-wing anti-Zionist antisemitism. In France, Holocaust survivor Jacques Givet published *The Left against Israel? An Essay on Neo-Anti-Semitism* in 1968 and the historian Léon Poliakov published *From Anti-Zionism to Antisemitism* in 1969.[9] Givet used the term 'neo-antisemitism', and the term had entered the language of the Jewish community by 1974, when the Anti-Defamation League in the US published *The New Anti-Semitism*.[10]

The UN General Assembly Resolution 3379 of November 1975 defining Zionism as 'a form of racism and racial discrimination' was a crystallizing moment in this period. David Cesarani describes how this played out in Britain:

> During the intense wave of anti-Zionism which swept British campuses in the late 1970s, the main attack stemmed from the equation of Zionism with racism and the association of Israel with South Africa. The invasion of Lebanon in 1982, however, triggered an avalanche of anti-Zionism which saw major innovations in the British context.[11]

Within Anglo Jewry, these arguments were circulated through articles in the *Jewish Chronicle*.[12] The Union of Jewish Students was formed in the 1970s partly in response to a wave of campus 'anti-Zionism'[13] which was seen as demonizing Jewish students, and the battle against perceived left-wing antisemitism in the student movement became a key element in Jewish student politics,[14] and was thus part of the apprenticeship of many subsequent leaders in the Jewish community.

The rise of antisemitism after 1990

It was in 1990 that the first sustained analysis of what was coming to be called the 'new antisemitism' was published: *Anti-Zionism and*

Antisemitism in the Contemporary World, edited by Robert Wistrich and published for the Institute of Jewish Affairs (then directed by Anthony Lerman, a contributor to the book).[15] Michael Whine of the Community Security Trust[16] describes the broad trend of antisemitic incidents in recent decades: a rise in the early 1990s, in the wake of desecration of Jewish graves at Carpentras, with the growth of the most violent sections of the far right, and the emergence of Islamism in the UK – followed by a drop in the later 1990s with prosecutions of the far right and a calming of the Middle East situation during the Madrid/Oslo period.

There was, however, a rise again from 2000 'as a consequence of the overspill of tension in the Middle East'.[17] This correlation with events in the Middle East is significant, and confirms the trend observed by Wistrich and others noted above. Whine shows that temporary fluctuations in rates of antisemitic incidents in the UK correlating with Middle Eastern events were first apparent in 1992. However, this meant that during the Madrid/Oslo period of relative peace, 'anti-Zionism went into remission',[18] and Jewish communal leadership to some extent turned its attention away from antisemitism towards the continuity concerns described in the last chapter.

However, the Al-Aqsa Intifada, which broke out in October 2000, to some extent reversed this trend. Writing about American Jewry, Raffel describes a reorientation of the community – particularly at the grassroots – to Israel and its defence in wake of the uprising.[19] In Britain, Whine notes that 'October 2000 proved to be a watershed with regard to [antisemitic] incidents. There appears to have been a genuine change, both qualitative and quantitative after this point.' This can be seen in the almost fourfold growth in synagogue desecrations between the year before and the year after that point, and in the much greater brutality of the acts of violence.[20] The All-Party Parliamentary Inquiry into Antisemitism similarly identified 2000 as a watershed: whereas the position of Jews in Britain had historically improved, 'there has been a reversal of that progress since the year 2000'.[21]

Pierre-André Taguieff, in the opening words of his influential *Rising from the Muck*, wrote that: 'Not since World War II have anti-Jewish expressions had such currency in France among so many social groups, or met so little intellectual and political resistance as they have since the fall of 2000.'[22] Laurence and Vaisse also describe 2000 as a 'pivotal' point in Muslim–Jewish relations in France. According to the figures of the CNCDH (Commission Nationale Consultative des Droits de l'Homme – National Advisory Commission of Human Rights), before 2000, racist (anti-Arab and anti-black) incidents were more numerous than antisemitic incidents; after 2000, the reverse was true. Before 2000, there were proportionally more antisemitic incidents in the US than France; after 2000, the reverse was true.[23] The extreme right was responsible for 90 per cent of antisemitic acts in the 1990s; Arab and Muslim perpetrators were responsible for 80 per cent in 2000.[24] Similarly, in Canada, Yousef Sandouga's firebombing of a synagogue in Edmonton on 1 November 2000 was a widely commented on symbol of the new configuration; Sandouga stated that he attacked the synagogue 'out of frustration with events in the Middle East'.[25]

The following year saw events in the Middle East being even more dramatically acted out elsewhere: the 9/11 Al-Qaeda attacks on New York and Washington. For Phyllis Chesler, the 1990s were still 'long before the emergence of the new anti-semitism'; the 'turning point' was 9/11.[26] Immediately preceding the 9/11 attacks was the NGO Forum Against Racism at Durban attached to the UN's World Conference Against Racism in August and September 2001. The Durban NGO Forum was dominated by protests against Israel and Zionism. For David Matas, Durban was 'a whole new experience, a landmark for the NGO world, an event of significance beyond the confines of the fight against racism'.[27]

The period from 2001 saw a number of high-profile antisemitic incidents in the UK and elsewhere, incidents which received unprecedented levels of coverage in the non-Jewish media. Whine writes:

Two synagogue desecrations during early 2002, in Finsbury Park and Swansea, gave rise to sympathetic media coverage, the like of which the Anglo-Jewish community has rarely seen ... Such acts inevitably lead us to question whether we are once again facing a rising tide of antisemitism, as some have suggested, or whether it is the intense media coverage of these incidents that is making us feel less secure as a community.[28]

Alongside these high-profile violent incidents, however, there were a number of reports of 'dinner party' or 'salon' antisemitism: the casual currency of anti-Jewish views, often linked to virulent anti-Israeli and anti-American sentiment, in 'respectable' liberal circles.[29] In December 2001, after Petronella Wyatt wrote in the *Spectator* that 'since September 11 anti-Semitism and its open expression has become respectable at London dinner tables',[30] Barbara Amiel reported that the French ambassador to London described Israel as 'that shitty little country' at a dinner party at her house.[31] Antisemitism was now emanating from the anti-racist left: in January 2002, the liberal *New Statesman* carried its 'Kosher

Conspiracy?' cover, showing an American flag pierced by a Star of David. In Spring 2003, leading Labour leftist Tam Dalyell spoke of a government in thrall to a 'Zionist cabal' in a *Vanity Fair* interview.[32] In July, *Observer* columnist Richard Ingrams wrote 'I have developed a habit when confronted by letters to the editor in support of the Israeli government to look at the signature to see if the writer has a Jewish name. If so, I tend not to read it.'[33]

It was during this period that former left-wing feminist Phyllis Chesler wrote the key text, *The New Anti-Semitism: The Current Crisis and What We Must Do About It*,[34] which she describes writing from September 2002 to March 2003: 'A fever burnt in me, the task gave me no rest.'[35] It was in the same period that, in France, Pierre-André Taguieff's concept of 'the new Judeophobia' appeared.[36] From June 2003 to September 2004, the Organization for Security and Co-operation in Europe (OCSE) hosted a series of conferences on antisemitism. At the February 2004 Brussels conference, Cobi Benatoff, president of the European Jewish Congress, dramatically declared:

> We bring a message today and that message is a warning cry, a warning to Europe. We Jews are not able to live our daily lives as other European citizens. Anti-Semitism and prejudice has returned. The monster is here with us again.[37]

The OCSE's Berlin Declaration in April 2004 turned this message into an official recognition of the new antisemitism:

> Recognizing that anti-Semitism, following its most devastating manifestation during the Holocaust, has assumed new forms and expressions, which, along with other forms of intolerance, pose a threat to democracy, the values of civilization and, therefore, to overall security in the OSCE region and beyond.[38]

In 2006–2007, there were a series of prominent affairs that continued to give the 'new antisemitism' a high profile in the Jewish community's public conversation, at a time when the Jewish 'blogosphere' was rapidly growing. Most significantly, two American academics, John Mearsheimer and Stephen Walt, published an article, 'The Israel lobby' in the British periodical, *London Review of Books*.[39] The pair claimed that pro-Israel lobbyists were essentially responsible for American foreign policy, causing America to act against its own interests, for example in invading Iraq. The text was seen by many in the Jewish community as giving a new academic and anti-Zionist veneer to older discourses around a 'Jewish lobby'. The widespread circulation of the Mearsheimer-Walt thesis, emanating from academic and liberal sources, but disseminated broadly in the anti-Zionist movement, exemplified, for many in the Jewish community the growing power of the new antisemitism.

New antisemitism as a discourse

As we can see from the preceding section, there was clearly a shift in the nature and intensity of antisemitism, particularly around the turning point of 2000/2001, which gave rise to claims for the existence of a 'new antisemitism'. However, for many of the advocates of this claim (and particularly its most influential advocates), it is striking how the 'new antisemitism' resembles the old. The discourse of new antisemitism often elaborates a theme whereby antisemitism is portrayed as an eternal presence in Jewish life (especially in Europe), and the 'new' antisemitism as merely the most recent appearance. While the appearance changes, the reality, it seems, remains unchanged.[40]

The academic Daniel Cohn-Sherbok articulates this understanding:

> We can thus see that in the modern world the scourge of anti-Semitism has not disappeared, despite the terrors of the Holocaust. Instead, throughout Western and Eastern Europe and extending to the United States, the flames of Judaeophobia have been kept alive. In the wake of the wars, instabilities and uprisings in the Middle East, Muslims today carry the banner of anti-Semitism and constitute a constant threat to Jewish survival.[41]

A similar thesis is also promoted by Abraham Foxman, the influential leader of the US Anti-Defamation League, who uses the phrase 'old poison in a new bottle',[42] and by the MP Denis MacShane, who says 'antisemitism never seems to grow old'.[43]

The thesis feeds directly into a strategy of insecurity, because it creates a direct line of continuity and equivalence from the medieval pogrom to the Shoah to the anti-Israeli activism and terror attacks of the present era, positioning Jews as eternally endangered and ill able to afford complacency and a sense of secure belonging in Europe. This is signalled by Chesler's phrase 'postmodern pogroms', making electronically circulated union resolutions equivalent to organized ancient anti-Jewish bloodletting. And it is signalled in the title of Abraham Foxman's influential *Never Again?*,[44] evoking the image of a new Shoah, further amplified by the presence of a Foreword by prominent Holocaust survivor Elie Wiesel.

Such images of the new antisemitism – or the old poison in new bottles – circulate widely across differing contexts. For example, Chesler's *The New Anti-Semitism* uses a number of sources of information, including academic and semi-academic sources, some affiliated to the Jewish community and others not, many based in the US but some in Europe. These include: the Anti-Defamation League (ADL), the Board of Deputies, HonestReporting.com, the Israel Ministry of Foreign Affairs, the Stephen Roth Institute and the Simon Wiesenthal Center. As another example, *The Deadliest Lies* by Abraham Foxman of the ADL has a foreword by George Schultz, the Republican former secretary of state (1982–9) and distinguished fellow of the Hoover Institute.

As a third example, another influential work on the new antisemitism is David Matas's *Aftershock*.[45] Matas is a leading member of B'nai B'rith in Canada, and his book is endorsed on the front cover by Natan Sharansky and on the back cover by Abe Foxman. Acknowledgements are made to the Middle East Center for Peace and the Jacob Blaustein Institute in Vienna. North American commentators such as Matas, Chesler and Foxman, often connected to the official communal infrastructure of American Jewry (e.g. the ADL), have shaped the terms of the debate globally, their work widely commented on in Jewish communal publications and the Jewish public spheres in the UK.

However, European sources have also been crucial, such as the OCSE conferences, Pierre-André Taguieff's concept of 'the new Judeophobia' and Cobi Benatoff's alarmist statements in France. The authority of figures like Taguieff and Finkielkraut in the global Jewish public sphere is bolstered by a perception that the situation in France represents a sort of high-tide mark to date for the new antisemitism. Significantly, American (and to a lesser extent Israeli) perceptions of the situation in continental Europe, and especially France, have figured prominently in the debate around the new antisemitism, particularly since the 'shitty little country' remark in late 2001.

Laurence and Vaisse present a number of examples of this. In the mid 2000s, the notion of 'Eurabia', a Europe becoming part of the Arab world, emerged in American conservative discourse.[46] American journalists responded to the 2005 riots in French housing estates as 'Islamists taking the streets of Paris' and a 'distinct form of jihad', even though the riots had little or no religious content and not all rioters were Muslim. An article in the American Jewish Committee's magazine *Commentary* claimed that there are 'dozens of "ungovernable" areas in France', while Bernard Lewis spoke of a 'reverse colonization' in France, which is soon to be 'Islamicized'.[47] Laurence and Vaisse conclude:

> American Jewish organizations have closely tracked the rise of anti-Semitism in France, and they have repeatedly voiced their preoccupations … [American critics] sometimes painted a portrait of a uniformly anti-Semitic France, where the Vichy past was resurfacing and where the 'Final Solution, Phase 2,' as one columnist put it, was underway.[48]

Sharon's government also intervened, making 'comments stressing the danger for Jews of remaining in France amid the growing Muslim population'. French emigration did increase: in 2004, 6–8 per cent said they were preparing to emigrate to Israel, while the actual rate doubled from 2001–2002 to around 2,000 a year. Both the attacks and their discursive amplification in such US and Israeli interventions have led to a rise in a sense of insecurity among French Jews, which is hard to disentangle from the strengthening of communal infrastructure: 'Neighborhood security groups were created, French emigration to Israel increased, and Jewish schools experienced a wave of new enrollments – from 16,000 in the late 1980s to 28,000 in 2002, accounting for one-quarter of Jewish school-children.'[49]

England has figured in the debate too, although to a much smaller extent. In 2002, a *Ha'aretz* article by David Landau, 'Jewish angst in Albion', was central in defining the new mood of insecurity in Britain, and in highlighting this to a global audience. The American Jewish Committee published Alvin H. Rosenfeld's *Anti-Zionism in Great Britain and Beyond: A 'Respectable' Anti-Semitism?* in 2004, noting allegedly antisemitic comments by poet Tom Paulin and columnist Richard Ingrams, as well as moves for an academic and cultural boycott of Israel; it also claimed bias against Israel in the BBC.[50] In 2007, the influential Vidal Sassoon International Center for the Study of Antisemitism in Jerusalem held a symposium on Islam, British Society and the Terrorist Threat, involving the neo-conservative UK Jewish columnist Melanie Phillips, highlighting Islamic antisemitism.[51] Two of the three Yale Initiative for the Interdisciplinary Study of Antisemitism Research Working Papers have focused on the UK.[52]

Anglo Jewish leaders have responded to these perceptions in ambivalent ways: defining Britain as a place of relative security in contrast to mainland Europe, while also invoking images and information from France to foster insecurity among British Jews. For example, Jonathan Sacks warned at the end of 2005 of a 'tsunami of antisemitism' sweeping the world.[53] In his evidence to the All-Party Parliamentary Inquiry into Antisemitism, Sacks similarly invoked the situation in France to describe the gravity of the threat, with an anecdote about a French family on holiday getting a call from their son: 'The time has come for us to leave and go to Israel. France is not safe for us any more.'[54] The contrast between relatively safe Britain and totally unsafe France, with France as a possible future for Britain, allows for a continuation of the English exceptionalism built into the Anglo Jewish liberal compromise that underpinned its security strategy, while nonetheless stressing the need to British Jews to shake off their complacency, to become more insecure.

The most widely circulating texts on the new antisemitism, such as those of Melanie Phillips or Chesler, tend to be the vaguest, most simplistic and most alarmist.[55] Chesler defining the new antisemitism:

> a virulent epidemic of violence, hatred, and lies that are being touted as politically correct. Islamic reactionaries and western intellectuals and progressives who may disagree on every other subject have agreed that Israel and America are the cause of all evil. Israel has fast become the Jew of the world – scorned, scapegoated, demonized and attacked.

She also calls its 'modern anti-semitism', tracing its development in the Arab world from 1908 onwards, epitomized by the riots in Palestine in the 1920s and by the Mufti of Jerusalem.[56] Chesler's periodization is confusing. She talks about the emergence of what she alternately calls 'modern pogroms' or 'postmodern pogroms': 'not like the pogroms of old in which synagogues were torched [etc., but] a pogrom of nonstop words and ideas, an exercise in total intimidation', for example the UN resolutions calling Zionism a form of racism. She talks of

> ideological and other kinds of terrorism against Jews, Israel and the United States ... During this period, the Russians and the Europeans commandeered the propaganda war against Israel. The Palestinian and Muslim terrorists took to the streets, so to speak.[57]

This sort of slippage (modern *and* postmodern, a century old *and* new, violent *and* discursive), as well as the alarming language, create a version of the new antisemitism which is not analytically helpful, but nevertheless *discursively productive*, in that it does considerable work in generating insecurity and thus mobilizing a response. Similarly, the widely circulating texts use images of antisemitism as a 'monster' (as in Cobi Benatoff's 'The monster is here with us again', quoted above) or a 'virus' (e.g. Sacks: 'Antisemitism is not a belief. It is a virus'[58]). Again, in this context, the new antisemitism is not something that can be analysed and understood, it is a disease to be eradicated, a terror to be feared.

These sorts of understandings of antisemitism generate a gallery of others who are positioned as the Jewish community's constitutive outside: an unholy alliance of Arab terrorists, leftists, neo-Nazis and the liberal media. The perpetrators of violent attacks on Jews, whether Islamist or from the fascist right, are prominent within this gallery; figures such as Osama bin Laden, the 7/7 bombers or Yousef Sandouga are constantly evoked in books such as Chesler's and Foxman's. However, taking a central position in this gallery of others, and exemplifying one of the key 'newnesses' of the new antisemitism, are liberal intellectuals. The image of the dinner party, as in Petronella Wyatt and Barabra Amiel's examples, recurs, as does that of the college campus. MacShane writes: 'Antisemitism was once called the socialism of fools. It is now the ideology of clever and determined men ... capable of taking different forms from the university campus to the upper-class dinner party.'[59] *Commentary*'s Gabriel Schoenfeld writes:

> today, the most vicious ideas about Jews are not primarily voiced by downtrodden and disenfranchised fringe elements of society but by its most successful, educated and 'progressive' members ... One is less likely to find anti-Semites today in beer halls and trailer parks than on college campuses and among the opinion makers of the media elite.

Or: 'the street-level scene is only the beginning; it is in the world of elite opinion and high politics that the nature of the European anti-Semitic movement becomes fully evident'.[60]

The identification of a novel form of respectable, liberal, intellectual antisemitism – albeit, as Schoenfeld notes, with deep roots in the Enlightenment and socialist tradition[61] – is not without some foundation.[62] However, one effect of a stress on this new formation is to endow the new antisemitism with a particular form of cultural power. A key term in Schoenfeld's formulation quoted above is 'the opinion makers of the media elite'. While the gallery of others evoked in the new antisemitism discourse links the dinner party antisemites to the bombers and jihadists, the image of the media is an image of the power of antisemitism. This feeds directly into a discourse of insecurity, allowing the new antisemitism discourse to be operationalized in legitimating particular forms of communal authority.[63]

Operationalizing the discourse

Alarmist language, vague definitions and a concentration on headline statistics rather than sophisticated analysis, along with the idea of the new antisemitism as merely old poison in new bottles and the image of Europe (as opposed to America and Israel) as a land eternally blighted by Jew-hatred: these elements have combined to create a sense of the European – and by extension the British – Jew today as fundamentally unsafe. All these themes, for example, are encapsulated in these quotations, from American Jewish commentator Charles Krauthammer, from Avi Beker of the World Jewish Congress, from the French commentator Alain Finkielkraut and from Abraham Foxman:

> In Europe, it is not very safe to be a Jew. What is odd is not the antisemitism of today, but its relative absence during the past half-century. That was the historical anomaly. Holocaust shame kept the demon corked. But now the atonement is passed.[64]

> these are the worst antisemitic days in Europe since the end of the second world war.[65]

> Political, social, cultural Europe is once more disfigured by this most ancient and vile prejudice ... And the Jews have a heavy heart. For the first time since the war they are afraid.[66]

> We live in tumultuous times. The continuing war on terror, unrest in the Middle East, and a faltering world economy are capturing headlines everywhere and contributing to a wide-spread sense of unease and anxiety ... The pattern is particularly strong in Europe, the historic breeding ground of anti-Semitism and the continent where, just sixty years ago, the greatest crime in history – the Holocaust – was perpetrated against the Jewish people.[67]

These claims that feelings of unsafety and fears of the danger of the recurrence of the Holocaust are prevalent within British Jewry have been harnessed, even fostered, by Anglo Jewry's communal leadership as a strategy to legitimate its claim to represent the community. In this section, therefore, we will examine the 'operationalization' of the new antisemitism discourse.

Even during the period when the strategy of security was still dominant, the Jewish community gradually developed its own 'defence' organizations. The Board of Deputies defence group and the Association of Jewish Servicemen quietly developed an infrastructure for intelligence and security against antisemitism in the post-war period. These efforts came to fruition in 1994 with the formation of the Community Security Trust (CST). The CST and its predecessors have collected statistics on antisemitism since 1984 and it acts as a watchdog against antisemitic discourse. It also provides security for Jewish events and trains security personnel, working closely with the police. It now has over fifty staff and over 3,000 volunteers. The CST also works alongside more activist organizations, such as Searchlight and its recent anti-BNP campaign Hope Not Hate.

The formation of the Union of Jewish Students (UJS) in 1973 was another important development in Anglo Jewry's battle with the new antisemitism. The UJS, along with the small Trotskyist group Socialist Organiser (now the Alliance for Workers Liberty), have regularly supported National Organisation of Labour Students (NOLS) candidates in National Union of Students (NUS) elections, and the NUS has tended to be strongly supportive of UJS campaigns against left and Islamist antisemitism. This alliance from the 1970s to the 1990s had crucial effects after 1997 with the election of the New Labour government. For example, Mike Gapes, chair of NOLS in 1976, later became an MP and was a vice chair of Labour Friends of Israel. John Mann, the chair in 1983–4, later, as an MP, took a leading role in combating antisemitism, chairing the All-Party Parliamentary Group against Antisemitism and in 2009 receiving the American Jewish Committee's Jan Karski Award in recognition of his commitment to fighting antisemitism. Stephen Twigg, NUS president 1990–92, subsequently became an MP and chair of Labour Friends of Israel. Lorna Fitzsimons, NUS president 1992–4, after her career as an MP became the CEO of the Britain Israel Communications and Research Centre (BICOM). Jim Murphy, NUS president 1994–6, also became an MP and another chair of Labour Friends of Israel. Murphy gave the keynote address at the parliamentary launch of the European Institute for the Study of Contemporary Anti-Semitism (EISCA) in 2008. Former members of Socialist Organiser have been involved in Engage, a campaign against left anti-Zionist antisemitism, and *Democratiya*, an online journal critical of various forms of left antisemitism.

Following the outbreak of the 2000 Intifada, another wave of institution building in support of Israel and against antisemitism took place: BICOM was founded in 2001; Engage was founded against academic boycotts in 2005; and the European Institute for the Study of Contemporary Antisemitism (EISCA) was founded in 2007 with close connections to the Board of Deputies. New coalitions and ad hoc campaigns also emerged: the Fair Play Campaign Group was established by the Board of Deputies of British Jews and the Jewish Leadership Council in December 2006 to coordinate activity against boycotts of Israel and other anti-Zionist campaigns. Focusing specifically on the academic boycott, the JLC and BICOM formed Stop The Boycott in 2007.[68]

In 2008, the Fair Play Campaign Group published a grassroots Israel activist pack, with a message from Board of Deputies President Henry Grunwald. In May 2002, an Israel Solidarity rally organized by the Board of Deputies in London was attended by between 30,000 and 55,000 people, addressed by Jonathan Sacks, Israeli Prime Minister Benjamin Netanyahu, Labour MP Peter Mandelson, and Conservative Deputy Leader and Shadow Foreign Secretary Michael Ancram.[69] All of this constituted a major area of communal activity, involving large numbers of members of the community.

This work also had an impact, for example, in helping to inform the work of the All-Party Parliamentary Inquiry into Antisemitism, to which the Chief Rabbi and the president of the Board, as well as representatives of the Community Security Trust, the Union of Jewish Students and Engage were all invited to give evidence. This also led to the global Inter-parliamentary Coalition for Combating Antisemitism, whose inaugural conference in London in January 2009 saw the adoption of the London Declaration on Combating Antisemitism, signed by parliamentarians from Germany, Canada, the US, Italy and elsewhere.

Although not specifically tied to the rise of the new antisemitism, another sign of the community's activity in highlighting insecurity was in the UK parliament's decision to establish an annual Holocaust Memorial Day staring on 27 January 2001. The day owed as much to global efforts to memorialize the Holocaust as it did to Jewish communal lobbying and not all British Jews supported the commemoration.[70] Nevertheless, communal bodies by and large welcomed the day and have fought hard to defend it from criticism from other communities that it monopolizes Jewish suffering. This willingness publicly to articulate Jewish insecurity through wielding the Holocaust as a pre-eminent symbol of suffering was an early indicator of the willingness of communal organizations to raise issues of antisemitism in the 2000s.

Challenging the discourse: against ethnic panic

Fairly early on in the history of the new antisemitism discourse voices began
to emerge within the Jewish community challenging it. In North America,
Leon Wieseltier warned against 'ethnic panic', concluding that the 'Jewish
genius for worry has served the Jews well, but Hitler is dead'.[71] In the UK,
Anthony Julius, writing in the *Guardian* at the start of 2002,[72] argued that
while there may be more Israel-related antisemitism now than in the Oslo
period, there is less than there was in the 1970s, the period of the UN
resolution, of the anti-Zionist attempts to ban university Jewish societies,
of a cult of the PLO and of Constituency Labour parties passing resolutions calling for the destruction of the Zionist entity: 'By any sensible
calculus of danger, English Jews are not in danger.'[73] This view is characterized by MP Denis MacShane as 'the Panglossian argument'.[74]

In an August 2002 article, 'Sense on antisemitism', in the influential
centre-left monthly magazine *Prospect*, Tony Lerman took issue with
excessive statements of Jewish insecurity. Significantly for our argument,
he placed these statements in a historical context, contrasting the Chief
Rabbi, Jonathan Sacks, who has articulated the dangers of the new
antisemitism, with his predecessor, Lord Jakobovits, who 'repeatedly
emphasized that antisemitism was in significant decline'.[75] The 'argument
begins', he wrote, with al Aqsa in September 2000, continued with Durban,
followed by 9/11:

> Some synagogues were torched and desecrated, and a small prefab-
> ricated synagogue in Manchester burned down. In April, the
> *Independent* published a front page picture of a desecrated synagogue
> in North London. With it ran the headline: 'A picture that tells a
> shocking story: the rise of antisemitism in Britain.' What is the expla-
> nation for, and evidence of, this alleged rise in antisemitism?[76]

Lerman argued, however, that far from auguring a new Holocaust, the
Middle East-linked antisemitism of today is radically different from
classical antisemitism.

> The mix of antisemitism and anti-Zionism in the Arab and Muslim
> worlds is different from traditional European antisemitism in two
> respects. First, the hostility to Jews is grounded in a real grievance and
> second, as a result, the antisemitic form in which this grievance is
> sometimes expressed is mutable: it can increase or decrease according
> to events. This makes it different from classic European anti-semitism,

which is largely grounded in myth and fantasy and not susceptible to such change.[77]

Why, he asked, has there been a rise in the 'new antisemitism' narrative? His first answer was defence of Israel. The state

> came into existence at the moment of greatest weakness for Jews, giving them a sense of security and pride. So the 'new antisemitism' is, in part, not new at all but rather a device for de-legitimizing criticism of Israel and a political weapon in a global propaganda battle.[78]

Jewish academic Brian Klug also challenged the new antisemitism discourse. In a 2003 issue of the journal *Patterns of Prejudice* (then published by the Institute for Jewish Policy Research), he wrote that 'the empirical evidence overwhelmingly supports the view that hostility towards Israel, at bottom, is not a new form of anti-Semitism; it is a function of a deep and bitter conflict'. Supporters of Palestine are 'not anti-Semitic'; 'they are just not being Jewish'. And 'the longer Israel is at loggerheads with the rest of the region, the more likely it is that anti-Semitism will take on a life of its own'.[79] Another Jewish academic, Neil Lazarus, more recently wrote of antisemitism as 'the Jewish addiction': 'The cry of anti-Semitism is wearing thin – even the rebranded, ready to go, even nastier "new" anti-Semitism is having little appeal to a new generation of Jews who do not remember the Holocaust.'[80]

The 'Livingstone formulation'

Around the same time as Lerman and Klug were writing, a new counter-discourse was emerging that claimed that the purpose of talk of a 'new antisemitism' was in fact to stifle criticism of Israel. Although almost every single commentator who has spoken of the new antisemitism – from Jonathan Sacks to Barbara Amiel to Abraham Foxman – has *defended* the right to criticize Israel (although they are often extremely circumscribed about the terms in which that criticism might be legitimate), the idea began to circulate that any criticism of Israel was immediately countered by such commentators with accusations of the new antisemitism.

Peter Pulzer documented some early formulation of this discourse. A 'senior *Guardian* journalist', according to the paper's Reader's Editor, Ian

Mayes, complained of the 'clearly orchestrated pressure to equate any criticism of the Israeli government with anti-Semitism'. The *Independent*'s Robert Fisk wrote that a 'vicious campaign of slander (of 'anti-Semitism') is now being used against anyone who dares to criticize Israeli politics'. Writing in the *Observer*, Peter Beaumont claimed that 'the charges of the new anti-Semitism should be rejected for what they are: an attempt to deflect criticism from the actions of an Israeli government by declaring criticism out of bounds'.[81] Pulzer commented:

> On the one hand Jews who individually or collectively support the [Israeli] state or its government's polices are delegitimized as 'the Jewish lobby'; on the other hand Jews are called on, in their capacity as Jews, to condemn the Sharon government. Peter Beaumont: 'The Jewish community worldwide must be honest too about what is really being done in Israel, ostensibly in its name.' This means that Jews, whether they like it or not, bear a collective guilt for the government of a state in which they do not live and in which they do not have a vote.[82]

He also summarized some of the responses in the mainstream media to the new antisemitism debate: it can pretend that it is simply a revival of fascism. According to Seamus Milne, 'all the evidence is that it is the far right, the traditional fount of anti-semitic poison, which has been responsible for attacks on both Muslim and Jewish targets in Europe'. Alternatively, it can assert that if antisemitism is not the fault of the far right, then its perpetrators should be pitied rather than countermined, as in Lindsay Hilsum's 2002 article, 'I am not an anti-Semite', in the *New Statesman*, describing French Muslim perpetrators as alienated and excluded. Or it can claim to see nothing wrong in cartoons that recall 'classic' antisemitism imagery, albeit veiled in irony, as in the case of defenders of the *New Statesman* kosher conspiracy cover.[83]

The philosopher Bernard Harrison also analyses these sorts of denial of the new antisemitism. 'Walt and Mearsheimer avail themselves of the familiar accusation that it is impossible to voice any criticism of Israel without being accused of anti-Semitism.' They also claim that 'concern about "the new anti-Semitism"' represents an entirely dishonest attempt by Jews supportive of the aims of the Israel lobby to smear pro-Palestinian journalists and intellectuals, including the authors:

> Israel's advocates, when pressed, claim that there is a 'new antisemitism' which they equate with criticism of Israel. Speaking as

a non-Jew, I have read most of what has been published so far on 'the new anti-Semitism,' most of it ... by Jews. None of this writing, to my knowledge, asserts equivalence between anti-Semitism and criticism of Israel ... The proposition that 'the Jews' try to represent all criticism of Israel as anti-Semitic is, of course, itself – in its own right, as it were – an anti-Semitic calumny.[84]

Scholar and activist David Hirsh has described the attempt to claim that complaints about instances of the new antisemitism are actually intended to muzzle criticism of Israel as 'the Livingstone Formulation', after one of its key articulators, then Mayor of London Ken Livingstone, who said in 2006 'for far too long the accusation of antisemitism has been used against anyone who is critical of the policies of the Israeli government'.[85] Hirsh defines the formulation as 'the claim that people are accused of antisemitism in order to delegitimize their criticisms of Israeli human rights abuses' – or '"crying Israel" in order to de-legitimize those who [are] concerned about [antisemitism]'.[86] The Livingstone Formulation, in other words, seeks to defuse the new antisemitism discourse by claiming that the new antisemitism is a fiction created by supporters of Jews to defend Israel.

At their most extreme, accusations of antisemitism and counter-accusations of using antisemitism to defend Israel are often the mirror image of each other. Sweeping statements that criticism of Israel are not antisemitic ignore the ways in which they sometimes can be. Sweeping statements that accusations of antisemitism are not cynical attempts to defend Israel ignore the ways in which such accusations of antisemitism can inhibit discussion of Israel. Both positions make it difficult to disentangle the complex relationship between Israel and antisemitism.

Challenging the discourse: Independent Jewish Voices

A line of argument similar to Lerman's was taken up in 2007 by the group Independent Jewish Voices (IJV). IJV was a network of Jewish individuals concerned about the ways in which the community was led and represented, and in particular about its support for Israel. Its starting point was a Declaration, 'A Time to Speak Out':

We are a group of Jews in Britain from diverse backgrounds, occupations and affiliations who have in common a strong commitment to social justice and universal human rights. We come together in the belief that the broad spectrum of opinion among the Jewish population of this country is not reflected by those institutions which claim authority to represent the Jewish community as a whole. We further believe that individuals and groups within all communities should feel free to express their views on any issue of public concern without incurring accusations of disloyalty.

We have therefore resolved to promote the expression of alternative Jewish voices, particularly in respect of the grave situation in the Middle East.[87]

The Steering Group of IJV included Brian Klug, Rabbi David Goldberg, Lady Ellen Dahrendorf, who is on the board of a number of Jewish communal bodies, including the Institute for Jewish Policy Research and the New Israel Fund, senior lawyer Sir Geoffrey Bindman, and high-profile academics such as Jacqueline Rose and Lynne Segal.

IJV was a contradictory formation. In one sense, it can be seen as an heir to the democratizing tradition in Anglo Jewish life, a tradition ironically exemplified in the 1917 and 1943 Zionist 'communal revolutions' discussed in chapter 1. In this sense, IJV gave organizational form to a strong belief within Anglo Jewry that the leadership did not adequately represent the diversity of the community. This belief can be seen, for example, in an interview with playwright Julia Pascal conducted by Nick Lambert in the early 2000s: 'The Jewish establishment is mainly male, middle-aged and rich. I am critical of the conservative voices of these self-proclaimed "leaders", who believe they can speak for the rest of us.'[88]

Comment is Free's editor, Georgina Henry,[89] introduced the IJV launch by explicitly drawing a comparison with the launch on the website the previous November of the New Generation Network (NGN), a group of mainly Asian figures calling for a rethink of the ways in which Britain's ethnic and faith communities are represented:

In a throwback to the colonial era, our politicians have chosen to appoint and work with a select band of representatives and by doing so treat minority groups as monolithic blocks, only interested in race or faith based issues rather than issues that concern us all, such as housing, transport, foreign policy and crime.

Unfortunately, many self-appointed community representatives have an incentive to play up their victimisation. This arrangement allows politicians to pass on the burden of responsibility to them and treat minorities as outsiders. MPs have increasingly sought to politicise problems of segregation, political apathy, criminality and poverty into problems of race and religion, and shift responsibility onto appointed gate-keepers rather than find ways of engaging with all Britons.

This brand of politics works against the very people it is meant to help. The gate-keepers have helped to polarise the debate on community cohesion by taking extreme positions and failing to reflect more progressive opinion from those they claim to represent. Sikhs, Muslims, Christians, Hindus and Jews all have long traditions and histories of progressive thought, self-criticism and change.[90]

This call clearly echoes the concerns of British Jews in 1917 and 1943 who sought to resist unrepresentative and reactionary leaderships in the Jewish community, and there is a sense that the IJV criticisms of the Board were in this tradition. They also resonated with criticisms of the Muslim Council of Britain, British Islam's main representative body, made around the same time, for example by the newly formed Sufi Muslim Council.[91]

In a second sense, however, we can see the IJV signatories as dominated by what Lambert calls the 'Western-intellectual Jews', 'thinkers' or the 'unplatformed': Jewish intellectuals who have an ambivalent relationship with the mainstream Jewish community and its organizations. This category, however, is itself fairly loose. At one end, it includes someone like Rabbi Elizabeth Tikvah Sarah of Brighton and Hove Progressive Synagogue, who is a radical voice *within* British progressive Judaism; at the other end, it includes people like Eric Hobsbawm or Harold Pinter, who, though born Jewish, have had no institutional affiliation with any Jewish communal group.[92]

The third, and perhaps more obvious, dimension of IJV was its position on Israel. The accusation levelled at the Anglo Jewish leadership was that the mantra of communal unity was deployed in order to protect Israel from criticism. However, it is probably more the case that Israel is used by the communal leadership to legitimate its authority. Lambert writes:

[A] favoured term among communal elites is the notion of 'undermining the community'. As communal funders are traditionally conservative-minded, they sense that this attempt to 'speak out' is also an attempt to undermine their control over the community. As dissenting Jewish intellectuals challenge the myth of communal consensus, they will usually face the wrath of communal leaders, who will publicise them as a threat to 'communal well-being', requiring measures to 'defend the community', which are designed to be at the expense of such Jewish intellectuals.[93]

Thus, while the Declaration was a general denunciation of the Anglo Jewish leadership, the companion pieces – by Brian Klug,[94] David Goldberg,[95] Gillian Slovo[96] and Anne Karpf[97] – concentrated almost exclusively on Israel, some raising comparisons between the state and apartheid South Africa.

Tony Lerman's contribution made the connection between the issue of Israel and the issue of antisemitism:

> The first fault-line is Israel. Since the second intifada started, the pro-Israel leaderships in Jewish communities urged Jews to close ranks and express complete solidarity with Israel. They tried to marginalise dissent, increasingly fostering a 'for us or against us' mentality. But deep dissatisfaction with this approach has grown ...
>
> The second fault-line is antisemitism. Pro-Israel and Zionist groups have interpreted intensified criticism of Israel and anti-Zionism as the expression of a 'new antisemitism'. The IJV initiative leans towards the view that this charge is far too often used in an attempt to stifle strong criticism of Israeli policies. Some of the strongest accusations are levelled at so-called 'left-liberal' Jewish critics who are being described as self-hating Jews or even 'Jewish antisemites'.[98]

The IJV declaration provoked a storm of criticism in the British Jewish community. One of the most vituperative critics was Melanie Phillips, who dubbed IJV 'Jews for Genocide' a cynical and mortal threat to Jewish security at a time when Islamists are calling for the extermination of the Jews.[99] Leftist Jewish voices also criticized IJV: Linda Grant, for example, argued that the preponderance of secular intellectuals among IJV signatories implied an abdication of responsibility from the work of encouraging debate on Israel among the mainstream Jewish community.[100] It is almost certainly the case that the overwhelming majority of grassroots members of the Jewish community was in fact broadly supportive of the state of Israel, even if not of all of its policies. As Geoffrey Alderman wrote in Comment is Free in response to IJV:

> After 1945, and in the wake of the shock of the Holocaust, Zionism – meaning support for the re-establishment of an independent Jewish state in Mandate Palestine – did however become the single most unifying force within the Jewish communities of the UK. This support is neither jingoistic nor uncritical. But it is real.
>
> As we read the petitions and statements signed by the glitterati of Anglo-Jewry we should take care not to permit ourselves to be

deceived by the actually small number of members of the Anglo-Jewish intelligentsia and showbiz industries who shamelessly exploit their media personae for the sole purpose of denouncing either specific Israeli governments or the state of Israel in general.

We would do better to recall that on 6 May 2002 Britain witnessed the largest demonstration of Jews and Jewesses that had ever been seen in the British Isles. This was at Trafalgar Square, and was in unequivocal support of the Jewish state.[101]

In a sense then the Board of Deputies and other mainstream communal organizations do represent the majority of the community's broad support for Israel and Zionism. That said, the problem with this form of representation is that it is a 'zero-sum' game: it does not recognize the existence of substantial minorities in opposition to it. In this respect the Board of Deputies, for all of its elected structure, fails to truly follow the parliamentary model as it has no room for an 'official opposition'.

At stake then in the IJV debate was the question of how and whether Jewish communal representation should be carried out. The IJV declaration was ambiguous on this point and it was never clear whether IJV were urging a revolution in representation, repudiating the concept of representation or declaring 'UDI' from the rest of the Jewish community. David Hirsh has dubbed the IJV-minded Jewish left as the 'new conservatives', arguing that:

> Traditionally, the Jewish leadership in Britain has been noted for its timidity in the face of antisemitism. When the fascists were on the rise in the 1970s, the Jewish left wanted to confront them while the apparently all-powerful Jewish troika, the Board of Deputies, the Chief Rabbi and the *Jewish Chronicle*, seemed to prefer the 'keep your heads down strategy'.
>
> A section of this Jewish left has now adopted the timid conservatism against which it used to rebel. The fire of 1968 has become a yearning to conform to those sections of the intelligentsia that understand Israel, and the Jews that 'support' it, as constituting a unique evil in the world and the greatest obstacle to world peace. It is a milieu that is increasingly ambivalent about the 'legitimacy' of Israel.[102]

It is certainly the case that disputing definitions and the prevalence of antisemitism within the Jewish community will inevitably raise parallels with the historical quietism of the Jewish communal leadership. In addition there are elements of the discourse of the IJV left that echo previous eras.[103] For example, in 2002 David Goldberg, Emeritus Rabbi of the Liberal Jewish Synagogue (which had previously been at the forefront of Anglicized opposition of Zionism) wrote that:

> By any objective criteria, the modern, acculturated, broadly accepted, successful Jew in the Western world has never had it so good. We should never cease to be vigilant about anti-semitism, but at present it is far easier and safer to be a Jew in Britain than a Muslim, a black person or an east European asylum seeker. I wish my co-religionists would remember that the next time they feel inclined to whinge about perceived anti-Israel media bias.[104]

Rabbi Goldberg could be accused here of wanting a return to an earlier communal language of security. Nonetheless, the 'new conservatives' label is inaccurate in other respects. For one thing, the IJV Jewish left is not conservative by any other definition. Further, for the most part IJV signatories do not seek to take over existing Jewish communal organizations, not even necessarily to challenge their existing leadership. Neither are they counselling quietism in public Jewish expression more generally.

What the 'new conservatives' term does effectively highlight though is how the leadership of the Jewish community, in publicly emphasizing antisemitism and defending Israel, had decisively turned away from the old strategy of security. The Jewish communal leadership had never demonstrated its adaptation to multicultural Britain more than in its propensity in the 2000s to draw attention to antisemitism through a strategy of insecurity. This does not mean, however, that challenges to the way the communal leadership has operationalized discourse about antisemitism and Israel necessarily derive from a desire to turn the clock back to the strategy of security (although for a small minority this might be the case). Rather, the leadership and its critics are *both* taking advantage of *different* possibilities that multiculturalism affords: one publicly to stress insecurity in order to legitimize its communal authority, the other to challenge the automatic right of communal elites to speak for others.

Beyond the new antisemitism?

For all the sound and fury that IJV generated, its impact was not revolutionary and it did not generate any substantial changes in the communal structure. In 2008, an edited Independent Jewish Voices anthology was published that set out in more detailed the position of various IJV contributors.[105] IJV holds semi-regular meetings and at the time of writing the declaration has over 600 signatories. IJV and other groups such as Jews for Justice for Palestinians (whose declaration has over 1,500 signatories) form a highly active opposition to automatic British Jewish support for Israel. Although they remain marginal to the Jewish community, there are signs that a more critical attitude to Israel might be taking shape within the mainstream of the community. Groups which are committed to peace and justice in the Middle East, such as the New Israel Fund and One Voice, have grown *within* the mainstream Jewish community. The progressive US lobbying group J Street in 2008 began to develop a self-identified 'pro-Israel' lobby that is nonetheless highly critical of the occupation, and at the time of writing confidential conversations are being held to investigate the feasibility of establishing a similar initiative in the UK.[106]

Just as significant was the fall-out from events in Israel in early 2009. The conflict in Gaza at the start of the year was a source of unease for many British Jews. The 11 January 2009 Israel solidarity rally, organized by the Board of Deputies in Trafalgar, was rebranded under the slogan 'Peace in Israel and Peace in Gaza', and attendance figures were considerably lower than at the 2002 event.[107] Rabbi Danny Rich, the chief executive of Liberal Judaism, made a public statement disassociating himself from the march, instead signing a call for a ceasefire with other faith leaders.[108] The event was also notable for the Jewdas hoax 'cancellation' discussed in the previous chapter.

The *Jewish Chronicle* published an article by Jonathan Freedland saying why he was not rallying for Israel in the context of the conflict in Gaza. He noted a letter published in the *Observer* on the same day by Jewish critics of the way Israel was prosecuting the conflict:

> The signatories were not the usual suspects; they could not be dismissed as marginal or, heaven forbid, 'self-hating' Jews.
>
> They included the leaders of Liberal and Reform Judaism in Britain, along with the pre-eminent British scholar of Jewish history, David Cesarani, and the architect of Holocaust Memorial Day, Michael Mitzman. Baroness Julia Neuberger was there, as was that indefatigable fighter against antisemitism, Shalom Lappin.
>
> They declared themselves to be 'profound and passionate supporters of Israel'. But they warned that Cast Lead 'could strengthen extremists, destabilise the region and ... threaten to undermine international support for Israel.[109]

The letter was significant, as it demonstrated a novel willingness of mainstream Jewish communal leaders to criticize Israel, publicly, during one its military campaigns.[110] In general, the UK Jewish leadership response to Operation Cast Lead was something of a debacle. The rally was held in part as a response to criticism that the communal response to the Lebanon war of summer 2006 – in which a small rally had been held at Jews' Free School – was too feeble. Following the war the Board of Deputies and the Jewish Leadership Council had promised that, in future, the community would be more robust and public in its defence of Israel.[111] Yet when it came to it, a broad-based rally was only made possible through frenzied behind-the-scenes negotiations and compromises[112] (such as setting up a phone number to donate money to Israeli and Palestinian hospitals). The Board and the JLC were caught between those who were unambiguously behind Israel's actions and those who were appalled by the assault on Sderot but highly ambivalent about the suffering incurred in Israel's response. The episode highlighted the often ignored fact that, as well as being criticized for being too pro-Israel and too willing to cry antisemitism, communal bodies are also vulnerable to criticism for not being forceful enough – for retaining too much of the strategy of insecurity.[113]

The right-wing politician Avigdor Lieberman's inclusion in the Israeli government after the April 2009 elections provoked further public criticisms from Anglo Jewry's leaders.[114] The Israeli elections were followed closely by the elections for the officers of the Board of Deputies, and it is possible that the revulsion towards Lieberman and concern at Israel's rightward turn had an impact on the results. The successful presidential candidate, Vivian Wineman, was a former chairman of British Friends of Peace Now and a founder of the British branch of the New Israel Fund. Another Peace Now leader, Laurence Brass, was elected unopposed as treasurer. Brass told the *Jewish Chronicle*:

> I shall never agree to give unquestioning support to the policies of the Israeli government at all times. While I am fully aware of the responsibilities of public office, I do not propose to suspend my commitment to human rights or sacrifice the principles on which I have campaigned for many years in order to blindly echo the Board's official line.[115]

Wineman himself provoked some controversy in July 2009 for an op-ed in the *Jerusalem Post* describing a report of antisemitism in Britain as 'misguided and alarmist'.[116] His op-ed described antisemitism, including anti-Zionist antisemitism, as a threat, but argued that it has not reached an epidemic level. He noted a number of causes for hope, such as a government fund for British–Israeli academic cooperation, the open friendship for Israel cultivated by the British government, and the All-Party Parliamentary Inquiry into Antisemitism. There have been other mainstream communal leaders – including those who are involved in the fight against antisemitism – who have similarly cautioned against the more extreme forms of rhetoric on antisemitism in the UK, pointing out that Jewish life in Britain remains strong.[117]

Conclusion

Whether or not concern about the new antisemitism is justified, the prevalence of the discourse illustrated the confidence of the Jewish leadership in articulating insecurity publicly in multicultural Britain. The discourse also entangled the community in impossibly complex questions of representation, leading to much bitterness and division. It is now clear that any Jewish organization that aspires to speak for British Jews or represent their interests will not be able to fulfil its mission without recognizing the inevitability that at least some Jews will disagree about issues of Israel and antisemitism.

As the 'Limmud generation' described in the previous chapter begins to enter communal leadership roles, it is possible that Jewish organizations will come to be led by people with a more sophisticated understanding of pluralism than has previously been the case. That generation will have to grapple with how far the strategy of insecurity that was hitherto so effective in producing action in the Jewish community may have outlived its usefulness. It may be that neither strategies of security or insecurity can mobilize community action while retaining community cohesion. In the next chapter we will consider the challenges the British Jewish community must face in the future.

Conclusion

The Future of Jewish Community in Multicultural Britain

A paradoxical community

This book has argued that the British Jewish community has, since 1990, implemented a series of important changes to its institutions and in a more nebulous way to its leaders' discourses and to its 'culture'. We are not arguing that the changes we discussed have transformed the entirety of the community. Indeed, assessing the significance of the changes we have discussed requires an appreciation of the complexity of the British Jewish community, since as Israel Finestein puts it: 'Tell tale signs of erosion and revival, of wide indifference, and wide enthusiasm for Jewish knowledge, offer at times a bewilderingly chequered communal picture.'[1]

Two apparent paradoxes are particularly important to consider: first, that the flourishing and renewal of British Jewish life has taken place alongside an increase in publicly articulated concerns about antisemitism. Second, that British Jewish life has been renewed despite the fact that many of the major deep-seated anachronisms, divisions and weaknesses of the community remain unreformed.

The first paradox is the easier to explain. Institutional renewal and discourse about antisemitism are linked by the strategy of insecurity we discussed in chapter 3. The willingness of communal leaders in the 1990s to articulate their concerns *internally* about the insecurity of British Jewish communal survival helped to pave the way for the articulation of their concerns *externally* about the insecurity of Anglo Jewry with regard to the 'new antisemitism' from 2000. The strategy, in both its internally and externally directed 'moments', stemmed from a fundamental shift in the position of Anglo Jewry with regard to multicultural Britain. The British Jewish community emerged during a time of official monoculturalism, in which it was difficult for minorities publicly to articulate their concerns and in which the communal leadership saw its primary task as facilitating the secure belonging of British Jews as British citizens. By the 1990s, the communal leadership finally felt able implicitly to embrace the possibilities that multiculturalism affords for articulating insecurity. In other words, the articulation of fears about antisemitism provides an implicit recognition that the British Jewish community had achieved security in a monocultural society, but would need to behave very differently in a multicultural one. Multiculturalism is itself paradoxical in that it endows the security necessary to express insecurity.

The second paradox lies in the simultaneously unreformed and renewed nature of the contemporary British Jewish community. In the late 1980s, an observer might have pointed to the following structural aspects of Anglo Jewry that urgently needed reform: over-dependence on a small number of donors; an oligarchical leadership structure; deep divisions between religious denominations; a chief rabbinate that only represented a minority of British Jews; a United Synagogue increasingly under the influence of right-wing orthodoxy; a Board of Deputies that did not represent the full spectrum of Anglo Jewish opinion. None of these issues have been addressed. The structure of the community remains divided, unrepresentative and prone to takeover by small, unrepresentative cliques. The renewal of Anglo Jewry has been directed more at the 'content' of the Jewish community and its institutions than at the community's organizational structure itself.

The history of the British Jewish community since the 1990s demonstrates that an unreformed and conservative establishment need not necessarily prevent communal renewal and dynamism. The continued survival and even flourishing of the United Synagogue shows what can be done when desire for change goes hand in hand with an equal desire for organizational continuity. The latter desire might be called conservatism, but it is a conservatism of a particular kind in which structures are protected while the functions of the organization are subject to renewal. Even when some communal structures are such an impediment to renewal that new structures have to be built, the new does not necessarily wipe away the old. In many ways the Limmud conference has been revolutionary within Anglo Jewry in its pluralism and its unabashed intellectualism, but even as its structure bypasses existing communal structural divisions, it has also helped to renew those very same structures.

The British Jewish community provides a reminder of the continued relevance of the sociological preoccupation with the unintended consequences of human action. As we argued in chapter 6, the more radical developments in the culture of British Jewry stemmed, at least in part, from more conservatively intended changes. The vision of Jewish continuity and identity set out by Jonathan Sacks, and initiatives such as Jewish Continuity was much more rigid than that of Jewdas and other Jewish arts and cultural practitioners, yet the two are linked by a shared desire for renewal.

These unintended consequences suggest that critiques of the conservatism of the British Jewish community need to be qualified. As progressive-minded British Jews, we share the concerns that the British Jewish community is hierarchical and oligarchical, that many of its institutions are unrepresentative, that open discussion of Israel is often made difficult, that right-wing orthodoxy is disproportionately influential and that cross-communal relations are often stymied by political divisions. We also recognize that despite these forbidding problems, the British Jewish community has nonetheless managed to renew itself in ways that make more critical and radical visions of Jewish identity much easier to pursue than was previously the case.

While it is tempting to yearn for a revolutionary moment in which the more archaic and oppressive structures of the community might be swept away, it is important to recognize the advantages of the kind of incremental changes that the community has seen: by ensuring that the outward institutional structures of the community remain intact, the renewal of the British Jewish community has proceeded in ways that are much more likely to carry the majority of British Jews with it. The high tolerance for anachronism in Anglo Jewry helps to retain the possibility for widespread communal change. While we can certainly appreciate the intense frustrations that lead to initiatives such as Independent Jewish Voices, there is still 'everything to play for' in mainstream communal activity.

The future of British Jewish community

Prognostications about the future of Jews and Judaism are always fraught with risk. As we saw in chapters 2 and 3, there is a long history of dire warnings about the survival of the Jewish people in general, and more particularly about the condition of Anglo Jewry. The experience of the British Jewish community since 1990 suggests that there is ground for cautious optimism about the future of Anglo Jewry. We do suggest though that there are a number of challenges that policy-makers and opinion formers in the British Jewish community would do well to attend to.

The continuing challenge of survival

Regardless of the significant improvements in the dynamism of British Jewish communal life, the continuity and survival of British Jewish community will continue to be an issue. As long as individuals in modern societies retain a choice as to how to behave and what to identify with, there will be no guarantees that individuals will remain Jewish. The concern for Jewish continuity/survival/renewal – call it what you will – has to be a permanent one. While there will never be a consensus as to how this can best be achieved, any vision for Anglo Jewry has to be operationalized through a dynamic self-renewing process of policy-making and implementation. However 'successful' particular strategies may be, at the very least such a process will help to guard against the dangers of stasis.

The challenge of survival also requires strategies to motivate renewal. As we have seen, the strategy of insecurity was effective at doing this in the early 1990s, but it may not be effective in the future. To some extent the strategy of security and the continuity consensus it engendered avoided difficult questions as to *why* Jewish life is worth continuing. For religious thinkers such as Jonathan Sacks these questions could be answered in theological terms, but for others such questions were much more awkward. Given the 'secular' character of much of the Jewish community and its leadership – secular at least in terms of not believing in divine commandments – the question of why Jewish life is valuable needs to be addressed. Can Fackenheim's eleventh commandment still resonate as the Holocaust recedes into history?

The challenge of demography

Aside from the challenge of survival, there are two demographic trends that present a serious challenge to the British Jewish community. One is the rapid growth of the British Haredi community as an increasingly significant proportion of British Jewry. The other is that the Israeli Jewish community will soon become the largest Jewish community in the world. Both demographic trends threaten to marginalize 'middle-of-the-road' Jewry both in terms of Britain and the wider world. In an Israel and a Diaspora increasingly dominated by conservative religious forces, the power of existing communal elites is likely to come under increasing challenge. The future of non-Haredi British Jewry within the Jewish world depends on the community 'punching above its weight' through providing sources of innovation such as Limmud to the Jewish world. It is also possible that the UK, like other Diaspora countries, may become something of a haven from a fundamentalist-dominated Israel. Certainly there is now a growing secular Israeli Diaspora worldwide, with a significant presence in London, although its connection to the British Jewish community is variable.

The challenge of community

In the introduction to this book we argued that the 'mainstream' of Anglo Jewry should be understood as being institutionally anchored in some way into a self-conscious Jewish community. Definitions of and identification with such communities are never homogeneous and there is no consensus as to what British Jewish community means and what its boundaries are. However, we would argue that, at least for the moment, the various definitions of community and its various institutions overlap closely enough so as to provide a kind of 'cluster' of spaces that constitute a British Jewish community. The paradoxical process of change in British Jewish community since 1990 has meant that the more radical and more conservative elements of Anglo Jewry – excluding the Haredi community – have retained a connection to each other, just about. The challenge of community in Anglo Jewry is how to retain this connectedness in such a way that the varying aspirations of different kinds of Jews can be satisfied without the community splitting irrevocably. The retention of some kind of overarching communal structure brings with it advantages in terms of economies of scale, to say nothing of theological concerns for the unity of Jewish 'peoplehood'.

One of the challenges to the Anglo Jewish structure stems from the increased vitality of the community. It is as yet unclear who is taking advantage of the new educational and cultural opportunities that have emerged. Do they include Jews who would otherwise be estranged from the community? Or is it simply that the most committed and interested Jews simply have more opportunities available than previously? It is a considerable challenge to bring the whole community along on any journey towards greater Jewish vitality in Britain. It may be that the division between 'seekers' and 'dwellers' (discussed in chapter 6) will become more pronounced, cross-cutting existing religious divisions.

As the 2001 census showed, Anglo Jewry is a heterogeneous community which, while concentrated in certain areas and among higher social classes, contains significant minorities from a diversity of demographic groups.[2] Any community of more than nominal heterogeneity faces challenges to ensure that its institutions are able to respond to the needs of different kinds of individuals. Whereas some initiatives that have taken place since 1990 have sought to reach out to previously excluded Jews – less involved unmarried young people in particular – others have a more ambiguous impact. Attempts to streamline and rationalize Jewish structures through mergers and redefining missions may exclude some kinds of Jews. The increased uptake of full-time Jewish day schooling creates new challenges in responding to the needs of the still substantial proportion of Jews whose children are educated outside the Jewish day school system. In searching for more effective and efficient ways of ensuring Jewish vitality and continuity, there are risks that those who persist in not taking advantages of the resultant opportunities may be marginalized.

The challenge of representation

It is inevitable that any minority community will in some way need to represent the interests of its members to the wider society and the state. Indeed, multiculturalism makes public representation ever more possible and ever more desirable. At the same time, in a multicultural society in which individuals have the freedom to choose identities and communities, it is also inevitable that representative bodies will be challenged by those who feel they do not represent their particular interests. The Board of Deputies and the Chief Rabbinate have faced persistent challenges to their authority throughout their existence. In the last few decades, though, their ability to weather these storms has decreased, while other bodies have come to engage in representative work, sometimes in conflict and sometimes in cooper-ation with previously hegemonic institutions.

There are real dilemmas here that are not easily resolved. While Independent Jewish Voices and other groups were perfectly correct in challenging the Board and other bodies' claims to represent the entirety of the Jewish community's views on Israel, it is also true that the Board probably does represent the majority of British Jews' supportive views on Israel more or less accurately. The Board's structures are democratic to a certain extent in that policy is made – officially at least – by deputies elected by synagogues and other bodies, but it does not represent secular Jews. Not even this limited democracy is present in other bodies such as the Jewish Leadership Council, which also engages in representative work. In any case, a fully democratic form of representation is difficult to envisage. Given that there are no agreed definitions of who a Jew is or any comprehensive lists of British Jews, there is no possibility of having a fully representative elected body.

One way of responding to the challenge of representation is for represen-tative bodies to be more modest in their claims to representation. Further, as has been suggested elsewhere, it may be more effective for representation to take place through a network of ad hoc temporary issue-based coalitions.[3] As Keith Kahn-Harris has suggested,[4] it may be advantageous for the community to embrace a more political structure that recognizes the existence of different bodies of opinion within the community. Politics is not necessarily antithetical to community if it is recognized that political differences are inescapable.

The challenge of Israel and antisemitism

Among the major sources of controversy in the contemporary British Jewish community are Israel and antisemitism. The two issues are closely connected, if not reducible to each other. The bitter divisions that followed the launch of Independent Jewish Voices and the anger directed at different parties in debates on Israel and antisemitism suggest that divisions over these issues are as potentially divisive as religious divisions. Such divisions may get much worse in the future. The increased presence of the right-wing Yisrael Beiteinu party in the Israeli government following the February 2009 elections may prefigure a future shift towards an unambiguously racist state policy. This would make the already strained attempts at maintaining community-wide 'solidarity' with Israel impossible as more hitherto 'mainstream' Jews join the ranks of those openly critical of the Israeli government. Conversely, were any future Israeli government to engage in a large-scale evacuation of the occupied territories, many orthodox Jews would also be fiercely critical.

The issue of antisemitism further complicates the problem. Definitions of antisemitism are the subject of strong disagreement. While there may be consensus as to the antisemitic nature of certain kinds of primarily violent acts, such as firebombings of synagogues, what constitutes antisemitic discourse is much more controversial. Further, even when there is agreement that certain acts are antisemitic, there is disagreement over how far and whether the community's distancing itself from Israel might be an effective or necessary response. It may well be that in order to maintain some level of agreement that would allow for a collective communal response to antisemitism, it would be necessary to expect cross-communal cooperation only on defence against the most obviously violent and unambiguous kinds, agreeing to differ on broader definitions. This seems unlikely as those who maintain a broader definition of antisemitism usually see proponents of more minimal definitions as endangering communal security.

The challenge of dialogue

The increased divisiveness of Israel and antisemitism and the continued religious divisions in the community are difficult or even impossible to resolve. In the face of this division one option might be for different wings of the community to go their separate ways and to cease to see themselves as one communal whole. Some writers have predicted that the Jewish people is likely to split in the near future, with divisions between orthodox and non-orthodox over 'who is a Jew?' being one of many sticking points.[5]

However, as long as there is some willingness for different kinds of Jews to see themselves as part of one people, then efforts will need to be made for Jews to interact across intra-communal boundaries. Limmud provides one model of how to do this, creating a pluralist space to which different kinds of Jews can contribute. The limitation of Limmud, though, is that it only allows simultaneous co-existence and does not require any participant to interact with anyone they do not agree with (although many of course do just that).

The challenge remains how to develop modes of *dialogue* between different camps. The Jewish community has made considerable strides in recent years in supporting inter-faith dialogue,[6] but *intra*-faith dialogue has barely been developed. The controversy that followed the publication of Sacks's letter to Dayan Padwa in 1997 led to an attempt to ease inter-denominational tensions. The so-called 'Stanmore Accords', signed in November 1998 by the leaders of the United Synagogue and the progressive movements, sought to prevent public battles between denominations. In the sense that the various battles fought in the 1990s have not recurred, the accords were successful. However, the accords did not lead to any substantial inter-denominational dialogue and the inter-communal committee envisaged by the accords has only rarely met. In any case, inter-denominational divisions are not the only ones in the Jewish community. The public abusiveness of many protagonists in conflicts about Israel and antisemitism suggests that there needs to be work done to develop a different tone in intra-Jewish debates.

Communities can be fraught and fractious spaces. How to balance the human need for fellowship with the endless diversity of human beings is an insoluble problem with which all communities grapple. But it is reasonable to hope that divisions within communities do not cause inordinate hurt to their members, and to do this, communities need to develop mechanisms through which disputes can be negotiated in ways that diffuse some of the resulting tension. One attempt to develop such mechanisms has been made by the project New Jewish Thought, which has pioneered intra-Jewish dialogue groups in the UK.[7]

The challenge of sustainability
Chief Rabbi Jonathan Sacks's induction in 1991 took place in the middle of a recession. Much of the renewal of the British Jewish community occurred during the latter part of the 1990s and during the noughties, in a

period of sustained economic growth. The impact of the recession that began in mid 2008, and that at the time of this book's writing appeared to be continuing, is so far unclear. In the US it appears that the recession, combined with losses sustained in the Madoff affair, has resulted in a period of mergers, renewed efforts to engage small donors and calls for higher ethical standards in Jewish communal life and fundraising.[8] In 2009, there were redundancies at UJIA and some other Jewish communal organizations, but so far no major losses of programmes or institutions. Indeed, two of the British Jewish community's most ambitious capital projects, the Jewish Community Secondary School and the building of the Jewish Community Centre in Hampstead, were launched in the teeth of the recession.

Since the 1990s, there have been persistent warnings that the community's reliance on a small number of donors, the expansion in Jewish day schooling and an increasingly ageing Jewish population were putting massive pressures on the Jewish community's financial resources and may not be ultimately sustainable. The 'gamble' implicit in the process of renewal was that the increased vitality of the Jewish community and the renewed involvement of preciously marginal Jews would bring in new sources of funding and commitment. So far, there has been no 'crash' and the process of renewal has not yet turned out to be a 'bubble'. Whether or not this situation will continue, questions of sustainability need to be raised if the community is to stay on a secure financial footing. Renewal's acid test must be whether it can survive whether or not the community's finances are healthy.

Learning from Anglo Jewry: the future of multiculturalism

Much of this book has detailed complex institutional changes that, while they may have had wide implications within the British Jewish community, were conducted with little apparent reference to wider circumstances. Not only have Jews often been suspicious of multicultural discourse, scholars interested in multiculturalism and minority issues in Britain have rarely considered the Jewish experience. We would contend that our research has raised issues that have important implications for multiculturalism in general and for other minorities in particular.[9] The politics of security – the insistence on secure British citizenship and belonging – came with a heavy price, including the hasty death of Yiddish culture, the missing cultural vitality that those groups marginalized from the community could have provided. Multiculturalism, in some ways, stems from the refusal of other minorities to pay that price.

Our research shows clearly that while communities may benefit from and adapt to multiculturalism, they do not necessarily concomitantly embrace multiculturalist discourse. We have argued that the strategy of insecurity and the changes that Anglo Jewry has witnessed since 1990 were founded on a shift from a model of leadership predicated on a monocultural Britain to one predicated on a multicultural Britain. This did not mean that British Jewish communal leaders moved any closer towards the kind of multicultural discourse that is prevalent in the academy.

The first years of the New Labour government elected in 1997 saw the emergence of a new articulation of multiculturalist thinking inflected by communitarian philosophy and tied to the promotion of a British patriotism which proudly focused on Britain as diverse and dynamic, and cool.[10] On a popular level, this new multicultural patriotism involved the branding exercise around the idea of 'cool Britannia' and the celebration of patriotic sporting figures, such as Kelly Holmes, Denise Lewis and Colin Jackson, whose family backgrounds were in the (post)colonial citizen migrants of the Windrush Generation. On an academic and policy level, this new multicultural patriotism was most clearly articulated in the Parekh Report, the Runnymede Trust's *Future of Multi-Ethnic Britain*, edited by the philosopher Bikhu Parekh in 2000.[11] The report followed multiculturalists in seeing cultural pluralism – the presence of different cultures – as an objective good. And, like many multiculturalists, it imagined cultural difference in terms of a patchwork or mosaic of different cultural or ethnic 'communities'. But it parted from most versions of multiculturalism by arguing that there was a need for a common culture *across* communities, based on dialogue and based on respect for basic universal rights, including the right of exit from one's cultural group. It articulated this tension between cultural difference and common culture through the idea of a *community of communities*. Sacks's book, *The Dignity of Difference*, published in 2002 but written largely between 1998 and 2001, resonated well with this moment. It argued that the classical liberal ideal of toleration was no longer enough; instead, a positive theology of difference was required, a more fundamental respect for the diversity that makes us human.[12]

This sort of multiculturalism was challenged in the early twenty-first century by a series of events that appeared to highlight some of the dangers of diverse society. These included the disturbances in northern towns in the summer of 2001, which were widely understood as 'race riots', pitching Asian Muslim youth against white society.[13] In July 2005, the London bombings raised the spectre of the 'homegrown terrorist': young British Muslims prepared to murder fellow British citizens on a mass scale. In the autumn of the same year the controversy over the publication of Danish cartoons satirizing the Islamic Prophet Mohammed raised questions over the extent to which cultural and religious sensitivities presented a limit to what were conceived of as traditionally British values of free speech – and the extent to which the tolerance of cultural and religious diversity was compatible with a liberal democratic order.

These events led to the articulation of a critique of multiculturalism from both the left and the right, including from commentators close to the New Labour project, and to the emergence of a policy language of 'integration' and 'cohesion' to replace it.[14] A series of reports – most notably the Community Cohesion Review Team report,[15] but also the Bradford Vision report,[16] the Oldham Independent Review,[17] the Burnley Task Force Report and the report of the Ministerial Group on Public Order and Community Cohesion[18] – identified white and non-white communities as living separate and parallel lives, and called for 'community cohesion' as a way forward. The new cohesion literature attacked what it described as a form of de facto apartheid generated by municipal multiculturalist strategies: in Trevor Phillips's memorable phrase, Britain was accused of 'sleep-walking into segregation'.[19] The new emphasis was on common bonds and on obligations, rather than rights, of groups. Within the Jewish community, this position was strongly argued by Melanie Phillips, who claimed that 'If citizenship is to mean anything at all, minorities must sign up to an overarching set of British values rooted in the culture of the majority ... The phrase "multicultural society" is a contradiction in terms because multiculturalism is a recipe for social disintegration.'[20]

After 7/7, the supposed demise of multiculturalism became an even more insistent theme in the media, and Gordon Brown began more strongly to assert the importance of a common Britishness.[21] Now, for Melanie Phillips, multiculturalism was no longer simply divisive, it was 'lethally divisive'.[22] The work of Jonathan Sacks reflected this shift. Sacks had already been criticized by ultra-orthodox rabbis for sections in The Dignity of Difference that, they alleged, implied that other faiths reflected spiritual truths that were equally as valid as Judaism's. He had been obliged to issue a revised version of the book that 'clarified' his position. The Home We Build Together, published in 2007, contained nothing that could be mistaken for multicultural relativism. Although maintaining the validity of difference, he argued that multiculturalism was divisive and that common culture and common values are needed to glue a diverse society together.[23] Ali Rattansi and Les Back et al.[24] have characterized this emergent discourse as a 'new assimilationism', while Arun Kundnani has called it 'the end of tolerance'.[25] Bagguley and Hussain have described it as a 'shift [to] an atavistic assimilationism that demands integration, reminiscent of the failed policies of the 1950s and 60s'.[26] Consequently, Shukra et al. argue that 'Current debates about race relations and immigration are caught in a conundrum: how to challenge the weaknesses of multiculturalism without reinforcing conditions for the rise of a new assimilationism?'[27] This conundrum illuminates a serious lacuna in multi-cultural discourse in attending to issues of communal survival, a gap which the Jewish experience dramatizes. As we argued in chapter 2, concerns about Jewish continuity, while they may often unduly dismiss anti-essentialist perspectives on identity, also call into question the long-term viability of those identities. There are no guarantees that a heterogeneous society made up of an endless play of hybrid identities will necessarily stay heterogeneous. Even if concerns for Jewish continuity have often been articulated in deeply conservative ways, the concerns should nonetheless be taken seriously. How might concerns for survival be re-articulated in anti-essentialist ways?

Similarly, the Anglo Jewish experience is revealing of the frequent limita-tions of concerns for 'difference'. Differences within communities need to be subject to as much attention as differences between communities. A multicultural society is one that is diverse on many levels, including commu-nities within communities. In this sense, policy-makers need to be more careful when talking about ethnic communities. As the sociologists Brian Alleyne and Clive Harris note, the centrality of 'community' can reinforce the notion of unalterable difference *between* and sameness *within* 'ethnic communities'. For Harris, this model cannot always accommodate the notion that differences *within* may be of greater significance than differences between; the notion of 'ethnic community' can obscure the complex social networks or webs of social relations, and conjunctures of the local and global, which make up diasporic peoples.[28]

The story we have told of Anglo Jewish community shows how community has been messy, contingent, fluid, evolving and contested – transformed through a series of 'communal revolutions' and through incre-mental reform. Drawing 'lessons' from the Jewish experience for other minorities is fraught with difficulty. Jews can at times be treated and may see themselves as a 'model minority' to which other groups should aspire, which may ignore the specificity of different groups' experiences and their different exposure to racism and discrimination[29] – as Geoffrey Alderman argued at the time, this was one of the problems of Lord Jakobovits's *From Doom to Hope*. Nevertheless, there remain some aspects of the British Jewish experience that may suggest lessons for others.

One of the most important lessons is that the communal leadership strategy that aimed to ensure the security of British Jews was perhaps too successful. While it helped to ensure that the British Jewish community became a prosperous and well-integrated one, the strategy also took a heavy toll on the community's intellectual and cultural vitality. The Anglo Jewish leadership's insistence on rapid anglicization of immigrants hastened the decline of Yiddish language and culture, helping to erode one of the world's most creative literatures.[30] In learning from Anglo Jewish 'success', its failures should also be borne in mind. For example, attempts to prevent extremism in Muslim communities should be subtle enough to recognize that the secure belonging of British Muslims should not require British Muslims similarly to abandon their cultural wealth.

The British Jewish experience also suggests that a systematic effort to develop policies for communal survival can pay dividends. The specificities of efforts to ensure Jewish continuity and renewal are less important here than the fact that a community-wide effort to change a community can work, at least to some extent. This is a valuable lesson, and something of which the Jewish community can be rightly proud.

The British Jewish community in turbulent times

If the politics of security came with a heavy price, the politics of insecurity come with a heavy price too. For sociologist Ulrich Beck, the theorist of postmodern risk society and its insecurities, we have moved from an age when politics was about the just distribution of goods to an age when politics is about the distribution of 'bads' – risks, dangers, threats.[31] If Beck is right, then the politics of the modern era was about making claims on entitlement to goods, and this was in some senses what the strategy of security was about: demonstrating that Jews were good, normal, secure British citizens with all the same rights. And, again if Beck is right, today's politics is about demonstrating insecurity, making a claim to safety needs, and this is what the new antisemitism discourse does.

However, Jane Franklin argues that there are two political responses to the proliferation of insecurity. One response, 'the politics of nostalgic community', is defensive: seeking to preserve that which once provided a secure backdrop to life.

> This politics appears to be a resistance to change. It builds on an idealized notion of community and encourages efforts to bring back the traditional family, reconstruct strong neighbourhoods and reassert

a kind of commonsense morality to hold it all together. It offers a way of imagining a secure society.[32]

There were elements of this politics of nostalgic community in the continuity agenda and in the Chief Rabbi's *Will We Have Jewish Grandchildren?* and *The Home We Build Together.*

The second path, in contrast, recognizes insecurity and seeks to construct a new politics to deal with it – venturing into the unknown, living creatively with risk, creating a shared recognition of the risks we face.[33] This is precisely the message with which we want to conclude this book. The Jewish 'renaissance' we saw in chapter 6 was predicated on exactly such a venture into the unknown. The model of Jewish community which emerges from that is based neither on asserting security nor on generating insecurity, but rather on creating a shared recognition of the risks we face, and of the possibilities we can generate beyond them.

What this means is a *dialogical community*: a community in dialogue internally, living with the differences and recognizing similarities with other groups – a Jewish community in dialogue with multiculturalism and with other multicultural communities. If the history of Anglo Jewry and its leadership tells us anything, it is that the community is at its most alive when problems are discussed and solutions debated openly. When Jewish community becomes a polyphony of contending voices, the resulting firmament generates creative solutions to the challenges of being a minority in multicultural Britain. Dialogue can be what ties a community together, what sustains it and what transforms it. We hope in this book to have encouraged this dialogue and we look forward to continuing it as the Jewish community proceeds further into an uncertain century.

Notes

Introduction

1 Hannah Neustatter, 'Demographic and other statistical aspects of Anglo Jewry', in *A Minority in Britain: Social Studies of the Anglo-Jewish Community*, ed. Maurice Freedman (London: Vallentine Mitchell, 1955), pp. 53–133.

2 David Graham, Marlena Schmool and Stanley Waterman, *Jews in Britain: A Snapshot from the 2001 Census* (London: Institute for Jewish Policy Research, 2007).

3 This and other non-English Jewish terms are explained in the glossary.

4 Figures derived from Rona Hart and Edward Kafka, 'Trends in British Synagogue Membership 1990–2005/6' (The Board of Deputies of British Jews, 2006). These and subsequent figures are rounded to whole numbers.

5 See, for example, Commission on Representation of the Interests of the British Jewish Community, *A Community of Communities* (London: Institute for Jewish Policy Research, 2000).

6 Peter Halfpenny and Margaret Reid, *The Financial Resources of the UK Jewish Voluntary Sector* (London: Institute for Jewish Policy Research, 2000).

7 Jon Stratton, 'Speaking as a Jew: on the absence of a Jewish speaking position in British Cultural Studies', *European Journal of Cultural Studies*, vol. 1, no. 3 (1998): 305–25.

8 See, for example, Avtar Brah, *Cartographies of Diaspora: Contesting Identities* (London: Routledge, 1996).

9 Mitchell B. Hart, 'The unbearable lightness of Britain', *Journal of Modern Jewish Studies*, vol. 6, no. 2 (2007): 155.

10 Geoffrey Alderman, 'Academic Duty and Communal Obligation: Some Thoughts on the Writing of Anglo-Jewish History' (London: Centre for Jewish Studies, School of Oriental and African Studies, University of London, Occasional Paper No. 1, 1994).

11 Jews were defined as an ethnic group under the 1976 Race Relations Act following the ruling in Seide v Gillette Industries (1980).

12 This is increasingly the term used in global Jewish policy making. See, for example, Ezra Kopelowitz and Menachem Reviv (eds), *Building Jewish*

Peoplehood: Challenges and Possibilities (Brighton, MA: Academic Studies Press, 2008).

13   Karen Brodkin, *How Jews Became White Folks and What That Says About Race in America* (New Brunswick, NJ: Rutgers University Press, 1998).

14   Eric S. Goldstein, *The Price of Whiteness: Jews, Race and Ethnic Identity* (Princeton, NJ: Princeton University Press, 2006), p. 221.

15   Sander L. Gilman, *Multiculturalism and the Jews* (New York: Routledge, 2006), p. xiii.

16   Immanuel Jakobovits, *From Doom to Hope: A Jewish View on 'Faith in the City', the Report of the Archbishop of Canterbury's Commission on Urban Priority Areas* (London: Office of the Chief Rabbi, January 1996).

17   Jonathan Sacks, *The Home We Build Together: Recreating Society* (London: Continuum, 2007).

18   Geoffrey Alderman, 'British Jews or Britons of the Jewish persuasion? The religious constraints of civic freedom', in *National Variations in Jewish Identity: Implications of Jewish Education* (Albany: State University of New York Press, 1999), pp. 125–36.

19   Howard M. Sachar, *Diaspora: An Inquiry into the Contemporary Jewish World* (New York: Perennial Library, 1986), p. 167.

20   Stephen Brook, *The Club: The Jews of Modern Britain* (London: Pan Books, 1990), pp. 411, 413, 434.

21   Howard Cooper and Paul Morrison, *A Sense of Belonging: Dilemmas of British Jewish Identity* (London: Weidenfeld and Nicolson, 1991), p. 97.

22   David Harvey, *The Condition of Postmodernity* (Oxford: Blackwell Publishers, 1990).

23   Gabe Mythen, *Ulrich Beck: A Critical Introduction to the Risk Society* (London: Pluto, 2004), pp. 1–2.

24   Quoted ibid., p. 2.

25   Quoted in Christopher Coker *Globalisation and Insecurity in the Twenty-First Century: NATO and the Management of Risk* (London: International Institute for Strategic Studies, Adelphi Papers no. 345, 2002), p. 59.

26   Zygmunt Bauman, *Postmodern Ethics* (Oxford: Blackwell, 1993), p. 235.

27   Max Weber, *The Sociology of Religion* (Boston: Beacon Press, 1963); Max Weber, *The Protestant Ethic and the Spirit of Capitalism* (London: Routledge, 1992). See also Brian Morris *Anthropological Studies of Religion: An Introductory Text* (Cambridge: Cambridge University Press, 1987).

28   For example, Peter Berger, *A Rumour of Angels: Modern Society and the Rediscovery of the Supernatural* (London: Pelican Books, 1971).

29   Grace Davie, *The Sociology of Religion* (London: Sage Publications, 2007).

30   For a selection of predictions about the future of religion, see Grace Davie, Paul Heelas and Linda Woodhead (eds), *Predicting Religion: Christian, Secular and Alternative Futures* (Aldershot: Ashgate, 2003).

31   Robert Putnam, *Bowling Alone: The Collapse and Revival of American Community* (New York: Touchstone, 2000).

Chapter 1

1   There is considerable historical debate over the Resettlement. Due to the opposition of the clergy, Cromwell stopped short of making a public declaration of the right of Jews to reside in the country; there was no Act of Parliament or equivalent. Some Anglo Jewish historians, most notably Lucien Wolf, have fitted Resettlement into a history of progressive and gradual opening up of civic rights for Jews, but the prevalence of antisemitic attacks on the Jews in the 1650s and the partialness of the terms of Readmission cast some doubt on this. See discussion by Ariel Hessayon, *From Expulsion (1290) to Readmission (1656): Jews and England* (public lecture Jewish Genealogical Society of Great Britain, October 2006 <http://www.gold.ac.uk/media/350th-anniversary.pdf>, accessed 8 February 2010). For the optimistic account, see Lucien Wolf, *Menassah ben Israel's Mission to Oliver Cromwell* (London: Macmillan, 1901).

2   Geoffrey Alderman, 'London Jewry and London Politics, 1889–1934', in Geoffrey Alderman (ed.), *Governments, Ethnic Groups and Political Representation: Comparative Studies on Governments and Non-Dominant Ethnic Groups in Europe, 1850–1940 Volume IV* (Dartmouth: European Science Foundation New York University Press Dartmouth, 1993), pp. 3–30 (8).

3   Howard Bloch, *Earlham Grove Shul* (London: West Ham and Upton Park Synagogue, 1997), p. 2; Aubrey Newman, *Migration and Settlement* (London: Jewish Historical Society of England, 1971); Aubrey Newman and Stephen Massil (eds), *Patterns of Migration, 1860–1914*, Proceedings of the International Academic Conference 1993, Jewish Historical Society of England and the Institute of Jewish Studies (London: University College London, 1996).

4   Quoted in Peter Ackroyd, *London: The Biography* (London: Chatto and Windus, 2001), p. 706, emphasis added. Initially, London's Jewish community – about two dozen Marrano households – did not support such a petition, devised by the leader of Amsterdam's Jewish community, Rabbi Menasseh ben Israel. 'In a manner reminiscent of succeeding generations of Anglo-Jewish leaders ... [t]hey wanted to be left alone, in obscurity; they certainly did not want any more Jews coming into the country, perhaps because they knew, and were fearful of, the ease with which anti-Jewish prejudices could be aroused' (Geoffrey Alderman, *The Jewish Community in British Politics*, Oxford: Clarendon, 1983, p. 2). Only war with Spain and consequent fear of persecution as Spaniards propelled them into 'coming out' as Jewish refugees.

5   Mark Levene, *War, Jews and the New Europe: The Diplomacy of Lucien Wolf 1914–1919* (Oxford: Oxford University Press, 1992), p. 4. On the 'Jewish liberal compromise', see Sharman Kadish, *Bolsheviks and British Jews* (London: Frank Cass, 1992), e.g. pp. 55–60, 132; Jonathan Hyman, *Jews in Britain During the Great War* (Manchester: University of Manchester Working Papers in Economic and Social History No. 51, 2001), e.g. p. 11. The phrase was coined by Steven Bayme.

180   Notes

6   Israel Finestein, 'Jewish emancipationists in Victorian England: self-imposed limits to assimilation', in Jonathan Frankel and Steven J. Zipperstein (eds), *Assimilation and Community: The Jews in Nineteenth-Century Europe* (Cambridge: Cambridge University Press, 1992), p. 43.
7   *Jewish Chronicle*, 25 June 1886
8   Quoted in the *Report of the All-Party Parliamentary Inquiry into Antisemitism* (London: The Stationary Office Limited, 2006,), p. 20, sect. 97.
9   Eugene C. Black, *The Social Politics of Anglo-Jewry 1880–1920* (Oxford: Blackwell, 1988), p. 302.
10 Alderman, *The Jewish Community*, p. 8.
11 Chaim Bermant, *The Jews* (London: Weidenfeld and Nicolson, 1977), p. 1.
12 Daniel Gutwein, *The Divided Elite: Economics, Politics and Anglo-Jewry 1882–1917* (Leiden: E.J. Brill, 1992), pp. 7–8.
13 Ibid., p. 9.
14 'Liberalism and Anglo Jewry', pp. 6–7, 'Communal Solidarity', p. 506. Quoted in Gutwein, *The Divided Elite*.
15 David Cesarani, 'The transformation of communal authority in Anglo-Jewry, 1914–1940', in D. Cesarani (ed.), *The Making of Modern Anglo-Jewry* (Oxford: Basil Blackwell, 1990), pp. 115–40 (115).
16 Hal M. Lewis, *Models and Meanings in the History of Jewish Leadership* (Lewiston NY: Edward Mellen Press, 2004), p. 279.
17 Ibid., pp. 283–4.
18 Ibid., pp. 284–5.
19 Bill Williams, 'Anti-semitism of tolerance: middle-class Manchester and the Jews, 1879–1900', in A.J. Kidd and K.W. Roberts (eds), *City, Class and Culture; Studies of Social Policy and Cultural Production in Victorian Manchester* (Manchester: Manchester University Press, 1985), pp. 74–102 (92).
20 William J. Fishman, *East End Jewish Radicals* (London: Duckworth, 1975); Ben Gidley, 'Citizenship and Belonging: East End Jewish Radicals 1903–1918' (University of London PhD thesis, 2003).
21 Julius Carlebach, *Karl Marx and the Radical Critique of Judaism* (London: Routledge and Kegan Paul, 1978), p. 18.
22 Alderman, *The Jewish Community*, pp. 51–2.
23 Judy Glasman, 'Architecture and anglicization: London synagogue building 1870–1900', *Jewish Quarterly*, vol. 34, no. 2 (1987): 19; Black, *The Social Politics of Anglo-Jewry*, pp. 217–20; C. Russell and H.S. Lewis, *The Jew in London: A Study of Racial Character and Present-day Conditions* (London: T. Fisher Unwin, 1900), pp. 101–6.
24 Quoted in Geoffrey Alderman, *Modern British Jewry* (Oxford: Clarendon, 1992), p. 144.
25 Ibid.
26 Ibid.
27 Quoted in Juliet Steyn, *The Jew: Assumptions of Identity* (London: Cassell, 1999), pp. 29–30.

28   Quoted in ibid., p. 36.

29   Stuart A. Cohen, 'Same places, different faces – a comparison of Anglo-Jewish conflicts over Zionism during Word War I and World War II', in Stuart A. Cohen and Eliezer Don-Yehiya (eds), *Conflict and Consensus in Jewish Political Life* (Ramat-Gan: Bar-Ilan University Press, 1986).

30   Bill Williams, '"East" and "West": class and community in Manchester Jewry, 1850–1914', in David Cesarani (ed.), *The Making of Modern Anglo-Jewry* (Oxford: Basil Blackwell, 1990), pp. 15–33 (20).

31   Ibid., p. 21.

32   Ibid., pp. 23–6.

33   Gutwein, *The Divided Elite*, pp. 11–12.

34   Kadish, *Bolsheviks and British Jews*; Hyman, *Jews in Britain During the Great War*; Gidley, 'Citizenship and Belonging'.

35   James Renton, *The Zionist Masquerade: The Birth of the Anglo-Zionist Alliance 1914–1918* (London: Palgrave Macmillan, 2007); Kadish, *Bolsheviks and British Jews*.

36   Ibid.; Renton, *The Zionist Masquerade*.

37   Israel Finestein, 'The changing governance of Anglo-Jewry, 1950–2000', in *Scenes and Personalities in Anglo-Jewry 1800–2000* (London: Vallentine Mitchell, [1999] 2002), pp. 6–7.

38   Cesarani, *The Making of Modern Anglo-Jewry*, p. 122.

39   Ibid., p. 123.

40   Williams, '"East" and "West"', p. 33.

41   Cesarani, *The Making of Modern Anglo-Jewry*, p. 139.

42   Ibid., p. 136.

43   Ibid., pp. 127–8.

44   Quoted in David Rosenberg, *Facing up to Antisemitism: How Jews in Britain Countered the Threats of the 1930s* (London: JCARP Publications, 1985), p. 5.

45   *Jewish Chronicle*, quoted in Rosenberg, *Facing up to Antisemitism*, pp. 34–5.

46   Cesarani, *The Making of Modern Anglo-Jewry*, pp. 126–8.

47   Quoted in Rosenberg, *Facing up to Antisemitism*, p. 11.

48   Ibid., p. 11.

49   Cesarani, *The Making of Modern Anglo-Jewry*, pp. 129–30; Henry Srebrnik, *London Jews and British Communism, 1935–1945* (London: Vallentine Mitchell, 1995); Rosenberg, *Facing up to Antisemitism*, pp. 51–60.

50   Cesarani, *The Making of Modern Anglo-Jewry*, pp. 129–30; Srebrnik, *London Jews and British Communism*; Rosenberg, *Facing up to Antisemitism*, p. 71.

51   Rosenberg, *Facing up to Antisemitism*, p. 71.

52   Meier Sompolinsky, *Britain and the Holocaust: The Failure of Anglo-Jewish Leadership?* (Brighton: Sussex Academic Press, 1999), p. 11.

53   Cohen, 'Same places, different faces', p. 68.

54   This time, Cohen suggests, the embattled anti-Zionists – Leonard Montefiore (Claude's son), Sir Robert Waley Cohen (president of the United Synagogue) and Neville Laski – were more pugnacious (ibid., pp. 72–3).

55   Ibid., p. 77.

56   Elaine R. Smith, 'Jews and politics in the East End of London, 1918–1939', in Cesarani, The Making of Modern Anglo-Jewry, pp. 141–62 (143–4).

57   Cohen, S.M. and L.J. Fein, 'From integration to survival: American Jewish anxieties in transition', Annals of the American Academy of Political and Social Science, no. 480 (1985): 75–88.

58   Israel Finestein, 'The changing governance of Anglo-Jewry', pp. 20–1.

59   However, it is important not to overstate this, as, for example, W.D. Rubinstein has done, in claiming that 'Since 1945 (and especially since about 1960) the formerly depressed eastern European migrants have moved *as a whole* into the upper-middle class and into the elites of most Western nations' (W.D. Rubinstein, The Left, The Right and the Jews (London: Croon Helm, 1982), p. 11). It should not be forgotten that there remain significant pockets of poverty in the Haredi population, as well as a significant numbers of members of the mainstream community who would better be described as working class or lower middle class. Even Rubinstein, writing in the 1980s, admits that British Jews 'probably retain a somewhat larger working-class sector than is the case among America's Jews' (ibid., p. 19).

60   Israel Finestein, 'A community of paradox: office, authority, and ideas in the changing governance of Anglo-Jewry', in Selwyn Ilan Troen (ed.), Jewish Centers and Peripheries: Europe between America and Israel Fifty Years after World War II (New Brunswick: Transaction Books, 1999), p. 255.

61   Ibid., p. ix.

62   Cesarani, The Making of Modern Jewry, p. 10.

63   A. Sivanandan, A Different Hunger: Writings on Black Resistance (London: Pluto, 1990); Paul Gilroy Black Britain: A Photographic History (London: Saqi Books, 1998).

64   Paul Gilroy 'There Ain't no Black in the Union Jack': The Cultural Politics of Race and Nation (Chicago: University of Chicago Press, 1991); Kobena Mercer, '1968: periodizing postmodern politics and identity', in Lawrence Grossberg, Cary Nelson and Paula Treichler (eds), Cultural Studies (New York and London: Routledge, 1992).

65   Working Party on Race Relations, Improving Race Relations: A Jewish Contribution (London: The Board of Deputies of British Jews, 1969).

66   Shalom Charikar, 'Confronting racism: a role for Jews', Jewish Socialist, no. 1 (1985): 15–16.

67   Anthony Lester (ed.), Essays and Speeches by Roy Jenkins (London: Collins, 1967), p. 267.

68   See Clive Harris, 'Beyond multiculturalism? Difference, recognition and social justice', Patterns of Prejudice, vol. 35, no. 1 (2001): 13–58; Arun Kundnani, The End of Tolerance: Racism in 21st Century Britain (London: Pluto, 2007), chap. 3.

69   David Cesarani, *The Jewish Chronicle and Anglo-Jewry, 1841–1991* (Cambridge: Cambridge University Press 1994), p. 241.
70   Quoted in Gemma Romain, *Connecting Histories: A Comparative Exploration of Afro-Caribbean and Jewish History and Memory in Modern Britain* (London: Routledge Kegan Paul, 2006), p. 232.
71   Romain, *Connecting Histories*, pp. 231–3; Chaim Bermant, *Lord Jacobovitz: An Authorized Biography of the Chief Rabbi* (London: Weidenfeld and Nicolson, 1990), p. 178.
72   Quoted in Romain, *Connecting Histories*, pp. 237–8.
73   David Rosenberg, 'An independent Jewish platform', *Jewish Socialist*, no.1 (1985): 11.
74   'We knew the level of antisemitic harassment, as did the monitors of the Board, but they were able to keep it a carefully guarded secret…' (ibid.).
75   Ibid.
76   Interview with David Rosenberg; Cesarani, *The Jewish Chronicle and Anglo-Jewry*, p. 242.
77   Lewis, *Models and Meanings in the History of Jewish Leadership*, pp. 206 n. 604.
78   Ibid., pp. 266–7.
79   Ibid., pp. 273–4.
80   Nick Lambert, *Jews and Europe in the Twenty-first Century* (London: Vallentine Mitchell, 2008), p. 82.
81   Quoted in ibid., p. 83.
82   Avraham Burg, *Brit Am, Covenant of the People: The Zionist Element. Draft Outline of the Policy of the Zionist Movement* (Jerusalem: Presented to the 33rd Zionist Congress, December 1997). An earlier version had been published by the Jewish Agency in 1995.
83   The diminished importance of encouraging *aliyah* in the Jewish Agency's activities was tacitly recognized in 2008 with the merger of the Jewish Agency's *aliyah* department in North America with the private organization Nefesh B'Nefesh. See Anshel Pfeffer 'Jerusalem and Babylon: the Jewish Agency's diminished role', *Haaretz*, 7 September 2008, <http://www.haaretz.com/ hasen/spages/1018435.html>, accessed 8 February 2010. Further, in January 2009 the US United Jewish Communities announced it was considering ending its exclusive funding arrangements with the Jewish Agency.
84   Interview, 29 November 2007.
85   Charley J. Levine, 'Interview with Jonathan Sacks', *Hadassah Magazine*, vol. 85, no. 1 (2003), <http://www.hadassah.org/news/content/per_hadassah/ archive/2003/03_AUG/interview.htm>, accessed 15 August 2008.
86   David Cesarani, 'Foreword', in Nick Lambert, *Jews and Europe in the Twenty-First Century*, p. 3.

Chapter 2

1   Jonathan Sacks, *Induction Address*, London, 1 September 1991, <http://www.chiefrabbi.org/sp-index.html>, accessed 22 August 2007.

2   Scott Lash, 'Reflexivity and its doubles: structure, aesthetics, community', in Ulrich Beck, Anthony Giddens and Scott Lash (eds), *Reflexive Modernization: Politics, Tradition and Aesthetics in the Modern Social Order* (Cambridge: Polity Press, 1994), pp. 110–73.

3   Hannah Neustatter, 'Demographic and other statistical aspects of Anglo-Jewry', in Maurice Freedman (ed.), *A Minority in Britain: Social Studies of the Anglo-Jewish Community* (London: Vallentine Mitchell, 1955), pp. 53–133.

4   Sonia L. Lipman and Vivian D. Lipman (eds), *Jewish Life in Britain: 1962–1977* (New York: K.G. Saur, 1981).

5   Stanley Waterman and Barry Kosmin, *British Jewry in the Eighties: A Statistical and Geographical Study* (London: Board of Deputies of British Jews, 1986); Marlena Schmool and Frances Cohen, *A Profile of British Jewry: Patterns and Trends at the Turn of the Century* (London: Board of Deputies of British Jews, 1998).

6   Barry Kosmin et al., *Highlights of the CJF 1990 National Jewish Population Survey* (New York: Council of Jewish Federations, 1991).

7   Ibid., p. 14.

8   This figure represented a considerable simplification of complex data and was challenged by the American Jewish sociologist Steven M. Cohen, who claimed the figure was nearer 41 per cent. See Steven M. Cohen, 'Why intermarriage may not threaten Jewish continuity', *Moment*, December (1994).

9   *To Renew and Sanctify: A Call to Action. The Report of the North American Commission on Jewish Identity and Continuity* (Council of Jewish Federations, November 1995), p. 1.

10   Jonathan Sacks, *Will We Have Jewish Grandchildren? Jewish Continuity and How to Achieve it* (Ilford: Valentine Mitchell, 1994), p. 18.

11   Ibid., pp. 18–19.

12   Such as the pioneering study of the Redbridge Jewish community: Barry Kosmin and Caren Levy, *Jewish Identity in an Anglo-Jewish Community: The Findings of the 1983 Redbridge Survey* (London: Research Unit Board of Deputies of British Jews, 1983).

13   S. Haberman, B.A. Kosmin and C. Levy, 'The size and structure of Anglo-Jewry' (London: Board of Deputies of British Jews, 1983). A more technical version of this paper was later published in the *Journal of the Royal Statistical Society*.

14   Geoffrey Alderman, *Modern British Jewry* (Oxford: Clarendon Press, 1998), pp. 321–2.

15   Interview with Barry Kosmin, 10 December 2007.

16   At the time a Labour MP and president of the Board of Deputies.

17   Stanley Kalms, *A Time for Change: United Synagogue Review* (London: The Stanley Kalms Foundation, 1992).

18 Stephen Miller and Marlena Schmool, 'Survey of Synagogue Members', in Kalms, *A Time for Change*.

19 Ibid., p. 97.

20 Sarah Bronzite et al., *Beyond the Synagogue: Report of the Working Group of the 'Missing' Generation* (London: The Reform Synagogues of Great Britain, 1995).

21 Ibid., p. 6.

22 Ibid.

23 The 1990s also saw research on teenagers and communal provision for them: Sandi Mann, *Through their Eyes: The Final Report of the North Manchester Jewish Youth Project Survey* (1995); Steve Miller, *Talkback Survey of Jewish Youth* (1997).

24 Judy Goodkin and Judith Citron, *Women in the Jewish Community: Review and Recommendations* (London: Women in the Community, 1994).

25 Marlena Schmool and Stephen Miller, *Women in the Jewish Community: Survey Report* (London: Women in the Community, 1994).

26 Jewish Educational Development Trust, *Securing our Future: An Inquiry into Jewish Education in the United Kingdom* (London: Jewish Educational Development Trust, 1992).

27 Ibid., p. iii.

28 Stephen Miller, Marlena Schmool and Anthony Lerman, *Social and Political Attitudes of British Jews: Some Key Findings of the JPR Survey* (London: Institute for Jewish Policy Research, 1996).

29 Ibid., p. 1.

30 Ibid., p. 3 (also for quotes in the rest of the paragraph).

31 *Long-Term Planning for British Jewry: Final Report and Recommendations*, Planning for Jewish Communities (London: Institute for Jewish Policy Research, 2003).

32 Ibid., p. 3.

33 These include: a report funded by Jewish Continuity on single unmarried Jews based on the 1995 JPR survey sample; *Beyond Belonging*, a 2004 report commissioned by the United Jewish Israel Appeal drawing on qualitative interviews with 'moderately engaged' Jews together with a quantitative survey of parents with children at Jewish schools; the Movement for Reform Judaism also published further qualitative research on eighteen to thirty-five-year-olds in 2006.

34 Graham et al., *Jews in Britain*.

35 Ibid., p. 9.

36 Manchester Jewish Community Project, Aston Business School Centre for Voluntary Action Research, 18 August 2004.

37 Christine Holman and Naomi Holman, *Torah, Worship and Acts of Loving Kindness: Baseline Indicators for the Charedi Community in Stamford Hill* (Leicester: De Montfort University, 2002).

38 Mitchell B. Hart, *Social Science and the Politics of Modern Jewish Identity* (Stanford, CA: Stanford University Press, 2000).

39   Ibid., p. 2.

40   Ibid., pp. 74–5.

41   See Sander Gilman, *The Jew's Body* (London: Routledge, 1991).

42   Bernard Wasserstein, *Vanishing Diaspora: The Jews in Europe since 1945* (London: Penguin, 1996).

43   Lila Corwin Berman, *Speaking of Jews: Rabbis, Intellectuals and the Creation of an American Public Identity* (Berkeley: University of California Press, 2009).

44   Ibid., p. 2.

45   Steven M. Cohen and Arnold M. Eisen, *The Jew Within: Self, Family and Community in America* (Bloomington: University of Indiana Press, 2000).

46   Jonathan Boyd (ed.), *The Sovereign and the Situated Self: Jewish Identity and Community in the 21st Century* (London: UJIA/Profile Books, 2003), p. 109.

47   Ibid, p. 1.

48   Ibid., p. 2.

49   As it turned out, when Steven Cohen and Keith Kahn-Harris replicated the methodology of the American study in *Beyond Belonging*, the UK Jewish community was found to be strikingly different from the US. Respect for tradition and community was much more important in the UK than in the US. Steven M. Cohen and Keith Kahn-Harris, *Beyond Belonging: The Jewish Identities of Moderately Engaged British Jews* (London: UJIA/Profile Books, 2004).

50   Among the rare exceptions are social science PhDs by Oliver Valins, Robert Ash and David Graham.

51   Some outmarried and highly assimilated Jews did appear in some studies, but were not the focus of those studies. Steven Cohen and Keith Kahn-Harris's report for the UJIA, *Beyond Belonging*, for example, did interview some involved outmarried Jews but the UJIA did not encourage any specific section on them. The various JPR surveys also included some outmarried Jews but they were rarely subject to specific sub-analyses.

52   Stephen Miller et al., 'The shape of Jews to come', *The Jewish Quarterly*, Spring (1989): 36.

53   Rabbi Jackie Tabbick, a UK Reform rabbi, is in the process of conducting PhD research on converts into the Reform movement.

54   Emma Klein, *Lost Jews: The Struggle for Identity Today* (London: Macmillan, 1996).

55   Zvi Bekerman and Ezra Kopelowitz (eds), *Cultural Education – Cultural Sustainability: Minority, Diaspora, Indigenous and Ethno-Religious Groups in Multicultural Societies* (New York: Routledge, 2008), p. 1.

56   Ibid.

57   See, for example, Jonathan Potter and Margaret Wetherell, *Discourse and Social Psychology: Beyond Attitudes and Behaviour* (London: Sage Publications, 1987).

58   Paul Gilroy, *The Black Atlantic: Modernity and Double Consciousness* (London: Verso, 1993).

59 See, for example, Avtar Brah and Anne E. Coombes, *Hybridity and Its Discontents: Politics, Science, Culture* (London: Routledge, 2000).

60 Caryn Aviv and David Shneer, *New Jews: The End of the Jewish Diaspora* (New York: New York University Press, 2005).

61 Ibid., p. 175.

62 See, for example, the various essays in Jonathan Boyarin and Daniel Boyarin, *Jews and Other Differences: The New Jewish Cultural Studies* (Minneapolis: University of Minnesota Press, 1997).

63 Charles S. Liebman, 'Jewish identity in transition: transformation or attenuation?', in Barry Kosmin, Kovacs Andras and Zvi Gitelman (eds), *New Jewish Identities: Contemporary Europe and Beyond* (Budapest: Central European University Press, 2003), pp. 341–50.

64 Riv-Ellen Prell, *Fighting to Become Americans: Assimilation and the Trouble between Jewish Women and Jewish Men* (Boston: Beacon Press, 1999).

65 See, for example, the contributions to Norman Kleeblatt (ed.), *Too Jewish?: Challenging Traditional Identities* (New York and New Brunswick, NJ: The Jewish Museum, New York and Rutgers University Press, 1996).

66 The various presenters on a panel entitled 'Intersecting and Mixed Heritage Identities', held at the July 2008 conferences 'Encounters and Intersections: Religion, Diaspora and Identities' held at St Catherine's College, Oxford, drew on ongoing research on a number of British mixed married families to demonstrate this.

67 Bruce Phillips, 'Assimilation, Transformation and the Long Range Impact of Intermarriage', *Contemporary Jewry*, vol. 25 (2005): 50–84; Steven M. Cohen, *A Tale of Two Jewries: The 'Inconvenient Truth' for American Jews* (New York: Jewish Life Network/Steinhardt Foundation, 2006).

68 Sylvia Barack Fishman, *Double or Nothing? Jewish Families and Mixed Marriage* (Lebanon, NH: Brandeis University Press, 2004).

69 For a taste of such complex debates see Shmuel Rosner, 'Reaching out to interfaith families', *Haaretz (English Edition)*, 22 September 2007, <http://www.haaretz.com/hasen/spages/905856.html>, accessed 8 February 2010; Anthony Weiss, 'Intermarriage Study Muddies Waters', *The Forward*, 12 December 2007, <http://www.forward.com/articles/12253/>, accessed 8 February 2010.

70 Cohen, *A Tale of Two Jewries*.

71 Erik H. Cohen, 'A questionable connection: community involvement and attitudes to intermarriage of young American Jews', *Jewish Journal of Sociology*, vol. 45, no. 1/2 (2003): 16.

72 Daniel Vulkan and David Graham, *Population Trends among Britain's Strictly Orthodox Jews* (London: Board of Deputies of British Jews, 2008).

73 Leon Symons, 'What baby boom? Board disputes birth statistics for UK Jews', *The Jewish Chronicle*, 23 May 2008, <http://www.thejc.com/home.aspx?ParentId=m11s18&SecId=18&AId=60254&ATypeId=1>, accessed 8 February 2010.

74   Women's Review Task Force, *Connection, Continuity and Community: British Jewish Women Speak Out* (London: Women's Review Task Force, 2009).

Chapter 3

1   David Vital et al., 'At the crossroads of history: is there a future for the Jewish people?', *The Jewish Quarterly*, Summer (1993): 29.
2   Simon Rawidowicz, 'Israel: the ever dying people', in *Studies in Jewish Thought* (Philadelphia: Jewish Publication Society of America, 1974), pp. 210–24.
3   Ibid., p. 223.
4   Zygmunt Bauman, *Modernity and Ambivalence* (Cambridge: Polity, 1991), p. 141.
5   Zygmunt Bauman, *Modernity and the Holocaust* (Cambridge: Polity, 1989), pp. 52–3.
6   Zygmunt Bauman, 'Allosemitism: premodern, modern, postmodern', in Brian Cheyette and Laura Marcus (eds), *Modernity, Culture and 'The Jew'* (Cambridge: Polity, 1991), p. 141.
7   Ibid., p. 107.
8   David Roskies, *Against the Apocalypse: Responses to Catastrophe in Modern Jewish Culture* (Cambridge: Harvard University Press, 1984), p. 62.
9   It should be noted, however, that most of the Conservative movement has always claimed that its version of Judaism is fully consistent with traditional *halacha*.
10   CAJE went out of business in 2009, in part as a consequence of the recession.
11   *A Time To Act: The Report of the Commission on Jewish Education in North America* (Commission on Jewish Education in North America, 1990).
12   Ibid., p. 15.
13   *To Renew and Sanctify: A Call to Action. The Report of the North American Commission on Jewish Identity and Continuity* (Council of Jewish Federations, 1995).
14   For a brief biography see <http://www.jewishagency.org/NR/exeres/3A39F51A-6C46-4F18-B21C-CC670A038F25>, accessed 15 November 2008.
15   John Dewey, *Democracy and Education: An Introduction to the Philosophy of Education* (New York: The Free Press, 1944).
16   Seymour Fox, 'The Vitality of Theory in Schwab's Conception of the Practical', *Curriculum Inquiry*, vol. 15, no. 1 (1985): 63–89.
17   Mordecai Kaplan, *Judaism as Civilization: Toward a Reconstruction of American-Jewish Life* (Philadelphia: Jewish Publication Society, 1994).
18   Seymour Fox, Israel Scheffler and Daniel Marom (eds), *Visions of Jewish Education* (Cambridge: Cambridge University Press, 2003).
19   Seymour Fox and William Novak, *Vision at the Heart: Lessons from Camp Ramah on the Power of Ideas in Shaping Educational Institutions* (Jerusalem: The Mandel Foundation, 2000).

20   Keith Kahn-Harris was a Jerusalem Fellow from 2001–2002, leaving one year early for personal reasons rather than objections to the programme's content or philosophy.

21   Ibid.

22   Chabad is a Hebrew acronym for Chochmah, Binah, Da'at – Wisdom, Understanding, and Knowledge. Lubavitch refers to the Russian town where it was based. The two terms are now used interchangeably (although originally Chabad referred to a wider movement of which Lubavitch was a part) but Chabad will be used in this book.

23   For a useful account of Chabad outreach activities see Sue Fishkoff, *The Rebbe's Army: Inside the World of Chabad-Lubavitch* (New York: Schoken Books, 2003). Our account of Chabad-Lubavitch also draws on an interview with Rabbi Tali Loewenthal, director of the Chabad Research Unit, 7 August 2008.

24   Indeed, some factions in Chabad have proclaimed him the Messiah, see: David Berger, *The Rebbe, the Messiah, and the Scandal of Orthodox Indifference* (Oxford: Littman Library, 2003).

25   Simon Rocker and Candice Krieger, 'Orthodox paying students to learn', *Jewish Chronicle*, 29 August 2008, p. 5.

26   Aaron Joshua Tapper, 'The cult of Aish HaTorah: Ba'alei Teshuva and the new religious movement phenomenon', *Jewish Journal of Sociology*, vol. 44, no. 1 (2002): 5–29.

27   MORI, *Independent Longitudinal Survey into the Results upon Jewish Continuity and Leadership Development Affected by: Aish Fellowships UK* (Market Opinion Research International, 2003). The research surveyed a random sample of 1993–2001 alumni of the Aish fellowship programme and found that 'of those participants who have married or become engaged since the Fellowships, 97% have chosen a Jewish partner'. However, given that the research could not tell how likely participants were to marry Jews if they had not attended the programme, the significance of this finding is unclear.

28   'Rabbi's departure leaves community divided', *Jewish Chronicle*, 24 November 2005.

29   Simon Rocker, 'Cambridge falls out over Mikvah plans', *Jewish Chronicle*, 19 September 2008.

30   Dana Gloger, 'Chabad campus role provokes row', *Jewish Chronicle*, 12 September 2008.

31   Miriam Shaviv, 'Outreach groups "target" JFS pupils', *Jewish Chronicle*, 3 May 2007.

32   Clifford Singer, 'Playing with fire', *Jewish Socialist*, October 2006.

33   Adam S. Ferziger, 'Between outreach and "inreach": redrawing the lines of the American Orthodox Rabbinate', *Modern Judaism*, vol. 25, no. 3 (2005): 237–63.

34   Miri Freud-Kandel, *Orthodox Judaism in Britain since 1913: An Ideology Forsaken* (Edgware: Vallentine Mitchell, 2006).

35   Meir Persoff, *Faith Against Reason: Religious Reform and the British Chief Rabbinate 1840–1990* (Edgware: Vallentine Mitchell, 2008).

36   See, for example, Jonathan Sacks, 'The Chabad approach to life', <http://www.chabad.org/therebbe/article_cdo/aid/691360/jewish/The-Chabad-Approach-to-Life.htm>, accessed 9 December 2008.

37   This inspiration has also extended to the non-orthodox movements. While the Reform movement has criticized Aish HaTorah, it has also attempted to emulate it in setting up its own outreach programmes. See Simon Rocker, 'Reform launches outreach arm as alternative to Aish', *The Jewish Chronicle*, 17 October 2008.

38   Sacks, *Will We Have Jewish Grandchildren?*

39   Ibid., p. 3.

40   Ibid., p. 19.

41   Ibid., p. 18.

42   Ibid., p. 2.

43   Ibid., p. 107.

44   Emil Fackenheim, *The Jewish Return into History: Reflections in the Age of Auschwitz and a New Jerusalem* (New York: Schoken Books, 1978), pp. 23–4.

45   Jon Stratton, *Coming Out Jewish* (London: Routledge, 2000).

46   Jack Wertheimer, 'Jews and the Jewish birthrate', *Commentary*, October (2005).

Chapter 4

1   Pp. 8–9.

2   Interview with Michael Sinclair, 6 December 2007.

3   Leslie Wagner, *Change in Continuity: Report of the Review into Jewish Continuity* (London: Jewish Continuity, 1996), p. 63.

4   Interview, 8 April 2008.

5   Interview with Michael Sinclair, 6 December 2007.

6   Interview with Clive Lawton, 15 January 2008.

7   Wagner, *Change in Continuity*, p. 64.

8   Jacqueline Goldberg and Barry Kosmin, *The Social Attitudes of Unmarried Young Jews in Contemporary Britain* (London: Institute for Jewish Policy Research in Association with JIA-Jewish Continuity, 1997).

9   Miri Freud-Kandel, *Orthodox Judaism in Britain since 1913: An Ideology Forsaken* (Edgware: Vallentine Mitchell, 2006).

10   Geoffrey Alderman, 'British Jewry: the disintegration of a community', in Leslie Stein and Steven M. Encel (eds), *Continuity, Commitment and Survival: Jewish Communities in the Diaspora* (Westport, CT: Praeger, 2003), pp. 49–65.

11   Jonathan Sacks, *One People? Tradition, Modernity, and Jewish Unity* (London: Littman Library of Jewish Civilization, 1993).

12   Ibid., p. 86.

13   Ibid., p. 213.

14   Ibid., p. 213.

15   Ibid., pp. 31–5.

16   Ibid., p. 6.

17   Geoffrey Alderman argues that the letter was leaked deliberately by sources inside the UOHC in order to teach Sacks a lesson for not heeding their entreaties not to attend the memorial. See Geoffrey Alderman, 'That letter … rabbinical politics and Jewish management', *Judaism Today*, Winter (1997).

18   Meir Persoff, 'Another Way, Another Time' (Context Statement in partial fulfilment of the requirements for the degree of Doctor of Philosophy by Public Works, Middlesex University, 2008), pp. 39–48.

19   Geoffrey Alderman, 'British Jewry', p. 59.

20   Interview with Michael Sinclair, 6 December 2007.

21   Interview with Clive Lawton, 15 January 2008.

22   Interview, 8 April 2008.

23   Including Keith Kahn-Harris who worked as a part-time research assistant from 1995.

24   Meir Persoff concurs and points out that Clive Marks, Jewish Continuity's treasurer and a major philanthropist, resigned his post after declining to ratify the budget. See Persoff, 'Another way, another time', p. 38.

25   Wagner, *Change in Continuity*, 3.33.

26   Ibid., 2.13.

27   Ibid., 3.53.

28   Ibid., 3.53.

29   Ibid., 4.11.

30   Ibid., 3.55.

31   Including Keith Kahn-Harris (until spring 1998).

32   Interview with Jonathan Ariel, 15 January 2008.

33   UJIA, *The Next Horizon* (London: UJIA, 2001).

34   Ibid., p. 9.

35   Ibid., p. 10.

36   Ibid., p. 12.

37   Steven M. Cohen and Keith Kahn-Harris, *Beyond Belonging: The Jewish Identities of Moderately Engaged British Jews* (London: UJIA/Profile Books, 2004).

38   A collection of papers from the conference was published as: Jonathan Boyd (ed.), *The Sovereign and the Situated Self: Jewish Identity and Community in the 21st Century* (London: UJIA/Profile Books, 2003).

39   Daniel Rose, 'The world of the Jewish youth movement', in *The Encyclopedia of Informal Education*, <http://www.infed.org/informaljewisheducation/jewish_youth_movements.htm>, accessed 8 February 2010.

40   Gaby Wine, 'UJIA refuses funding for "political" Beitar', *Jewish Chronicle*, 23 April 2004, p. 17.

41   Private information.

42   Max Weber, *The Theory of Social and Economic Organisation*, ed. Talcott Parsons (New York: Free Press, 1964).

Chapter 5

1   For a discussion of the relative merits of outreach to the margins and to those already engaged, see Jack Wertheimer, Charles S. Liebman and Steven Cohen, 'How to save American Jews', *Commentary*, vol. 101, no. 1 (1996): 47–51.

2   Margaret Harris, *Organising God"s Work: Challenges for Churches and Synagogues* (London: Macmillan, 1998). A dramatic recent example is the controversy within the Bevis Marks Sephardic synagogue in 2009 over the rabbi's participation in an anti-usury campaign, sharply opposed by many of the synagogue's lay leaders (see John McManus, 'Rabbi quits job over City protest', BBC, 16 October 2009 <http://news.bbc.co.uk/1/hi/uk/8311904.stm>, accessed 8 February 2010.)

3   Calvin Trillin, 'Drawing the line', *The New Yorker*, 12 December 1994; Robert Ash, 'Mountains suspended by a hair: Eruv, a symbolic act by which a legal fiction of community is established', DPhil thesis submitted at the University of Leicester, May 2000.

4   Jonathan Sacks, *Community of Faith* (London: Orion, 1995).

5   'Vision and Mission', <http://www.theus.org.uk/the_united_synagogue/about_the_us/vision_and_mission/>, accessed 29 June 2009.

6   See for example Miri Freud-Kandel, *Orthodox Judaism in Britain since 1913: An Ideology Forsaken* (Edgware: Vallentine Mitchell, 2006); Meir Persoff, *Faith Against Reason: Religious Reform and the British Chief Rabbinate 1840–1990* (Edgware: Vallentine Mitchell, 2008).

7   Interview with Saul Zneimer, 10 April 2008.

8   Persoff, *Faith Against Reason*.

9   Bayfield was chief executive of the movement from 1994 to 2007 before the position of head of movement and chief executive were separated. The following quotations are taken from an interview with Tony Bayfield which took place on 19 March 2008.

10   Justin Wise, *Getting in Touch: 18–35 Project Report* (London: Movement for Reform Judaism, June 2006).

11   Ibid., p. 28.

12   'A Statement on "Communal Collaboration"', 11 September 2008 <http://news.reformjudaism.org.uk/press-releases/a-statement-on-qcommunal-collaborationq.html>, accessed 10 August 2009.

13   Commission on Jewish Schools, *The Future of Jewish Schools* (London: Jewish Leadership Council, 2008).

14   Rona Hart, Marlena Schmool and Frances Cohen, *Jewish Education at the Crossroads* (London: The Board of Deputies of British Jews Community Research Unit, 2001).

15   Yaacov Lehman, *Let my People Know: Proposals for the Development of Jewish Education* (London: Office of the Chief Rabbi, 1971), p. 5.

16   Helena Miller, 'Meeting the challenge: the Jewish schooling phenomenon in the UK', *Oxford Review of Education*, vol. 27, no. 4 (2001): 501–13 (507).

17   Alex Pomson, '"Dorks with yarmulkes": an ethnographic inquiry into the surprised embrace of parochial day schools by liberal American Jews', in Zvi Bekerman and Ezra Kopelowitz (eds), *Cultural Education – Cultural Sustainability: Minority, Diaspora, Indigenous and Ethno-Religious Groups in Multicultural Societies* (New York: Routledge, 2008), pp. 305–21.

18   Marie Parker-Jenkins, 'Achieving cultural sustainability? The phenomenon of Jewish and Muslim schools in England and Wales', in Zvi Bekerman and Ezra Kopelowitz (eds), *Cultural Education-Cultural Sustainability: Minority, Diaspora, Indigenous and Ethno-Religious Groups in Multicultural Societies* (New York: Routledge, 2008), pp. 51–68.

19   Miller, 'Meeting the challenge', p. 507.

20   The government's support for faith schools was affirmed in the report 'Faith in the System' (London: Department for Children, Schools and Families, 2007).

21   Geoffrey Short, *Responding to Diversity? An Initial Investigation into Multicultural Education in Jewish Schools in the United Kingdom* (London: Institute for Jewish Policy Research, 2002).

22   Miriam Shaviv, 'Outreach groups "Target JFS Pupils"', *Jewish Chronicle*, vol. 4 (2007): 3.

23   Jonathan Sacks, 'A bad ruling at a bad time: To confuse religion and race is a mistake', *Jewish Chronicle*, 2 July 2009, <http://www.thejc.com/articles/a-bad-ruling-a-bad-time-to-confuse-religion-and-race-a-mistake>, accessed 8 February 2010.

24   Simon Rocker, 'JFS: what's next', *Jewish Chronicle*, 2 July 2009, <http://www.thejc.com/articles/jfs-whats-next>, accessed 8 February 2010.

25   The full supreme court judgment can be found at <http://www.bailii. org/uk/cases/UKSC/2009/15.html>, accessed 19 February 2010.

26   Simon Hochhauser, 'US and JFS orthodoxy is inclusive', *Jewish Chronicle*, 6 August 2009, <http://www.thejc.com/articles/us-and-jfs-orthodoxy-inclusive>, accessed 10 February 2010.

27   Simon Rocker, 'School entry rules "fiasco"', *Jewish Chronicle*, 18 September 2009, <http://www.thejc.com/news/uk-news/school-entry-rules-fiasco>, accessed 8 February 2010.

28   'Admissions', <http://www.jfs.brent.sch.uk/admissions.aspx>, accessed 16 September 2009.

29   Ibid.

30   See for example: Jonathan Freedland, 'JFS: Why are no heads rolling?', *Jewish Chronicle*, 7 January 2010, <http://www.thejc.com/comment/columnists/25785/jfs-why-are-no-heads-rolling>, accessed 3 March 2010; Geoffrey Alderman, 'In defeat JFS still won't learn', *Jewish Chronicle*, 22 December 2010.

31   Simon Rocker, 'JFS fight collapses as board retreats'. *Jewish Chronicle*, 7 January 2010, <http://www.thejc.com/news/uk-news/25818/jfs-%EF% AC%81ght-collapses-board-retreats>, accessed 3 March 2010.

32   Naftali Brawer and Michael Harris, 'Schools: we must face new reality', *Jewish Chronicle*, 14 January 2010, <http://www.thejc.com/comment/comment/26013/schools-we-must-face-new-reality>, accessed 3 March 2010.
33   Simon Rocker, 'US rabbis squabble over JFS', *Jewish Chronicle*, 21 January 2010, <http://www.thejc.com/news/uk-news/26280/us-rabbis-squabble-over-jfs>, accessed 3 March 2010.
34   Stephen Miller, *The Impact of Jewish Education on the Religious Behaviour and Attitudes of British Secondary School Pupils*, ed. J Aviad, vol. 3, *Studies in Jewish Education* (Jerusalem: Hebrew University Press, 1988).
35   Geoffrey Short, 'The role of education in Jewish Continuity: a response to Jonathan Sacks', *British Journal of Religious Education*, vol. 27, no. 3 (2005): 262.
36   Helena Miller, 'Meeting the challenge', p. 510.
37   Oliver Valins, Barry Kosmin and Jacqueline Goldberg, *The Future of Jewish Schooling in the United Kingdom* (London: Institute for Jewish Policy Research, 2001).
38   Commission on Jewish Schools, *The Future of Jewish Schools*, p. 61.
39   Editorial, *Jewish Chronicle*, 26 October 2007: 34.
40   Benjamin Perl, 'Our children are getting a raw deal', *Jewish Chronicle*, 16 April 2009, <http://www.thejc.com/articles/our-children-are-getting-a-raw-deal>, accessed 8 February 2010.
41   Israel Finestein, *Scenes and Personalities in Anglo-Jewry 1800–2000* (London: Vallentine Mitchell, 2002), p. 26.
42   Commission on Representation of the Interests of the British Jewish Community, *A Community of Communities* (London: Institute for Jewish Policy Research, 2000).
43   The Board also faced another challenge to its status as Anglo Jewry's sole representative body with the formation of the London Jewish Forum in 2006 to run representative and coordination activities in London.
44   The system is mitigated to some extent by ad *personam* members not having a vote in the election of new members. In addition, some of the members representing organizations are elected by more or less broad constituencies.
45   Interview with Jeremy Newmark, 7 March 2008.
46   Jonathan D. Sarna, 'American Jews in the new millennium', in Yvonne Yasbeck Haddad, Jane I. Smith and John L. Esposito (eds), *Religion and Immigration: Christian, Jewish and Muslim Experiences in the United States* (Walnut Creek, CA: Altamira Press, 2003).

Chapter 6

1   Janet Levin, 'Multiculturalism – a mistake?', *Jewish Renaissance*, July (2008): 6.
2   In the late 1990s the Spiro Institute underwent an acrimonious internal split, with founders Robin and Nitza Spiro going on to found the Spiro Ark and the remainder of the organization transforming itself into the London Jewish

Cultural Centre. Both institutions continue to flourish – a testament to the expanded 'market' for adult education and Jewish cultural activities.

3   Matthew Kalman, 'The making of New Moon', unpublished document, 2009.

4   From 'Building Jewish life', <http://www.jcclondon.org.uk/Vision.html>, accessed 2 June 2009.

5   <http://www.moishehouse.org/about.asp>, accessed 1 October 2009.

6   <http://jewdas.org/news/hoax_admission.htm>, accessed 2 June 2009.

7   Much of the historical information about Limmud comes from 'History of Limmud (abridged)' in the 2007 *Limmud Conference Handbook*, pp. 327–34.

8   Limmud's mission statement was first published in 1995 and has evolved over time. The version quoted here comes from <http://www.limmud.org/home/about/mission/>, accessed 4 June 2009.

9   See Clive Lawton, 'In defence of the Beth Din', TotallyJewish.com, 30 June 2005, <http://www.totallyjewish.com/news/lawton/?content_id=1024>, accessed 8 February 2010.

10   Jonathan Boyd, 'In search of underlying principles: the case of Limmud', unpublished document, June 2006, p. 19.

11   Ibid., p. 26.

12   For a while in the 1990s the orthodox-led Encounter Conference attempted to develop a non-pluralist alternative to Limmud. Despite high attendances it did not survive in the long term.

13   See, for example, Isi Leibler, 'Don't give a platform to Israel-bashing', 30 January 2008, <http://web.israelinsider.com/Views/12602.htm>, accessed 4 June 2009.

14   Keith Harris, 'Exploring Jewish space: a critique of Limmud', in Robert Rabinowitz, *New Voices in Jewish Thought* (London: Limmud Publications, 1998), pp. 39–54.

15   From 'Mission statement', <http://www.jewishrenaissance.org.uk/>, accessed 10 June 2009.

16   Asher D. Biemann, 'The problem of tradition and reform in Jewish Renaissance and Renaissancism', *Jewish Social Studies*, vol. 8, no. 1 (2001): 58–87.

17   Michael Lerner, *Jewish Renewal: A Path to Healing and Transformation* (New York: Grosset/Putnam, 1994); Edward Feld, *The Spirit of Renewal: Crisis and Response in Jewish Life* (Woodstock, Vermont: Jewish Lights Publishing, 1991); Mordecai Kaplan, *Judaism as Civilization: Toward a Reconstruction of American-Jewish Life* (Philadelphia: Jewish Publication Society, 1994); Simon Rawidowicz, 'Israel: the ever dying people', in *Studies in Jewish Thought* (Philadelphia: Jewish Publication Society of America, 1974), pp. 210–24.

18   Ruth Ellen Gruber, *Virtually Jewish: Reinventing Jewish Culture in Europe* (Berkeley: University of California Press, 2002).

19   Interview with Jonathan Sacks, 3 March 2008.

20   The irony of Sacks praising an event that his Beth Din has compelled him *not* to attend is palpable; it does suggest, however, that Sacks would *like* to attend should communal politics be different.
21   Jonathan Sacks, 'Jewish discontinuity', in Stephen W. Massil (ed.), *The Jewish Year Book 1996* (London: Vallentine Mitchell, 1996).
22   Sue Fishkoff, *The Rebbe's Army: Inside the World of Chabad-Lubavitch* (New York: Schoken Books, 2003).
23   Yoel Finkelman, 'On the limits of American Jewish social engineering: ironic reflections of Prof. Mordecai M. Kaplan and R. Aharon Kotler', *Contemporary Jewry*, vol. 28 (2008): 58–83.
24   Steven Windmueller, 'The second American Jewish revolution', *Journal of Jewish Communal Service*, vol. 82, no. 3 (2007): 252–60.
25   Jonathan D. Sarna, 'American Jews in the new millennium', in Yvonne Yasbeck Haddad, Jane I. Smith and John L. Esposito (eds), *Religion and Immigration: Christian, Jewish and Muslim Experiences in the United States* (Walnut Creek, CA: Altamira Press, 2003), pp. 121–2.
26   Myrella Cohen, 'After the "Preston Report"', in Stephen W. Massil (ed.), *The Jewish Year Book 1997* (London: Vallentine Mitchell, 1997).
27   'Who we are – UJIA lay leaders', <http://www.ujia.org/who-we-are/whos-who/1096/ujia-lay-leaders/>, accessed 12 June 2009.
28   Women's Review Task Force, *Connection, Continuity and Community: British Jewish Women Speak Out* (London: Women's Review Task Force, 2009).
29   Accurate as of June 2009.
30   Yaacov Wise, 'Majority of Jews will be ultra-orthodox by 2050', press release (Manchester: University of Manchester, 2007). See also Eric Kaufmann, *Demographic Radicalization? The Religiosity-Fertility Nexus and Politics* (London: Birkbeck School of Politics and Sociology, 2009).
31   Steven M. Cohen and Keith Kahn-Harris, *Beyond Belonging: The Jewish Identities of Moderately Engaged British Jews* (London: UJIA/Profile Books, 2004).
32   Gerald Ronson, 'Introduction, *JCOSS Jewish Community Secondary School: A Multi-Million Pound Outreach Project* (JCOSS, 2008), p. 5.
33   See, for example, Steven M. Cohen and Ari Y. Kelman, *Cultural Events and Jewish Identities: Young Adult Jews in New York* (New York: The National Foundation for Jewish Culture, 2005).

Chapter 7
1   Unfortunately, Anthony Julius's monumental *Trials of the Diaspora: A History of Anti-Semitism in England* (Oxford: Oxford University Press, 2010), which deals with many of the issues discussed in this chapter, was published just as the proofs of this book were being finalized. We note here that although Julius does not use the term 'new antisemitism' he does argue that, post-1967, an insidious 'anti-Zionist antisemitism' has emerged in England.

2   For example, Anthony Lerman, 'Sense on antisemitism', in Paul Ignaski and
     Barry Kosmin (eds), *A New Antisemitism? Debating Judeophobia in 21st-
     century Britain* (London: Profile Books/JPR, 2003), pp. 54–67; Brian Klug,
     'The collective Jew: Israel and the new anti-Semitism', *Patterns of Prejudice*,
     vol. 37, no. 2 (2003); Brian Klug 'The myth of the new anti-semitism', *The
     Nation*, 2 February 2004; Brian Klug, 'Israel, antisemitism and the left', *Red
     Pepper*, 24 November 2005.

3   See, for example, Paul Iganski, Vicky Kielinger and Susan Paterson, *Hate
     Crimes Against London's Jews: An Analysis of Incidents Recorded by the
     Metropolitan Police Service 2001–2004* (London: Institute for Jewish Policy
     Research, 2005).

4   Cf. Michel Foucault, *Power/Knowledge: Selected Interviews* (New York:
     Pantheon, 1980); Judith Butler, *Gender Trouble* (New York: Routledge,
     1990); Norman Fairclough, *Language and Power* (London: Longman,
     1989).

5   *The New Anti-Semitism: The Official Protests of the British and American
     Jewish Communities* (London: The Press Committee of the Jewish Board
     of Deputies 1921).

6   Cecil Roth, *The Jew as British Citizen: Three Centuries of Achievement*
     (Jewish Historical Society of England, 1936), p. 3.

7   Robert S. Wistrich, 'Left-wing anti-Zionism in Western societies', in Robert S.
     Wistrich (ed.), *Anti-Zionism and Antisemitism in the Contemporary World*
     (London, Macmillan, 1990), pp. 46–52 (49).

8   Ibid, pp. 50–1; David Cesarani, 'Anti-Zionism in Britain, 1922–2002:
     Continuities and Discontinuities', in Jeffrey Herf (ed.), *Anti-Semitism and
     Anti-Zionism in Historical Perspective: Convergence and Divergence* (London:
     Routledge, 2007), pp. 115–44 (129).

9   Both cited in Pierre-André Taguieff, *Rising from the Muck: The New Anti-
     Semitism in Europe* (Chicago: Ivan R. Dee, 2004), p. 62.

10   Arnold Forster and Benjamin Epstein, *The New Anti-Semitism* (New York:
     McGraw-Hill, 1974).

11   David Cesarani, 'The perdition affair', in Robert S. Wistrich (ed.), *Anti-
     Zionism and Antisemitism in the Contemporary World* (London: Macmillan,
     1990), pp. 53–60 (53).

12   For example, articles by Max Beloff (21 November 1969) and Robert Wistrich
     (20 December 74) identifying convergence between New Left and Palestinian
     causes, as a danger to Israel and world Jewry – David Cesarani, *Reporting Anti-
     Semitism: The Jewish Chronicle* (Southampton: University of Southampton,
     1993), p. 36.

13   Cesarani, 'The perdition affair', p. 53; Cesarani, 'Anti-Zionism in Britain', p.
     130.

14   See testimony of Mitch Simmons to the All-Party Parliamentary Inquiry into
     Antisemitism, Transcript of Oral Evidence, Session One, 6 February 2006, All-
     Party Parliamentary Group Against Antisemitism, p. 13.

15   Wistrich, *Anti-Zionism and Antisemitism in the Contemporary World.*

16   Michael Whine, 'Antisemitism on the streets', in Ignaski and Kosmin, *A New Antisemitism?*, pp. 23–37.
17   Ibid., p. 28.
18   Cesarani, 'Anti-Zionism in Britain', p. 132.
19   Martin J. Raffel, 'History of Israel advocacy', in Alan Mittleman, Jonathan D. Sarna and Robert Licht (eds), *Jewish Polity and American Civil Society: Communal Agencies and Religious Movements in the American Public Sphere* (Lanham: Rowman and Littlefield, 2002), pp. 161–73.
20   Whine, 'Antisemitism on the streets', p. 31.
21   *Report of the All-Party Parliamentary Inquiry into Antisemitism* (London: The Stationary Office Limited, 2006,), p. 5, sect. 17.
22   Taguieff, *Rising from the Muck*, p. 3.
23   Jonathan Laurence and Justin Vaisse, *Integrating Islam: Political and Religious Challenges in Contemporary France* (Washington DC: Brookings Institute Press, 2006), p. 222.
24   With just 15–35 per cent attributed to the right (ibid., p. 230).
25   Quoted in David Matas, *Aftershock: Anti-Zionism and Antisemitism* (Toronto: The Dundurn Group, 2005), p. 8.
26   Phyllis Chesler, *The New Anti-Semitism: The Current Crisis and What We Must Do About It* (San Francisco: Jossey-Bass, 2003), p. 58.
27   Matas, *Aftershock*, p. 13.
28   Whine, 'Antisemitism on the streets', p. 23.
28   Paul Ignaski and Barry Kosmin, 'Editors' introduction', in Ignaski and Kosmin, *A New Antisemitism?*, p. 8; Gabriel Schoenfeld, *The Return of Anti-Semitism* (London: Politico's, 2005), pp. 95–6.
30   Petronella Wyatt, 'Poisonous prejudice', *The Spectator*, 8 December 2001.
31   Barbara Amiel, 'Islamists overplay their hand but London salons don't see it', *Daily Telegraph*, 17 December 2001. See also Ignaski and Kosmin, 'Editors' introduction'.
32   'Dalyell's "Jewish cabal" remark denied', BBC News Online, 4 May 2003 <http://news.bbc.co.uk/1/hi/uk_politics/2999219.stm>, accessed 8 February 2010.
33   Richard Ingrams, 'I'm still on the train', *The Observer*, 13 July 2003, <http://www.guardian.co.uk/politics/2003/jul/13/alistairdarling.guardiancolumnists>, accessed 8 February 2010.
34   Chesler, *The New Anti-Semitism*.
35   Ibid., p. vii.
36   *La nouvelle judéophobia* [*The new Judeophobia*] (Paris: Mille et une Nuits, 2002). Cf. Laurence and Vaisse, *Integrating Islam*, p. 65.
37   Elaine Sciolino, 'Jewish leaders appeal to E.U. to stamp out Anti-Semitism', *New York Times*, 19 February 2004.
38   Berlin Declaration (Second OSCE Conference on Anti-Semitism, Berlin, 28–2 April 2004).
39   John Mearsheimer and Stephen Walt, 'The Israel lobby', *London Review of Books*, vol. 28, no. 6 (2006), <http://www.lrb.co.uk/v28/n06/mear01_.html>, accessed 8 February 2010.

40   Hirsh describes this sort of account as an 'ahistorical, essentialist' under-
      standing of antisemitism. See David Hirsh, *Anti-Zionism and Antisemitism:
      Cosmopolitan Reflections* (New Haven: YIISA Occasional Papers, 2007), pp.
      19–25.

41   Daniel Cohn-Sherbok, *Anti-Semitism: A History* (Thrupp: Sutton Publishing,
      2002), p. 324.

42   Abraham H. Foxman, *The Deadliest Lies: The Israel Lobby and the Myth
      of Jewish Control* (London: Palgrave Macmillan, 2007), p. 39.

43   Dennis MacShane, *Globalising Hatred: The New Antisemitism* (London:
      Weidenfeld and Nicolson, 2008), p. 3.

44   Abraham H. Foxman, *Never Again? The Threat of the New Anti-Semitism*
      (San Francisco: HarperSanFrancisco, 2003).

45   Matas, *Aftershock.*

46   The term 'Eurabia' was coined by Bat Ye'or. See: *Eurabia: The Euro-Arab Axis*
      (Madison, NJ: Fairleigh Dickinson University Press, 2005).

47   Laurence and Vaisse, *Integrating Islam*, p. 3.

48   Ibid., p. 231.

49   Ibid., pp. 228–32.

50   Alvin H. Rosenfeld, *Anti-Zionism in Great Britain and Beyond: A 'Respectable'
      Anti-Semitism?*(New York: American Jewish Committee, 2004).

51   Melanie Phillips, Robert Wistrich and Isi Leibler, *Islam, British Society and the
      Terrorist Threat*, Posen Paper (Jerusalem: Vidal Sassoon Center for the Study
      of Antisemitism, Hebrew University of Jerusalem, 2007).

52   David Hirsh, *Anti-Zionism and Antisemitism*; Shalom Lappin, *This Green and
      Pleasant Land: Britain and the Jews* (New Haven: YIISA Working Papers,
      2008).

53   'Warning of anti-Semitic tsunami', BBC News Online, 1 January 2006,
      <http://news.bbc.co.uk/1/hi/uk/4573052.stm>, accessed 1 October 2009.

54   Jonathan Sacks, 'A new antisemitism?', in Ignaski and Kosmin, *A New
      Antisemitism?*, pp. 38 ff. (39).

55   Examples of key texts on the new antisemitism which allow for much greater
      complexity include Gabriel Schoenfeld, *The Return of Anti-Semitism* and
      especially Bernard Harrison, *The Resurgence of Anti-Semitism: Jews, Israel, and
      Liberal Opinion* (London: Roman and Littlefield, 2006). Needless to say, these
      are much further down the bestseller list than books such as Phyllis Chesler's
      or Melanie Phillips's.

56   Chesler, *The New Anti-Semitism*, pp. 3–4, 43–52.

57   Ibid., pp. 53, 55.

58   Jonathan Sacks, 'A new antisemitism?', p. 45. The All-Party Parliamentary
      Inquiry into Antisemitism noted that 'Many of those who gave evidence
      described antisemitism in terms of a constantly mutating virus' (*Report of the
      All-Party Parliamentary Inquiry into Antisemitism*, p. 5, sect. 18). Interestingly,
      although then they minimized antisemitism (see above, chapter 1), the
      communal leadership responding to fascism in the 1930s 'constantly likened
      [it] to a disease; a formulation that denied the applicability of a rigorous

social scientific analysis seeking to locate antisemitism as a phenomenon rooted in social, political, economic and cultural relationships in the society in which it emerged' (David Rosenberg, 'An independent Jewish platform', *Jewish Socialist*, no.1 (1985), pp. 31–2).

59   MacShane, *Globalising Hatred*, p. 12.

60   Schoenfeld, *The Return of Anti-Semitism*, pp. 3, 74.

61   Ibid., pp. 4, 85.

62   See Harrison, *The Resurgence of Anti-Semitism* for a very good analysis of this.

63   It is also worth considering the extent to which the image of the opinion-shaping omnipotence of the liberal elite mirrors the new antisemites' own image of an omnipotent Jewish/Zionist lobby. Indeed, bastions of the mainstream media, such as the BBC or the *New York Times*, are as likely to be identified from different quarters as entangled in the tentacles of the Zionist lobby or as part of the liberal anti-Zionist hegemony. Schoenfeld: 'The *Economist* represents the liberal establishment, as does the British Broadcasting Company (BBC), which uses television transmissions worldwide to paint an utterly lopsided picture in which the Jewish state's most dangerous enemies are presented as well-intentioned gentlemen and the Israelis themselves as demons' (*The Return of Anti-Semitism*, pp. 90–1).

64   Quoted in Lerman, 'Sense on antisemitism', p. 54.

65   Ibid., p. 57.

66   Quoted in Radu Iaonid, 'Foreword', in Pierre-André Taguieff, *Rising from the Muck*, p. xiv.

67   Foxman, *Never Again?*, pp. 1–3.

68   David Newman, 'Britain and the Academic Boycott of Israel', *Israel Journal of Foreign Affairs*, vol. 2, no. 2 (2008).

69   'Thousands come to support Israel', BBC News Online, 6 May 2002 <http://news.bbc.co.uk/1/hi/uk/1970028.stm>, accessed 8 February 2010; Claire Hills, '"In support of peace and solidarity"', BBC News Online, 6 May 2002 <http://news.bbc.co.uk/1/hi/uk/1971299.stm>, accessed 8 February 2010.

70   Judith Berman, 'Holocaust commemorations of London and Anglo-Jewish (dis-)unity', *Journal of Modern Jewish Studies*, vol. 3, no. 1 (2004): 51–72.

71   'Against the ethnic panic of American Jews: Hitler is dead', *The New Republic*, 27 May 2002.

72   Anthony Julius, 'Don't panic', 1 February 2002, revised as 'Is there anything "new" in the new antisemitism?', in Ignaski and Kosmin, *A New Antisemitism?*, pp. 68–75 (71).

73   Ibid., p. 73. However, in 2003, when Julius's essay was collected in Ignaski and Kosmin's, *A New Antisemitism?*, he added: 'I could, of course, be wrong, and since I wrote [the] earlier version of this piece … , things indeed have got worse' (p. 75).

74   MacShane, *Globalising Hatred*, p. 5.

75   Reprinted in Lerman, 'Sense on antisemitism', p. 55.

76   Ibid., p. 56.

77   Ibid., pp. 60–1.

78   Ibid., pp. 62–3.

79   Brian Klug, 'The collective Jew'. A version was published in the American left liberal weekly, *The Nation*, as 'The myth of the new Anti-Semitism', 2 February 2004, <http://www.thenation.com/doc/20040202/klug>, accessed 8 February 2010.

80   Neil Lazarus, 'The Jewish addiction', in Danny Ben-Moshe and Zohar Segev (eds), *Israel, The Diaspora and Jewish Identity* (Eastbourne: Sussex Academic Press, 2007), pp. 22–7 (26).

81   Peter Pulzer, 'The new antisemitism, or when is a taboo not a taboo?', in Ignaski and Kosmin, *A New Antisemitism?*, pp. 83–4.

82   Ibid., pp. 84–5.

83   Ibid., pp. 86–7.

84   Harrison, *The Resurgence of Anti-Semitism*, pp. 200–2.

85   Ken Livingstone, 'An attack on voters' rights', *The Guardian*, 1 March 2006, <http://society.guardian.co.uk/localgovt/comment/0,,1720439,00.html>, accessed 8 February 2010.

86   Hirsh, *Anti-Zionism and Antisemitism*, pp. 54, 58.

87   'A time to speak out: Independent Jewish Voices', Independent Jewish Voices <http://jewishvoices.squarespace.com/declaration-2/>, accessed 8 February 2010.

88   Nick Lambert, *Jews and Europe in the Twenty-first Century* (London: Vallentine Mitchell, 2008), pp. 69–70.

89   Georgina Henry, 'This week on Comment is free', 5 February 2007 <http://www.guardian.co.uk/commentisfree/2007/feb/05/post1046>, accessed 8 February 2010.

90   New Generation Network, 'Race and faith: a new agenda', 20 November 2006 <http://www.guardian.co.uk/commentisfree/2006/nov/20/whyweneedanewdiscourseon>, accessed 8 February 2010.

91   See BBC Radio 4, 'World This Weekend', 9 July 2006; Dominic Casciani, 'Analysis: taking on extremists', BBC News Online, 14 August 2006, <http://news.bbc.co.uk/1/hi/uk_politics/4791847.stm>, accessed 8 February 2010; John Ware, 'MCB in the dock', *Prospect*, 16 December 2006 <http://www.prospectmagazine.co.uk/2006/12/mcbinthedock/>.

92   Keith Kahn-Harris was initially a signatory to the IJV declaration but removed himself soon after publication. See: 'The problem with dialogue', *New Jewish Thought*, 2 September 2007, <http://www.newjewishthought.org/2007/09/the-problem-with-dialogue/>, accessed 8 February 2010.

93   Lambert, *Jews and Europe in the Twenty-first Century*, p. 85.

94   Brian Klug, 'Who speaks for Jews in Britain', guardian.co.uk, 5 February 2007, <http://www.guardian.co.uk/commentisfree/2007/feb/05/holdjewishvoices>, accessed 8 February 2010.

95   David Goldberg, 'Israel and the A-word', guardian.co.uk, 5 February 2007,<http://www.guardian.co.uk/commentisfree/2007/feb/05/holdjewishvoices5>, accessed 8 February 2010.

96   Gillian Slovo, 'Our responsibility towards others', guardian.co.uk, 6 February 2007, <http://www.guardian.co.uk/commentisfree/2007/feb/06/holdjewishvoices7>, accessed 8 February 2010.

97   Anne Karpf, 'Children of the Holocaust', guardian.co.uk, 7 February 2007, <http://www.guardian.co.uk/commentisfree/2007/feb/07/holdjewishvoices4>, accessed 8 February 2010.

98   Tony Lerman, 'Reflecting the reality of Jewish diversity', guardian.co.uk, 6 February 2007, <http://www.guardian.co.uk/commentisfree/2007/feb/06/holdjewishvoices8>, accessed 8 February 2010.

99   Melanie Phillips, 'Jews for genocide', 8 February 2007, <http://www.melaniephillips.com/diary/?p=1458>, accessed 1 October 2009.

100   Linda Grant, 'Other voices, other lives', *The Guardian*, 7 February 2007, <http://www.guardian.co.uk/commentisfree/2007/feb/07/othervoicesotherlives>, accessed 1 October 2009.

101   Geoffrey Alderman, 'Who really speaks for Jews in Britain?', guardian.co.uk, 6 February 2007, <http://www.guardian.co.uk/commentisfree/2007/feb/06/holdjewishvoices9>, accessed 10 February 2010.

102   David Hirsh, 'Radical 68ers have become the new conservatives of the Jewish community in Britain', *Engage*, 13 August 2006, <http://www.engageonline.org.uk/blog/article.php?id=578>, accessed 1 October 2009. The article preceded the IJV declaration but it later came to be used frequently to describe many of its signatories.

103   Historically, a minority of the post-war Jewish leadership combined criticism of Israel with downplaying antisemitism in the UK: Chief Rabbi Immanuel Jakobovits was a prominent example.

104   David Goldberg. 'Let's Have a Sense of Proportion', *Guardian Weekly*, 31 January 2002.

105   Anne Karpf et al. (eds), *A Time to Speak Out: Independent Jewish Voices on Israel, Zionism and jewish Identity* (London: Verso, 2008).

106   Private information.

107   'Rally message is "Yes to peace"' *Jewish Chronicle*, 15 January 2009, <http://www.thejc.com/news/uk-news/rally-message-yes-peace>, accessed 10 February 2010.

108   '"Rally cancelled" message exposed as a hoax', *Jewish Chronicle*, 9 January 2009, <http://www.thejc.com/news/israel-news/rally-cancelled%E2%80%99 99-message-exposed-a-hoax>, accessed 10 February 2010; 'Faith leaders demand UK action on Gaza', Christian Aid press release January 2009, <http://www.christianaid.org.uk/pressoffice/pressreleases/Index/implement-ceasefire-now-Gaza-crisis.aspx>, accessed 10 February 2010.

109   Jonathan Freedland, 'Why I did not "rally for Israel"', *Jewish Chronicle*, 14 January 2009, <http://www.thejc.com/comment/columnists/why-i-did-not-rally-israel>, accessed 10 February 2010. See 'Israel, we support you – but hear our plea', *The Observer*, 11 January 2009, <http://www.guardian.co.uk/world/2009/jan/11/gaza-israelandthepalestinians>, accessed 10 February 2010.

110 See Keith Kahn-Harris, 'British Jews and Israel: a new relationship?,' guardian.co.uk, 13 January 2009, <http://www.guardian.co.uk/commentisfree/2009/jan/13/judaism-israelandthepalestinians>, accessed 10 February 2010.

111 Henry Grunwald, 'If Israel enters Gaza, Anglo-Jewry will be ready', *The Jewish Chronicle*, 29 February 2008.

112 Private information.

113 See, for example, Lappin, *This Green and Pleasant Land*.

114 Simon Rocker, 'Lieberman's success horrifies UK leaders', *Jewish Chronicle*, 12 February 2009, <http://www.thejc.com/news/uk-news/liebermans-success-horri%EF%AC%81es-uk-leaders>, accessed 10 February 2010.

115 Simon Rocker, 'Peace activist Wineman snatches Board presidency in close-run poll', *Jewish Chronicle*, 21 May 2009, <http://www.thejc.com/news/uk-news/peace-activist-wineman-snatches-board-presidency-close-run-poll>, accessed 10 February 2010. See also Geoffrey Alderman, 'Can the Board speak for us all?', *Jewish Chronicle*, 9 July 2009, <http://www.thejc.com/comment/columnists/can-board-speak-us-all>, accessed 10 February 2010.

116 Vivian Wineman, 'Right of Reply: British criticism of Israel is nothing special', *Jerusalem Post*, 27 July 2009, <http://www.jpost.com/servlet/Satellite?cid=1248277904878&pagename=JPArticle per cent2FshowFull>, accessed July 2009. See also Jonathan Hoffman, 'The status of Israel and of Jews in the UK: "Darkness closing" or "business as usual"?', *Jerusalem Post*, 1 August 2009, <http://www.jpost.com/servlet/Satellite?cid=1248277944837 &pagename=JPost/JPArticle/ShowFull>, accessed August 2009; Simon Rocker, 'Deputies in row over how to treat hate', *Jewish Chronicle*, 6 August 2009, <http://www.thejc.com/news/uk-news/deputies-row-over-how-treat-hate>, accessed 8 February 2010.

117 See, for example, Dave Rich, 'Britain is a good place to be Jewish', Haaretz online (English edition), 21 August 2008, <http://www.haaretz.com/hasen/spages/1013644.html>, accessed 8 February 2010.

Conclusion

1 Israel Finestein, *Scenes and Personalities in Anglo-Jewry 1800–2000* (London: Vallentine Mitchell, 2002), p. 1.

2 David Graham, Marlena Schmool and Stanley Waterman, *Jews in Britain: A Snapshot from the 2001 Census* (London: Institute for Jewish Policy Research, 2007).

3 Commission on Representation of the Interests of the British Jewish Community, *A Community of Communities* (London: Institute for Jewish Policy Research, 2000).

4 Keith Kahn-Harris, 'What is British Jewish politics', *Zeek*, 30 June 2009, <http://www.jewcy.com/post/what_british_jewish_politics>, accessed June 2009.

5 Samuel Freedman, *Jew vs Jew: The Struggle for the Soul of American Jewry* (New York: Touchstone, 2000).

6   Keith Kahn-Harris, *Communities in Conversation: Jewish Involvement in Inter Faith Activities in the UK* (London: The Board of Deputies of British Jews Community Research Unit, 2009), <http://www.boardofdeputies.org.uk/file/CommunitiesInConversation.pdf>, accessed 8 February 2010.

7   Keith Kahn-Harris, *New Jewish Thought Policy Paper 2: An Experiment in Dialogue* (London: New Jewish Thought, 2008), <http://www.newjewishthought.org/wp-content/uploads/2009/09/An-Experiment-in-Dialogue2.pdf>, accessed 8 February 2010.

8   Jonathan D. Sarna, *The Economic Downturn and the Future of Jewish Communities* (London: Institute for Jewish Policy Research, September 2009).

9   For an overview of the sociological relevance of the Jewish experience to other minorities, see Harriet Hartman and Debra Kaufman, 'Decentering the study of Jewish identity: opening the dialogue with other religious groups', *Sociology of Religion*, vol. 67, no. 4 (2006): 365–85.

10   Huw Beynon and Lou Kushnick, 'Cool Britannia or cruel Britannia? Racism and New Labour', in Leo Panitch and Colin Leys (eds), *Socialist Register 2003. Fighting Identities: Race, Religion and Ethno-nationalism* (London: Merlin Press, 2003).

11   Bikhu Parekh, *The Future of Multi-Ethnic Britain – The Parekh Report* (London: Runnymede Trust, 2000).

12   Jonathan Sacks, *The Dignity of Difference: How to Avoid the Clash of Civilizations*, 2nd edn (London: Continuum, 2003).

13   V. Kalra, 'Riots, Race and Reports: Denham, Cantle, Oldham and Burnley Inquiries', *Sage Race Relations Abstracts*, vol. 27, no. 4 (2002): 20–30.

14   Yasmin Alibhai-Brown, *After Multiculturalism* (London: The Foreign Policy Centre, 2000); D. Goodhart, 'Too diverse', *Prospect*, 20 February 2004, <http://www.prospectmagazine.co.uk/2004/02/toodiverse/>, accessed 8 February 2010; Tom Baldwin, '"I want an integrated society with a difference": An interview with Trevor Phillips', *Times*, 3 April 2004.

15   Ted Cantle, *Community Cohesion: A Report of the Independent Review Team* (London: Home Office, 2001).

16   Herman Ouseley, *Community Pride not prejudice* (Bradford: Bradford Vision, 2000).

17   David Ritchie, *The Oldham Independent Review Panel Report* (Oldham: Oldham Independent Review, 2001).

18   John Denham, *Building Cohesive Communities: A Report of the Ministerial Group on Public Order and Community Cohesion* (London: Home Office, 2002).

19   'Britain "sleep-walking to segregation"', *The Guardian*, 19 September 2005, <http://www.guardian.co.uk/world/2005/sep/19/race.socialexclusion>, accessed 8 February 2010.

20   'The need to defend the nation', *Daily Mail*, 5 April 2004 <http://www.melaniephillips.com/articles-new/?p=212>, accessed 8 February 2010.

21 'The future of Britishness', speech to Fabian Society, 14 January 2006 <http://www.fabians.org.uk/events/speeches/the-future-of-britishness>, accessed 8 February 2010.

22 'This lethal moral madness', *Daily Mail*, 14 July 2005 <http://www.melaniephillips.com/articles-new/?p=342>, accessed 8 February 2010.

23 Jonathan Sacks, *The Home We Build Together: Recreating Society* (London: Continuum, 2007).

24 Ali Rattansi, 'Who's British? *Prospect* and the New Assimilationism', in R. Berkeley (ed.), *Cohesion, Community and Citizenship* (London: The Runnymede Trust, 2002); Les Back et al., 'New Labour's white heart: politics, multiculturalism and the return of assimilation', *The Political Quarterly*, vol. 73, no. 4 (2002): 445–54; Les Back et al., 'The return of assimilationism: race, multiculturalism and New Labour', *Sociological Research Online*, vol. 7, no. 2, <http://www.socresonline.org.uk/7/2/back.html>, accessed 8 February 2010.

25 Arun Kundnani, *The End of Tolerance* (London: Pluto, 2007).

26 Paul Bagguley and Yasmin Hussain, 'Conflict and cohesion: constructions of 'community' around the 2001 "riots"', in S. Herbrechter and M. Higgins. (eds), *Returning (to) Communities. Theory, Culture and Political Practice of the Communal* (London: Rodopi, 2006), p. 4; see also Jon Burnett, 'Community, cohesion and the state', *Race and Class*, vol. 45, no. 3 (2004): 1–18; Jonny Burnett and Dave Whyte (2004) 'New Labour's new racism', *IRR News*, October, <http://www.irr.org.uk/2004/october/ak000008.html>, accessed 8 February 2010.

27 Kalbir Shukra et al., 'Race, social cohesion and the changing politics of citizenship', *London Review of Education*, vol. 2, no. 3 (2004): 187–95 (192).

28 Brian Alleyne, 'The idea of community as epistemological obstacle', Beyond Difference: Racial and Ethnic Studies Into the Millennium Seminar, Race and Ethnic Relations Unit, South Bank University, London, 20 September 2000; Clive Harris, 'Beyond multiculturalism? Difference, recognition and social justice', *Patterns of Prejudice*, vol. 35, no. 1 (2001): 13–58. These sorts of points can be related to critiques developed within feminism by groups such as Southall Black Sisters, whose politics has developed in struggle against patriarchal community leaders in minority communities. For Uma Narayan, for example, the notion of community imposes on members of a culture the 'values and practices [of] specific *privileged* groups within the community as values of the "culture" as a whole' (Uma Narayan, *Dislocating Cultures: Identities, Traditions, and Third World Feminism* (London: Routledge, 1997): 15).

29 Eric S. Goldstein, *The Price of Whiteness: Jews, Race and Ethnic Identity* (Princeton, NJ: Princeton University Press, 2006).

30 Leonard Prager, *Yiddish Culture in Britain: A Guide* (Frankfurt: Verlag Peter Lang, 1990).

31 Ulrich Beck, *Risk Society: Towards a New Modernity* (London: Sage, 1992).
32 Jane Franklin, 'Introduction', in Jane Franklin (ed.), *The Politics of Risk Society* (Cambridge: Polity/IPPR, 1998), p. 2.
33 Ibid., pp. 2–4.

Bibliography

Ackroyd, Peter, *London: The Biography* (London: Chatto and Windus, 2001).
'Against the ethnic panic of American Jews: Hitler is dead', *The New Republic*, 27 May 2002.
Alderman, Geoffrey, *The Jewish Community in British Politics* (Oxford: Clarendon, 1983).
—, *Modern British Jewry* (Oxford: Clarendon, 1992).
—, 'London Jewry and London Politics, 1889–1934', in Geoffrey Alderman (ed.), *Governments, Ethnic Groups and Political Representation: Comparative Studies on Governments and Non-Dominant Ethnic Groups in Europe, 1850–1940 Volume IV* (Dartmouth: European Science Foundation New York University Press Dartmouth, 1993), pp. 3–30.
—, 'Academic Duty and Communal Obligation: Some Thoughts on the Writing of Anglo-Jewish History' (London: Centre for Jewish Studies, School of Oriental and African Studies, University of London, Occasional Paper No. 1, 1994).
—, 'That letter … rabbinical politics and Jewish management', *Judaism Today*, Winter (1997).
—, *Modern British Jewry* (Oxford: Clarendon Press, 1998).
—, 'British Jews or Britons of the Jewish Persuasion? The Religious Constraints of Civic Freedom', in *National Variations in Jewish Identity: Implications of Jewish Education* (Albany: State University of New York Press, 1999), pp. 125–36.
—, 'British Jewry: the disintegration of a community', in Leslie Stein and Steven M. Encel (eds), *Continuity, Commitment and Survival: Jewish Communities in the Diaspora* (Westport, CT: Praeger, 2003), pp. 49–65.
—, 'Who really speaks for Jews in Britain?', guardian.co.uk, 6 February 2007, <http://www.guardian.co.uk/commentisfree/2007/feb/06/holdjewishvoices9>, accessed 10 February 2010.
—, 'Can the Board speak for us all?', *Jewish Chronicle*, 9 July 2009, <http://www.thejc.com/comment/columnists/can-board-speak-us-all>, accessed 10 February 2010.
—, 'In defeat JFS still won't learn', *Jewish Chronicle*, 22 December 2010.

Alibhai-Brown, Yasmin, *After Multiculturalism* (London: The Foreign Policy Centre, 2000).

Alleyne, Brian, 'The idea of community as epistemological obstacle', Beyond Difference: Racial and Ethnic Studies Into the Millennium Seminar, Race and Ethnic Relations Unit, South Bank University, London, 20 September 2000.

All-Party Parliamentary Group against Antisemitism, *Report of the All-Party Parliamentary Inquiry into Antisemitism* (London: The Stationary Office Limited, 2006).

Amiel, Barbara, 'Islamists overplay their hand but London salons don't see it', *Daily Telegraph*, 17 December 2001.

Ash, Robert, 'Mountains suspended by a hair: Eruv, a symbolic act by which a legal fiction of community is established', DPhil thesis submitted at the University of Leicester, May 2000.

Aviv, Caryn and Shneer, David, *New Jews: The End of the Jewish Diaspora* (New York: New York University Press, 2005).

Back, Les et al., 'New Labour's white heart: politics, multiculturalism and the return of assimilation', *The Political Quarterly*, vol. 73, no. 4 (2002): 445–54.

Back, Les et al., 'The return of assimilationism: race, multiculturalism and New Labour', *Sociological Research Online*, vol. 7, no. 2, <http://www.socresonline.org.uk/7/2/back.html>, accessed 8 February 2010.

Bagguley, Paul and Hussain, Yasmin, 'Conflict and cohesion: constructions of 'community' around the 2001 "riots"', in S. Herbrechter and M. Higgins. (eds), *Returning (to) Communities. Theory, Culture and Political Practice of the Communal* (London: Rodopi, 2006), p. 4

Baldwin, Tom, '"I want an integrated society with a difference": An interview with Trevor Phillips', *Times*, 3 April 2004.

Bat Ye'or, *Eurabia: The Euro-Arab Axis* (Madison, NJ: Fairleigh Dickinson University Press, 2005).

Bauman, Zygmunt, *Modernity and the Holocaust* (Cambridge: Polity, 1989).

—, 'Allosemitism: premodern, modern, postmodern', in Brian Cheyette and Laura Marcus (eds), *Modernity, Culture and 'The Jew'* (Cambridge: Polity, 1991)

—, *Modernity and Ambivalence* (Cambridge: Polity, 1991).

—, *Postmodern Ethics* (Oxford: Blackwell, 1993).

Beck, Ulrich, *Risk Society: Towards a New Modernity* (London: Sage, 1992).

Bekerman, Zvi and Kopelowitz, Ezra (eds), *Cultural Education – Cultural Sustainability: Minority, Diaspora, Indigenous and Ethno-Religious Groups in Multicultural Societies* (New York: Routledge, 2008).

Berger, David, *The Rebbe, the Messiah, and the Scandal of Orthodox Indifference* (Oxford: Littman Library, 2003).

Berlin Declaration (Second OSCE Conference on Anti-Semitism, Berlin, 28–2 April 2004).

Berman, Judith, 'Holocaust commemorations of London and Anglo-Jewish (dis-) unity', *Journal of Modern Jewish Studies*, vol. 3, no. 1 (2004): 51–72.

Berman, Lila Corwin, *Speaking of Jews: Rabbis, Intellectuals and the Creation of an American Public Identity* (Berkeley: University of California Press, 2009).

Bermant, Chaim, *The Jews* (London: Weidenfeld and Nicolson, 1977).

—, *Lord Jacobovitz: An Authorized Biography of the Chief Rabbi* (London: Weidenfeld and Nicolson, 1990).

Beynon, Huw and Kushnick, Lou, 'Cool Britannia or cruel Britannia? Racism and New Labour', in Leo Panitch and Colin Leys (eds), *Socialist Register 2003. Fighting Identities: Race, Religion and Ethno-nationalism* (London: Merlin Press, 2003).

Biemann, Asher D., 'The problem of tradition and reform in Jewish Renaissance and Renaissancism', *Jewish Social Studies*, vol. 8, no. 1 (2001): 58–87.

Black, Eugene C., *The Social Politics of Anglo-Jewry 1880–1920* (Oxford: Blackwell, 1988)

Bloch, Howard, *Earlham Grove Shul* (London: West Ham and Upton Park Synagogue, 1997).

Boyarin, Jonathan and Boyarin, Daniel, *Jews and Other Differences: The New Jewish Cultural Studies* (Minneapolis: University of Minnesota Press, 1997).

Boyd, Jonathan (ed.), *The Sovereign and the Situated Self: Jewish Identity and Community in the 21st Century* (London: UJIA/Profile Books, 2003).

—, 'In search of underlying principles: the case of Limmud', unpublished document, June 2006, p. 19.

Brah, Avtar, *Cartographies of Diaspora: Contesting Identities* (London: Routledge, 1996).

Brah, Avtar and Coombes, Anne E., *Hybridity and Its Discontents: Politics, Science, Culture* (London: Routledge, 2000).

Brawer, Naftali and Harris, Michael, 'Schools: we must face new reality', *Jewish Chronicle*, 14 January 2010, <http://www.thejc.com/comment/comment/26013/schools-we-must-face-new-reality>, accessed 3 March 2010.

'Britain "sleep-walking to segregation"', *The Guardian*, 19 September 2005, <http://www.guardian.co.uk/world/2005/sep/19/race.socialexclusion>, accessed 8 February 2010.

Brodkin, Karen, *How Jews Became White Folks and What That Says About Race in America* (New Brunswick, NJ: Rutgers University Press, 1998).

Bronzite, Sarah et al., *Beyond the Synagogue: Report of the Working Group of the 'Missing' Generation* (London: The Reform Synagogues of Great Britain, 1995).

Brook, Stephen, *The Club: The Jews of Modern Britain* (London: Pan Books, 1990).

Brown, Gordon, 'The future of Britishness', speech to Fabian Society, 14 January 2006 <http://www.fabians.org.uk/events/speeches/the-future-of-britishness>, accessed 8 February 2010.

Burg, Avram, *Brit Am, Covenant of the People: The Zionist Element. Draft Outline of the Policy of the Zionist Movement* (Jerusalem: Presented to the 33rd Zionist Congress, December 1997).

Burnett, Jon, 'Community, cohesion and the state', *Race and Class*, vol. 45, no. 3 (2004): 1–18.

Burnett, Jonny and Whyte, Dave, 'New Labour's new racism', *IRR News*, October, <http://www.irr.org.uk/2004/october/ak000008.html>, accessed 8 February 2010.

Butler, Judith, *Gender Trouble* (New York: Routledge, 1990).

Cantle, Ted, *Community Cohesion: A Report of the Independent Review Team* (London: Home Office, 2001).

Carlebach, Julius, *Karl Marx and the Radical Critique of Judaism* (London: Routledge and Kegan Paul, 1978).

Casciani, Dominic, 'Analysis: Taking on extremists', BBC News Online, 14 August 2006, <http://news.bbc.co.uk/1/hi/uk_politics/4791847.stm>, accessed 8 February 2010.

Cesarani, David, 'The transformation of communal authority in Anglo-Jewry, 1914–1940', in D. Cesarani (ed.), *The Making of Modern Anglo-Jewry* (Oxford: Basil Blackwell, 1990), pp. 115–40.

— (ed.), *The Making of Modern Anglo-Jewry* (Oxford: Basil Blackwell, 1990).

—, 'The perdition affair', in Robert S. Wistrich (ed.), *Anti-Zionism and Antisemitism in the Contemporary World* (London: Macmillan, 1990), pp. 53–60 (53).

—, *Reporting Anti-Semitism: The Jewish Chronicle* (Southampton: University of Southampton, 1993).

—, *The Jewish Chronicle and Anglo-Jewry, 1841–1991* (Cambridge: Cambridge University Press, 1994).

—, 'Anti-Zionism in Britain, 1922–2002: Continuities and Discontinuities', in Jeffrey Herf (ed.), *Anti-Semitism and Anti-Zionism in Historical Perspective: Convergence and Divergence* (London: Routledge, 2007), pp. 115–44 (129).

—, 'Foreword', in Nick Lambert, *Jews and Europe in the Twenty-First Century* (London: Vallentine Mitchell, 2008).

Charikar, Shalom, 'Confronting racism: a role for Jews', *Jewish Socialist* no. 1 (1985): 15–16.

Chesler, Phyllis, *The New Anti-Semitism: The Current Crisis and What We Must Do About It* (San Francisco: Jossey-Bass, 2003).

Cohen, Erik H., 'A questionable connection: community involvement and attitudes to intermarriage of young American Jews', *Jewish Journal of Sociology*, vol. 45, no. 1/2 (2003): 16.

Cohen, Myrella, 'After the "Preston Report"', in Stephen W. Massil (ed.), *The Jewish Year Book 1997* (London: Vallentine Mitchell, 1997).

Cohen, Steven M., 'Why intermarriage may not threaten Jewish continuity', *Moment*, December (1994).

—, *A Tale of Two Jewries: The 'Inconvenient Truth' for American Jews* (New York: Jewish Life Network/Steinhardt Foundation, 2006).

Cohen, Steven M. and Eisen, Arnold M., *The Jew Within: Self, Family and Community in America* (Bloomington: University of Indiana Press, 2000).

Cohen, Steven M. and Kahn-Harris, Keith, *Beyond Belonging: The Jewish Identities of Moderately Engaged British Jews* (London: UJIA/Profile Books, 2004).

Cohen, Steven M. and Kelman, Ari Y., *Cultural Events and Jewish Identities: Young Adult Jews in New York* (New York: The National Foundation for Jewish Culture, 2005).

Cohen, Stuart A., 'Same places, different faces – a comparison of Anglo-Jewish conflicts over Zionism during Word War I and World War II', in Stuart A. Cohen and Eliezer Don-Yehiya (eds), *Conflict and Consensus in Jewish Political Life* (Ramat-Gan: Bar-Ilan University Press, 1986).

Cohn-Sherbok, Daniel, *Anti-Semitism: A History* (Thrupp: Sutton Publishing, 2002).

Coker, Christopher, *Globalisation and Insecurity in the Twenty-First Century: NATO and the Management of Risk* (London: International Institute for Strategic Studies, Adelphi Papers no. 345, 2002).

Commission on Jewish Education in North America, *A Time To Act: The Report of the Commission on Jewish Education in North America* (Commission on Jewish Education in North America, 1990).

Commission on Jewish Schools, *The Future of Jewish Schools* (London: Jewish Leadership Council, 2008).

Commission on Representation of the Interests of the British Jewish Community, *A Community of Communities* (London: Institute for Jewish Policy Research, 2000).

Cooper, Howard and Morrison, Paul, *A Sense of Belonging: Dilemmas of British Jewish Identity* (London: Weidenfeld and Nicolson, 1991).

Council of Jewish Federations, *To Renew and Sanctify: A Call to Action. The Report of the North American Commission on Jewish Identity and Continuity* (Council of Jewish Federations, November 1995).

'Dalyell's "Jewish cabal" remark denied', BBC News Online, 4 May 2003 <http://news.bbc.co.uk/1/hi/uk_politics/2999219.stm>, accessed 8 February 2010.

Denham, John, *Building Cohesive Communities: A Report of the Ministerial Group on Public Order and Community Cohesion* (London: Home Office, 2002).

Department for Children, Schools and Families, 'Faith in the System" (London: Department for Children, Schools and Families, 2007).

Dewey, John, *Democracy and Education: An Introduction to the Philosophy of Education* (New York: The Free Press, 1944).

Editorial, *Jewish Chronicle*, 26 October 2007: 34.

Fackenheim, Emil, *The Jewish Return into History: Reflections in the Age of Auschwitz and a New Jerusalem* (New York: Schoken Books, 1978).

Fairclough, Norman, *Language and Power* (London: Longman, 1989).

Feld, Edward, *The Spirit of Renewal: Crisis and Response in Jewish Life* (Woodstock, Vermont: Jewish Lights Publishing, 1991).

Ferziger, Adam S., 'Between outreach and "inreach": redrawing the lines of the American Orthodox Rabbinate', *Modern Judaism*, vol. 25, no. 3 (2005): 237–63.

Finestein, Israel, 'Jewish emancipationists in Victorian England: self-imposed limits to assimilation', in Jonathan Frankel and Steven J. Zipperstein (eds), *Assimilation and Community: The Jews in Nineteenth-Century Europe* (Cambridge: Cambridge University Press, 1992).

—, 'A community of paradox: office, authority, and ideas in the changing governance of Anglo-Jewry', in Selwyn Ilan Troen (ed.), *Jewish Centers and Peripheries: Europe between America and Israel Fifty Years after World War II* (New Brunswick: Transaction Books, 1999).

—, 'The changing governance of Anglo-Jewry, 1950–2000', in *Scenes and Personalities in Anglo-Jewry 1800–2000* (London: Vallentine Mitchell, [1999] 2002).

—, *Scenes and Personalities in Anglo-Jewry 1800–2000* (London: Vallentine Mitchell, 2002).

Finkelman, Yoel, 'On the limits of American Jewish social engineering: ironic reflections of Prof. Mordecai M. Kaplan and R. Aharon Kotler', *Contemporary Jewry*, vol. 28 (2008): 58–83.

Fishkoff, Sue, *The Rebbe's Army: Inside the World of Chabad-Lubavitch* (New York: Schoken Books, 2003).

Fishman, Sylvia Barack, *Double or Nothing? Jewish Families and Mixed Marriage* (Lebanon, NH: Brandeis University Press, 2004).

Fishman, William J., *East End Jewish Radicals* (London: Duckworth, 1975).

Forster, Arnold and Epstein, Benjamin, *The New Anti-Semitism* (New York: McGraw-Hill, 1974).

Foucault, Michel, *Power/Knowledge: Selected Interviews* (New York: Pantheon, 1980).

Fox, Seymour, 'The Vitality of Theory in Schwab's Conception of the Practical', *Curriculum Inquiry*, vol. 15, no. 1 (1985): 63–89.

Fox, Seymour and Novak, William, *Vision at the Heart: Lessons from Camp Ramah on the Power of Ideas in Shaping Educational Institutions* (Jerusalem: The Mandel Foundation, 2000).

Fox, Seymour, Scheffler, Israel and Marom, Daniel (eds), *Visions of Jewish Education* (Cambridge: Cambridge University Press, 2003).

Foxman, Abraham H., *Never Again? The Threat of the New Anti-Semitism* (San Francisco: HarperSanFrancisco, 2003).

—, *The Deadliest Lies: The Israel Lobby and the Myth of Jewish Control* (London: Palgrave Macmillan, 2007).

Foxman, Abraham H. and Freud-Kandel, Miri, *Orthodox Judaism in Britain since 1913: An Ideology Forsaken* (Edgware: Vallentine Mitchell, 2006).

Franklin, Jane, 'Introduction', in Jane Franklin (ed.), *The Politics of Risk Society* (Cambridge: Polity/IPPR, 1998).

Freedland, Jonathan, 'Why I did not "rally for Israel"', *Jewish Chronicle*, 14 January 2009, <http://www.thejc.com/comment/columnists/why-i-did-not-rally-israel>, accessed 10 February 2010.

—, 'JFS: Why are no heads rolling?', *Jewish Chronicle*, 7 January 2010, <http://www.thejc.com/comment/columnists/25785/jfs-why-are-no-heads-rolling>, accessed 3 March 2010.

Freedman, Samuel, *Jew vs Jew: The Struggle for the Soul of American Jewry* (New York: Touchstone, 2000).

Gidley, Ben, 'Citizenship and belonging: East End Jewish radicals 1903–1918' (University of London PhD thesis, 2003).

Gilman, Sander, *The Jew's Body* (London: Routledge, 1991).

—, *Multiculturalism and the Jews* (New York: Routledge, 2006).

Gilroy, Paul, *'There Ain't no Black in the Union Jack'*: *The Cultural Politics of Race and Nation* (Chicago: University Of Chicago Press, 1991).

—, *The Black Atlantic: Modernity and Double Consciousness* (London: Verso, 1993).

—, *Black Britain: A Photographic History* (London: Saqi Books, 1998).

Glasman, Judy, 'Architecture and anglicization: London synagogue building 1870–1900', *Jewish Quarterly*, vol. 34, no. 2 (1987): 16–21.

Gloger, Dana, 'Chabad campus role provokes row', *Jewish Chronicle*, 12 September 2008.

Goldberg, David, 'Let's Have a Sense of Proportion', *Guardian Weekly*, 31 January 2002.

—, 'Israel and the A-word', guardian.co.uk, 5 February 2007, <http://www.guardian.co.uk/commentisfree/2007/feb/05/holdjewishvoices5>, accessed 8 February 2010.

Goldberg, Jacqueline and Kosmin, Barry, *The Social Attitudes of Unmarried Young Jews in Contemporary Britain* (London: Institute for Jewish Policy Research in Association with JIA-Jewish Continuity, 1997).

Goldstein, Eric S., *The Price of Whiteness: Jews, Race and Ethnic Identity* (Princeton, New Jersey: Princeton University Press, 2006).

Goodhart, D., 'Too diverse', *Prospect*, 20 February 2004, <http://www.prospect-magazine.co.uk/2004/02/toodiverse/>, accessed 8 February 2010.

Goodkin, Judy and Citron, Judith, *Women in the Jewish Community: Review and Recommendations* (London: Women in the Community, 1994).

Graham, David, Schmool, Marlena and Waterman, Stanley, *Jews in Britain: A Snapshot from the 2001 Census* (London: Institute for Jewish Policy Research, 2007).

Grant, Linda, 'Other voices, other lives', *Guardian*, 7 February 2007, <http://www.guardian.co.uk/commentisfree/2007/feb/07/othervoicesother-lives>, accessed 1 October 2009.

Gruber, Ruth Ellen, *Virtually Jewish: Reinventing Jewish Culture in Europe* (Berkeley: University of California Press, 2002).

Grunwald, Henry, 'If Israel enters Gaza, Anglo-Jewry will be ready', *The Jewish Chronicle*, 29 February 2008.

Gutwein, Daniel, *The Divided Elite: Economics, Politics and Anglo-Jewry 1882–1917* (Leiden: E.J. Brill, 1992).

Haberman, S., Kosmin, B.A. and Levy, C., 'The size and structure of Anglo-Jewry' (London: Board of Deputies of British Jews, 1983).

Halfpenny, Peter and Reid, Margaret, *The Financial Resources of the UK Jewish Voluntary Sector* (London: Institute for Jewish Policy Research, 2000).

Harris, Clive, 'Beyond multiculturalism? Difference, recognition and social justice', *Patterns of Prejudice*, vol. 35, no. 1 (2001): 13–58.

Harris, Keith, 'Exploring Jewish space: a critique of Limmud', in Robert Rabinowitz, *New Voices in Jewish Thought* (London: Limmud Publications, 1998), pp. 39–54.

Harris, Margaret, *Organising God's Work: Challenges for Churches and Synagogues* (London: Macmillan, 1998).

Harrison, Bernard, *The Resurgence of Anti-Semitism: Jews, Israel, and Liberal Opinion* (London: Roman and Littlefield, 2006).

Hart, Mitchell B., *Social Science and the Politics of Modern Jewish Identity* (Stanford, CA: Stanford University Press, 2000).

—, 'The unbearable lightness of Britain', *Journal of Modern Jewish Studies*, vol. 6, no. 2 (2007): 155.

Hart, Rona and Kafka, Edward, 'Trends in British Synagogue Membership 1990–2005/6' (The Board of Deputies of British Jews, 2006).

Hart, Rona, Schmool, Marlena and Cohen, Frances, *Jewish Education at the Crossroads* (London: The Board of Deputies of British Jews Community Research Unit, 2001).

Hartman, Harriet and Kaufman, Debra, 'Decentering the study of Jewish identity: opening the dialogue with other religious groups', *Sociology of Religion*, vol. 67, no. 4 (2006): 365–85.

Harvey, David, *The Condition of Postmodernity* (Oxford: Blackwell Publishers, 1990).

Henry, Georgina, 'This week on Comment is free', 5 February 2007 <http://www.guardian.co.uk/commentisfree/2007/feb/05/post1046>, accessed 8 February 2010.

Hessayon, Ariel, *From Expulsion (1290) to Readmission (1656): Jews and England*, public lecture Jewish Genealogical Society of Great Britain, October 2006 <http://www.gold.ac.uk/media/350th-anniversary.pdf>, accessed 8 February 2010.

Hills, Claire, '"In support of peace and solidarity"', BBC News Online, 6 May 2002 <http://news.bbc.co.uk/1/hi/uk/1971299.stm>, accessed 8 February 2010.

Hirsh, David, 'Radical 68ers have become the new conservatives of the Jewish community in Britain', *Engage*, 13 August 2006, <http://www.engageonline.org.uk/blog/article.php?id=578>, accessed 1 October 2009.

—, *Anti-Zionism and Antisemitism: Cosmopolitan Reflections* (New Haven: YIISA Occasional Papers, 2007), pp. 19–25.

Hochhauser, Simon, "US and JFS orthodoxy is inclusive", *Jewish Chronicle*, 6 August 2009, <http://www.thejc.com/articles/us-and-jfs-orthodoxy-inclusive>, accessed 10 February 2010.

Hoffman, Jonathan, 'The status of Israel and of Jews in the UK: "Darkness closing" or "business as usual"?', *Jerusalem Post*, 1 August 2009, <http://www.jpost.com/servlet/Satellite?cid=1248277944837&pagename=JPost/JPArticle/ShowFull>, accessed August 2009.

Holman, Christine and Holman, Naomi, *Torah, Worship and Acts of Loving Kindness: Baseline Indicators for the Charedi Community in Stamford Hill* (Leicester: De Montfort University, 2002).

Hyman, Jonathan, *Jews in Britain During the Great War* (Manchester: University of Manchester Working Papers in Economic and Social History No. 51, 2001).

Iaonid, Radu, 'Foreword', in Pierre-André Taguieff, *Rising from the Muck: The New Anti-Semitism in Europe* (Chicago: Ivan R. Dee, 2004), p. xiv.

Ignaski, Paul and Kosmin, Barry, 'Editors' Introduction', in Paul Ignaski and Barry Kosmin (eds), *A New Antisemitism? Debating Judeophobia in 21st-century Britain* (London: Profile Books/JPR 2003), p. 8.

Ignaski, Paul, Kielinger, Vicky and Paterson, Susan, *Hate Crimes Against London's Jews: An Analysis of Incidents Recorded by the Metropolitan Police Service 2001–2004* (London: Institute for Jewish Policy Research, 2005).

Independent Jewish Voices, 'A time to speak out: Independent Jewish Voices', Independent Jewish Voices <http://jewishvoices.squarespace.com/declaration-2/>, accessed 8 February 2010.

Ingrams, Richard, 'I'm still on the train', *The Observer*, 13 July 2003, <http://www.guardian.co.uk/politics/2003/jul/13/alistairdarling.guardiancolumnists>, accessed 8 February 2010>

Institute for Jewish Policy Research, *Long-Term Planning for British Jewry: Final Report and Recommendations*, Planning for Jewish Communities (London: Institute for Jewish Policy Research, 2003).

'Israel, we support you – but hear our plea', *The Observer*, 11 January 2009, <http://www.guardian.co.uk/world/2009/jan/11/gaza-israelandthepalestinians>, accessed 10 February 2010.

Jakobovits, Immanuel, *From Doom to Hope: A Jewish View on 'Faith in the City', the Report of the Archbishop of Canterbury's Commission on Urban Priority Areas* (London: Office of the Chief Rabbi, January 1996).

Jewish Board of Deputies, *The New Anti-Semitism: The Official Protests of the British and American Jewish Communities* (London: The Press Committee of the Jewish Board of Deputies 1921).

Jewish Community Centre for London, 'Building Jewish life', <http://www.jcclondon.org.uk/Vision.html>, accessed 2 June 2009.

Jewish Educational Development Trust, *Securing our Future: An Inquiry into Jewish Education in the United Kingdom* (London: Jewish Educational Development Trust, 1992).

Julius, Anthony, 'Don't panic', *Guardian*, 1 February 2002, revised as 'Is there anything "new" in the new antisemitism?', in Paul Ignaski and Barry Kosmin (eds), *A New Antisemitism? Debating Judeophobia in 21st-century Britain* (London: Profile Books/JPR 2003), pp. 68–75.

—, *Trials of the Diaspora: A History of Anti-Semitism in England* (Oxford: Oxford University Press, 2010).

Kadish, Sharman, *Bolsheviks and British Jews* (London: Frank Cass, 1992).

Kahn-Harris, Keith, *New Jewish Thought Policy Paper 2: An Experiment in Dialogue* (London: New Jewish Thought, 2008), <http://www.newjewishthought.org/wp-content/uploads/2009/09/An-Experiment-in-Dialogue2.pdf>, accessed 8 February 2010.

—, 'British Jews and Israel: a new relationship?,' guardian.co.uk, 13 January 2009, <http://www.guardian.co.uk/commentisfree/2009/jan/13/judaism-israelandthepalestinians>, accessed 10 February 2010.

—, 'What is British Jewish politics', *Zeek*, 30 June 2009, <http://www.jewcy.com/post/what_british_jewish_politics>, accessed June 2009.

—, *Communities in Conversation: Jewish Involvement in Inter Faith Activities in the UK* (London: The Board of Deputies of British Jews Community Research Unit, 2009), <http://www.boardofdeputies.org.uk/file/Communities InConversation.pdf>, accessed 8 February 2010.

Kalman, Matthew, 'The making of New Moon', unpublished document, 2009.

Kalms, Stanley, *A Time for Change: United Synagogue Review* (London: The Stanley Kalms Foundation, 1992).

Kalra, Virinder, 'Riots, Race and Reports: Denham, Cantle, Oldham and Burnley Inquiries', *Sage Race Relations Abstracts*, vol. 27, no. 4 (2002): 20–30.

Kaplan, Mordecai, *Judaism as Civilization: Toward a Reconstruction of American-Jewish Life* (Philadelphia: Jewish Publication Society, 1994).

Karpf, Anne, 'Children of the Holocaust', guardian.co.uk, 7 February 2007, <http://www.guardian.co.uk/commentisfree/2007/feb/07/holdjewishvoices4>, accessed 8 February 2010.

Karpf, Anne et al. (eds), *A Time to Speak Out: Independent Jewish Voices on Israel, Zionism and Jewish Identity* (London: Verso, 2008).

Kaufmann, Eric, *Demographic Radicalization? The Religiosity-Fertility Nexus and Politics* (London: Birkbeck School of Politics and Sociology, 2009).

Kleeblatt, Norman (ed.), *Too Jewish?: Challenging Traditional Identities* (New York and New Brunswick, NJ: The Jewish Museum, New York and Rutgers University Press, 1996).

Klein, Emma, *Lost Jews: The Struggle for Identity Today* (London: Macmillan, 1996).

Klug, Brian, 'The collective Jew: Israel and the new anti-Semitism', *Patterns of Prejudice*, vol. 37, no. 2 (2003).

—, 'The myth of the new anti-semitism', *The Nation*, 2 February 2004.

—, 'Israel, antisemitism and the left', *Red Pepper*, 24 November 2005.

—, 'Who speaks for Jews in Britain', guardian.co.uk, 5 February 2007, <http://www.guardian.co.uk/commentisfree/2007/feb/05/holdjewishvoices>, accessed 8 February 2010.

Kopelowitz, Ezra and Reviv, Menachem (eds), *Building Jewish Peoplehood: Challenges and Possibilities* (Brighton, MA: Academic Studies Press, 2008).

Kosmin, Barry and Levy, Caren, *Jewish Identity in an Anglo-Jewish Community: The Findings of the 1983 Redbridge Survey* (London: Research Unit Board of Deputies of British Jews, 1983).

Kosmin, Barry et al., *Highlights of the CJF 1990 National Jewish Population Survey* (New York: Council of Jewish Federations, 1991).

Kundnani, Arun, *The End of Tolerance: Racism in 21st Century Britain* (London: Pluto, 2007).

Lambert, Nick, *Jews and Europe in the Twenty-first Century* (London: Vallentine Mitchell, 2008).

Lappin, Shalom, *This Green and Pleasant Land: Britain and the Jews* (New Haven: YIISA Working Papers, 2008).

Lash, Scott, 'Reflexivity and its doubles: structure, aesthetics, community', in Ulrich Beck, Anthony Giddens and Scott Lash (eds), *Reflexive Modernization: Politics, Tradition and Aesthetics in the Modern Social Order* (Cambridge: Polity Press, 1994), pp. 110–73.

Laurence, Jonathan and Vaisse, Justin, *Integrating Islam: Political and Religious Challenges in Contemporary France* (Washington DC: Brookings Institute Press, 2006).

Lawton, Clive, 'In defence of the Beth Din', TotallyJewish.com, 30 June 2005, <http://www.totallyjewish.com/news/lawton/?content_id=1024>, accessed 8 February 2010.

Lazarus, Neil, 'The Jewish addiction', in Danny Ben-Moshe and Zohar Segev (eds), *Israel, The Diaspora and Jewish Identity* (Eastbourne: Sussex Academic Press, 2007), pp. 22–7.

Lehman, Yaacov, *Let my People Know: Proposals for the Development of Jewish Education* (London: Office of the Chief Rabbi, 1971).

Leibler, Isi, 'Don't give a platform to Israel-bashing', 30 January 2008, <http://web.israelinsider.com/Views/12602.htm>, accessed 4 June 2009.

Lerman, Anthony, 'Sense on antisemitism', in Paul Ignaski and Barry Kosmin (eds), *A New Antisemitism? Debating Judeophobia in 21st-century Britain* (London: Profile Books/JPR, 2003) [originally published in *Prospect* August 2002], pp. 54–67.

—, 'Reflecting the reality of Jewish diversity', guardian.co.uk, 6 February 2007, <http://www.guardian.co.uk/commentisfree/2007/feb/06/holdjewishvoices8>, accessed 8 February 2010.

Lerner, Michael, *Jewish Renewal: A Path to Healing and Transformation* (New York: Grosset/Putnam, 1994).

Lester, Anthony (ed.), *Essays and Speeches by Roy Jenkins* (London: Collins, 1967).

Levene, Mark, *War, Jews and the New Europe: The Diplomacy of Lucien Wolf 1914–1919* (Oxford: Oxford University Press, 1992).

Levin, Janet, 'Multiculturalism – a mistake?', *Jewish Renaissance*, July (2008): 6.

Levine, Charley J., 'Interview with Jonathan Sacks', *Hadassah Magazine*, vol. 85, no. 1 (2003), <http://www.hadassah.org/news/content/per_hadassah/archive/2003/03_AUG/interview.htm>, accessed 15 August 2008.

Lewis, Hal M., *Models and Meanings in the History of Jewish Leadership* (Lewiston NY: Edward Mellen Press, 2004).

Liebman, Charles S., 'Jewish identity in transition: transformation or attenuation?', in Barry Kosmin, Kovacs Andras and Zvi Gitelman (eds), *New Jewish Identities: Contemporary Europe and Beyond* (Budapest: Central European University Press, 2003), pp. 341–50.

Limmud Conference, 'History of Limmud (abridged)', in *Limmud Conference Handbook* (2007), pp. 327–34.

Lipman, Sonia L. and Lipman, Vivian

Livingstone, Ken, 'An attack on voters' rights', *The Guardian*, 1 March 2006, <http://society.guardian.co.uk/localgovt/comment/0,,1720439,00.html>, accessed 8 February 2010.

MacShane, Dennis, *Globalising Hatred: The New Antisemitism* (London: Weidenfeld and Nicolson, 2008).

Mann, Sandi, *Through their Eyes: The Final Report of the North Manchester Jewish Youth Project Survey* (1995).

Matas, David, *Aftershock: Anti-Zionism and Antisemitism* (Toronto: The Dundurn Group, 2005).

Mearsheimer, John and Walt, Stephen, 'The Israel lobby', *London Review of Books*, vol. 28, no. 6 (2006), <http://www.lrb.co.uk/v28/n06/mear01_.html>, accessed 8 February 2010.

Mercer, Kobena, '1968: periodizing postmodern politics and identity', in Lawrence Grossberg, Cary Nelson and Paula Treichler (eds), *Cultural Studies* (New York and London: Routledge, 1992).

Miller, Helena, 'Meeting the challenge: the Jewish schooling phenomenon in the UK', *Oxford Review of Education*, vol. 27, no. 4 (2001): 501–13.

Miller, Stephen, *The Impact of Jewish Education on the Religious Behaviour and Attitudes of British Secondary School Pupils*, ed. J Aviad, vol. 3, *Studies in Jewish Education* (Jerusalem: Hebrew University Press, 1988).

Miller, Stephen and Schmool, Marlena, 'Survey of Synagogue Members', in Stanley Kalms, *A Time for Change: United Synagogue Review* (London: The Stanley Kalms Foundation, 1992).

Miller, Stephen, Schmool, Marlena and Lerman, Anthony, *Social and Political Attitudes of British Jews: Some Key Findings of the JPR Survey* (London: Institute for Jewish Policy Research, 1996).

Miller, Stephen et al., 'The shape of Jews to come', *The Jewish Quarterly*, Spring (1989).

Miller, Steve, *Talkback Survey of Jewish Youth* (1997).

MORI, *Independent Longitudinal Survey into the Results upon Jewish Continuity and Leadership Development Affected by: Aish Fellowships UK* (Market Opinion Research International, 2003).

Movement for Reform Judaism, 'A Statement on "Communal Collaboration"', 11 September 2008 <http://news.reformjudaism.org.uk/press-releases/a-statement-on-qcommunal-collaborationq.html>, accessed 10 August 2009.

Mythen, Gabe, *Ulrich Beck: A Critical Introduction to the Risk Society* (London: Pluto, 2004), pp. 1–2.

Narayan, Uma, *Dislocating Cultures: Identities, Traditions, and Third World Feminism* (London: Routledge, 1997)

Neustatter, Hannah, 'Demographic and other statistical aspects of Anglo Jewry', in Maurice Freedman (ed.), *A Minority in Britain: Social Studies of the Anglo-Jewish Community* (London: Vallentine Mitchell, 1955), pp. 53–133.

New Generation Network, 'Race and faith: a new agenda', 20 November 2006 <http://www.guardian.co.uk/commentisfree/2006/nov/20/whyweneedanewdiscourseon>, accessed 8 February 2010.

Newman, Aubrey. *Migration and Settlement* (London: Jewish Historical Society of England, 1971).

Newman, Aubrey and Massil, Stephen (eds), *Patterns of Migration, 1860–1914*, Proceedings of the International Academic Conference 1993, Jewish Historical Society of England and the Institute of Jewish Studies (London: University College London, 1996).

Newman, David, 'Britain and the Academic Boycott of Israel', *Israel Journal of Foreign Affairs*, vol. 2, no. 2 (2008).

Ouseley, Herman, *Community Pride not Prejudice* (Bradford: Bradford Vision, 2000).

Parekh, Bikhu, *The Future of Multi-Ethnic Britain – The Parekh Report* (London: Runnymede Trust, 2000).

Parker-Jenkins, Marie, 'Achieving cultural sustainability? The phenomenon of Jewish and Muslim schools in England and Wales', in Zvi Bekerman and Ezra Kopelowitz (eds), *Cultural Education-Cultural Sustainability: Minority, Diaspora, Indigenous and Ethno-Religious Groups in Multicultural Societies* (New York: Routledge, 2008).

Perl, Benjamin, "Our children are getting a raw deal", *Jewish Chronicle*, 16 April 2009, <http://www.thejc.com/articles/our-children-are-getting-a-raw-deal>, accessed 8 February 2010.

Persoff, Meir, *Faith Against Reason: Religious Reform and the British Chief Rabbinate 1840–1990* (Edgware: Vallentine Mitchell, 2008).

—, 'Another Way, Another Time' (Context Statement in partial fulfilment of the requirements for the degree of Doctor of Philosophy by Public Works, Middlesex University, 2008).

Pfeffer, Anshel, 'Jerusalem and Babylon: The Jewish Agency's Diminished Role', *Haaretz*, 7 September 2008,<http://www.haaretz.com/hasen/spages/1018435.html>, accessed 8 February 2010.

Phillips, Bruce, 'Assimilation, Transformation and the Long Range Impact of Intermarriage', *Contemporary Jewry*, vol. 25 (2005): 50–84.

Phillips, Melanie, 'The need to defend the nation', *Daily Mail*, 5 April 2004 <http://www.melaniephillips.com/articles-new/?p=212>, accessed 8 February 2010.

—, 'This lethal moral madness', *Daily Mail*, 14 July 2005 <http://www.melaniephillips.com/articles-new/?p=342>, accessed 8 February 2010.

—, 'Jews for genocide', 8 February 2007, <http://www.melaniephillips.com/diary/?p=1458>, accessed 1 October 2009.

Phillips, Melanie, Wistrich, Robert and Leibler, Isi, *Islam, British Society and the Terrorist Threat*, Posen Paper (Jerusalem: Vidal Sassoon Center for the Study of Antisemitism, Hebrew University of Jerusalem, 2007).

Pomson, Alex, '"Dorks with yarmulkes": an ethnographic inquiry into the surprised embrace of parochial day schools by liberal American Jews', in Zvi Bekerman and Ezra Kopelowitz (eds), *Cultural Education-Cultural Sustainability: Minority, Diaspora, Indigenous and Ethno-Religious Groups in Multicultural Societies* (New York: Routledge, 2008), pp. 305–21.

Potter, Jonathan and Wetherell, Margaret, *Discourse and Social Psychology: Beyond Attitudes and Behaviour* (London: Sage Publications, 1987).

Prager, Leonard, *Yiddish Culture in Britain: A Guide* (Frankfurt: Verlag Peter Lang, 1990).

Prell, Riv-Ellen, *Fighting to Become Americans: Assimilation and the Trouble between Jewish Women and Jewish Men* (Boston: Beacon Press, 1999).

'The problem with dialogue', *New Jewish Thought*, 2 September 2007, <http://www.newjewishthought.org/2007/09/the-problem-with-dialogue/>, accessed 8 February 2010.

Pulzer, Peter, 'The new antisemitism, or when is a taboo not a taboo?', in Paul Ignaski and Barry Kosmin (eds), *A New Antisemitism? Debating Judeophobia in 21st-century Britain* (London: Profile Books/JPR, 2003), pp. 83–4.

'Rabbi's departure leaves community divided', *Jewish Chronicle*, 24 November 2005.

'"Rally cancelled" message exposed as a hoax', *Jewish Chronicle*, 9 January 2009, <http://www.thejc.com/news/israel-news/rally-cancelled%E2%80%99-message-exposed-a-hoax>, accessed 10 February 2010.

'Rally message is "Yes to peace"' *Jewish Chronicle*, 15 January 2009, <http://www.thejc.com/news/uk-news/rally-message-yes-peace>, accessed 10 February 2010.

Rattansi, Ali, 'Who's British? *Prospect* and the New Assimilationism', in R. Berkeley (ed.), *Cohesion, Community and Citizenship* (London: The Runnymede Trust, 2002).

Rawidowicz, Simon, 'Israel: the ever dying people', in *Studies in Jewish Thought* (Philadelphia: Jewish Publication Society of America, 1974), pp. 210–24.

Renton, James, *The Zionist Masquerade: The Birth of the Anglo-Zionist Alliance 1914–1918* (London: Palgrave Macmillan, 2007).

Rich, Dave, 'Britain is a good place to be Jewish', Haaretz online (English edition), 21 August 2008, <http://www.haaretz.com/hasen/spages/1013644.html>, accessed 8 February 2010.

Ritchie, David, *The Oldham Independent Review Panel Report* (Oldham: Oldham Independent Review, 2001).

Rocker, Simon, 'Cambridge falls out over Mikvah plans', *Jewish Chronicle*, 19 September 2008.

—, 'Reform launches outreach arm as alternative to Aish', *The Jewish Chronicle*, 17 October 2008.

—, 'Deputies in row over how to treat hate', *Jewish Chronicle*, 6 August 2009, <http://www.thejc.com/news/uk-news/deputies-row-over-how-treat-hate>, accessed 8 February 2010.

—, 'Lieberman's success horrifies UK leaders', *Jewish Chronicle*, 12 February 2009, <http://www.thejc.com/news/uk-news/liebermans-success-horri%EF%AC%81es-uk-leaders>, accessed 10 February 2010.

—, 'Peace activist Wineman snatches Board presidency in close-run poll', *Jewish Chronicle*, 21 May 2009, <http://www.thejc.com/news/uk-news/peace-activist-wineman-snatches-board-presidency-close-run-poll>, accessed 10 February 2010.

—, '"JFS: what"s next", *Jewish Chronicle*, 2 July 2009, <http://www.thejc.com/articles/jfs-whats-next>, accessed 8 February 2010.

—, "School entry rules '"fiasco'"'", *Jewish Chronicle*, 18 September 2009, <http://www.thejc.com/news/uk-news/school-entry-rules-fiasco>, accessed 8 February 2010.

Rocker, Simon and Krieger, Candice, 'Orthodox paying students to learn', *Jewish Chronicle*, 29 August 2008, p. 5.

—, 'JFS fight collapses as board retreats'. *Jewish Chronicle*, 7 January 2010, <http://www.thejc.com/news/uk-news/25818/jfs-%EF%AC%81ght-collapses-board-retreats>, accessed 3 March 2010.

—, 'US rabbis squabble over JFS', *Jewish Chronicle*, 21 January 2010, <http://www.thejc.com/news/uk-news/26280/us-rabbis-squabble-over-jfs>, accessed 3 March 2010.

Romain, Gemma, *Connecting Histories: A Comparative Exploration of Afro-Caribbean and Jewish History and Memory in Modern Britain* (London: Routledge Kegan Paul, 2006), p. 232.

Ronson, Gerald, 'Introduction', *JCOSS Jewish Community Secondary School: A Multi-Million Pound Outreach Project* (JCOSS, 2008), p. 5.

Rose, Daniel, 'The world of the Jewish youth movement', in *The Encyclopedia of Informal Education*, <http://www.infed.org/informaljewisheducation/jewish_youth_movements.htm>, accessed 8 February 2010.

Rosenberg, David, *Facing up to Antisemitism: How Jews in Britain Countered the Threats of the 1930s* (London: JCARP Publications, 1985).

—, 'An independent Jewish platform', *Jewish Socialist*, no.1 (1985): 11.

Rosenfeld, Alvin H., *Anti-Zionism in Great Britain and Beyond: A 'Respectable' Anti-Semitism?* (New York: American Jewish Committee, 2004).

Roskies, David, *Against the Apocalypse: Responses to Catastrophe in Modern Jewish Culture* (Cambridge, MA: Harvard University Press, 1984)

Rosner, Shmuel, 'Reaching out to interfaith families', *Haaretz (English Edition)*, 22 September 2007, <http://www.haaretz.com/hasen/spages/905856.html>, accessed 8 February 2010.

Roth, Cecil, *The Jew as British Citizen: Three Centuries of Achievement* (Jewish Historical Society of England, 1936), p. 3.

Rubinstein, W.D., *The Left, The Right and the Jews* (London: Croon Helm, 1982).

Russell, C. and Lewis, H.S., *The Jew in London: A Study of Racial Character and Present-day Conditions* (London: T. Fisher Unwin, 1900)

Sachar, Howard M., *Diaspora: An Inquiry into the Contemporary Jewish World* (New York: Perennial Library, 1986).

Sacks, Jonathan, *Induction Address*, London, 1 September, 1991, <http://www.chiefrabbi.org/sp-index.html>, accessed 22 August 2007.

—, *Will We Have Jewish Grandchildren? Jewish Continuity and How to Achieve it* (Ilford: Valentine Mitchell, 1994), p. 18.

—, *Community of Faith* (London: Orion, 1995).

—, 'Jewish discontinuity', in Stephen W. Massil (ed.), *The Jewish Year Book 1996* (London: Vallentine Mitchell, 1996).

—, 'A new antisemitism?', in Paul Ignaski and Barry Kosmin (eds), *A New Antisemitism? Debating Judeophobia in 21st-century Britain* (London: Profile Books/JPR, 2003), p. 39.

—, *The Dignity of Difference: How to Avoid the Clash of Civilizations*, 2nd edn (London: Continuum, 2003).

—, *The Home We Build Together: Recreating Society* (London: Continuum, 2007).

—, 'The Chabad approach to life', <http://www.chabad.org/therebbe/article_cdo/aid/691360/jewish/The-Chabad-Approach-to-Life.htm>, accessed 9 December 2008.

Sarna, Jonathan D., 'American Jews in the new millennium', in Yvonne Yasbeck Haddad, Jane I. Smith and John L. Esposito (eds), *Religion and Immigration: Christian, Jewish and Muslim Experiences in the United States* (Walnut Creek, CA: Altamira Press, 2003).

—, *The Economic Downturn and the Future of Jewish Communities* (London: Institute for Jewish Policy Research, September 2009).

Schmool, Marlena and Cohen, Frances, *A Profile of British Jewry: Patterns and Trends at the Turn of the Century* (London: Board of Deputies of British Jews, 1998).

Schmool, Marlena and Miller, Stephen, *Women in the Jewish Community: Survey Report* (London: Women in the Community, 1994).

Schoenfeld, Gabriel, *The Return of Anti-Semitism* (London: Politico's, 2005).

Sciolino, Elaine, 'Jewish leaders appeal to E.U. to stamp out Anti-Semitism', *New York Times*, 19 February 2004.

Shaviv, Miriam, 'Outreach groups "target" JFS pupils', *Jewish Chronicle*, 3 May 2007.

Short, Geoffrey, *Responding to Diversity? An Initial Investigation into Multicultural Education in Jewish Schools in the United Kingdom* (London: Institute for Jewish Policy Research, 2002).

—, 'The role of education in Jewish Continuity: a response to Jonathan Sacks', *British Journal of Religious Education*, vol. 27, no. 3 (2005).

Shukra, Kalbir et al., 'Race, social cohesion and the changing politics of citizenship', *London Review of Education*, vol. 2, no. 3 (2004): 187–95 (192).

Singer, Clifford, 'Playing with fire', *Jewish Socialist*, October 2006.

Sivanandan, A., *A Different Hunger: Writings on Black Resistance* (London: Pluto, 1990).

Slovo, Gillian, 'Our responsibility towards others', guardian.co.uk, 6 February 2007, <http://www.guardian.co.uk/commentisfree/2007/feb/06/holdjewishvoices7>, accessed 8 February 2010.

Smith, Elaine R., 'Jews and politics in the East End of London, 1918–1939', in David Cesarani (ed.), *The Making of Modern Anglo-Jewry* (Oxford: Oxford University Press, 1990), pp. 141–62.

Sompolinsky, Meier, *Britain and the Holocaust: The Failure of Anglo-Jewish Leadership?* (Brighton: Sussex Academic Press, 1999).

Srebrnik, Henry, *London Jews and British Communism, 1935–1945* (London: Vallentine Mitchell, 1995).

Steyn, Juliet, *The Jew: Assumptions of Identity* (London: Cassell, 1999).

Stratton, Jon, 'Speaking as a Jew: on the absence of a Jewish speaking position in British Cultural Studies', *European Journal of Cultural Studies*, vol. 1, no. 3 (1998): 305–25.

—, *Coming Out Jewish* (London: Routledge, 2000).

Symons, Leon, 'What baby boom? Board disputes birth statistics for UK Jews', *The Jewish Chronicle*, 23 May 2008, <http://www.thejc.com/home.aspx?ParentId=m11s18&SecId=18&AId=60254&ATypeId=1>, accessed 8 February 2010.

Taguieff, Pierre-André, *La nouvelle judéophobia* [*The new Judeophobia*] (Paris: Mille et une Nuits, 2002).

—, *Rising from the Muck: The New Anti-Semitism in Europe* (Chicago: Ivan R. Dee, 2004).

Tapper, Aaron Joshua, 'The cult of Aish HaTorah: Ba'alei Teshuva and the new religious movement phenomenon', *Jewish Journal of Sociology*, vol. 44, no. 1 (2002): 5–29.

'Thousands come to support Israel', BBC News Online, 6 May 2002 <http://news.bbc.co.uk/1/hi/uk/1970028.stm>, accessed 8 February 2010.

Trillin, Calvin, 'Drawing the line', *The New Yorker*, 12 December 1994.

UJIA, *The Next Horizon* (London: UJIA, 2001).

—, 'Who we are – UJIA lay leaders', <http://www.ujia.org/who-we-are/whos-who/1096/ujia-lay-leaders/>, accessed 12 June 2009.

Valins, Oliver, Kosmin, Barry and Goldberg, Jacqueline, *The Future of Jewish Schooling in the United Kingdom* (London: Institute for Jewish Policy Research, 2001).

Vital, David et al., 'At the crossroads of history: is there a future for the Jewish people?', *The Jewish Quarterly*, Summer (1993): 29

Vulkan, Daniel and Graham, David, *Population Trends among Britain's Strictly Orthodox Jews* (London: Board of Deputies of British Jews, 2008).

Wagner, Leslie, *Change in Continuity: Report of the Review into Jewish Continuity* (London: Jewish Continuity, 1996), p. 63.

Ware, John, 'MCB in the dock', *Prospect*, 16 December 2006, <http://www.prospect-magazine.co.uk/2006/12/mcbinthedock/>, accessed 8 February 2010.

'Warning of anti-Semitic tsunami', BBC News, 1 January 2006, <http://news.bbc.co.uk/1/hi/uk/4573052.stm>, accessed 1 October 2009.

Wasserstein, Bernard, *Vanishing Diaspora: The Jews in Europe since 1945* (London: Penguin, 1996).

Waterman, Stanely and Barry Kosmin, Barry, *British Jewry in the Eighties: A Statistical and Geographical Study* (London: Board of Deputies of British Jews, 1986).

Weber, Max, *The Theory of Social and Economic Organisation*, ed. Talcott Parsons (New York: Free Press, 1964).

Weiss, Anthony, 'Intermarriage Study Muddies Waters', *The Forward*, 12 December 2007, <http://www.forward.com/articles/12253/>, accessed 8 February 2010.

Wertheimer, Jack, 'Jews and the Jewish birthrate', *Commentary*, October (2005).

Wertheimer, Jack, Liebman, Charles S. and Cohen, Steven, 'How to save American Jews', *Commentary*, vol. 101, no. 1 (1996): 47–51.

Whine, Michael, 'Antisemitism on the streets', in Paul Ignaski and Barry Kosmin (eds), *A New Antisemitism? Debating Judeophobia in 21st-century Britain* (London: Profile Books/JPR, 2003), pp. 23–37.

Williams, Bill, 'Anti-semitism of Tolerance: Middle-Class Manchester and the Jews, 1879–1900', in A.J. Kidd and K.W. Roberts (eds), *City, Class and Culture; Studies of Social Policy and Cultural Production in Victorian Manchester* (Manchester: Manchester University Press, 1985), pp. 74–102.

—, '"East" and "West": class and community in Manchester Jewry, 1850–1914', in David Cesarani (ed.), *The Making of Modern Anglo-Jewry* (Oxford: Basil Blackwell, 1990), pp. 15–33.

Windmueller, Steven, 'The second American Jewish revolution', *Journal of Jewish Communal Service*, vol. 82, no. 3 (2007): 252–60.

Wine, Gaby, 'UJIA refuses funding for "political" Beitar', *Jewish Chronicle*, 23 April 2004, p. 17.

Wineman, Vivian, 'Right of Reply: British criticism of Israel is nothing special', *Jerusalem Post*, 27 July 2009, <http://www.jpost.com/servlet/Satellite?cid=1248277904878&pagename=JPArticle per cent2FshowFull>, accessed July 2009.

Wise, Justin, *Getting in Touch: 18–35 Project Report* (London: Movement for Reform Judaism, June 2006).

Wise, Yaacov, 'Majority of Jews will be ultra-orthodox by 2050', press release (Manchester: University of Manchester, 2007).

Wistrich, Robert S., 'Left-wing anti-Zionism in Western societies', in Robert S. Wistrich (ed.), *Anti-Zionism and Antisemitism in the Contemporary World* (London, Macmillan, 1990), pp. 46–52 (49).

Wolf, Lucien, *Menassah ben Israel's Mission to Oliver Cromwell* (London: Macmillan, 1901).

Women's Review Task Force, *Connection, Continuity and Community: British Jewish Women Speak Out* (London: Women's Review Task Force, 2009).

Working Party on Race Relations, *Improving Race Relations: A Jewish Contribution* (London: The Board of Deputies of British Jews, 1969).

Wyatt, Petronella, 'Poisonous prejudice', *The Spectator*, 8 December 2001.

Glossary

Agunah	Literally 'chained woman'. Term for a woman who is forced to stay married to her husband. In Jewish law a husband grants his wife a bill of divorce, or *get*, which a woman should normally accept of her own free will. If a husband chooses not to grant his wife a divorce, the marriage stays valid and any remarriage by the wife would be illegitimate. Children of such an illegitimate marriage would be classified as *mamzerim*, or bastards, and under Jewish law would only be entitled to marry other *mamzerim*. Progressive Jews have abandoned both this aspect of marriage law as well as the law of the *mamzer*, but orthodox bodies, despite many attempts, have not yet found a universally accepted solution to the problem.
Aliyah	Literally 'ascent'. Term widely used in Jewish circles for emigration by Jews to Israel.
Ashkenazi	Term for Jews who trace their ancestry from the Jewish communities of Central, Eastern and Northern Europe.
Baal Teshuvah	Literally 'master of return/repentance'. Term used to describe Jews who have adopted orthodox observance, either after growing up in a secular or progressive background or after straying from the orthodox path.
Beit Midrash	Literally 'house of explanation/interpretation'. Term for study hall in a synagogue or other institution, sometimes applied more generally to an institution of Jewish learning.
Beth Din	Literally 'house of judgement'. Term for a rabbinic court, traditionally made up of three rabbis.

Chanukah	Also known as the Festival of Lights. An eight-day winter holiday commemorating the rededication of the Temple in Jerusalem at the time of the Maccabean Revolt of the second century BCE. Celebrated with the lighting of an eight-branched candelabra or *Chanukiah*, the eating of oily foods and with the giving of gifts.
Chavruta	From the Aramaic for 'friend'. Term used for the traditional Jewish method of study of texts in pairs, the method used in *yeshivot* and adopted cross-communally in the UK by Limmud's Chavruta Project.
Cheder	Literally 'room'. Term used for elementary religious education classes. In the UK and many other Diaspora countries today, the term is generally applied to supplementary Jewish schooling for those attending non-Jewish schools.
Halacha	Literally 'path/way'. Jewish religious law.
Haredi	Literally 'trembling or fearful'. Term for the most self-consciously traditional and observant stream of Judaism, whose followers generally try to minimize contact with the culture of other streams of Judaism and non-Jews. It has its origins in eighteenth and nineteenth-century Eastern Europe.
Havurah	Literally 'fellowship'. Term used to describe small groups that meet together for prayer, study and other observance.
Kashrut	The system of Jewish dietary laws, based on biblical laws. Food that is fit for Jewish consumption under these laws is known as *kosher* in English.
Khevre	Yiddish term for fraternity.
Kollel	A *yeshivah* for married men.
Macher	Yiddish term literally meaning 'doer'. Used by English-speaking Jews to describe those involved as activists within Jewish organizations.
Masorti	Literally 'traditional'. Term used in the UK, Israel and elsewhere for what is known in the US and Canada as Conservative Judaism.
Midrash	Literally 'explanation/interpretation'. Term used for collections of rabbinic homilies (from the second century CE onwards) that employ particular hermeneutics to create biblical exegesis, either legal or non-legal. More broadly, and especially in contemporary times, this term

	may also refer to any sort of Jewish interpretation of the biblical text that is not explicitly related to Jewish law.
Mikvah	Jewish ritual bath.
Purim	Literally 'lots'. A festival commemorating the deliverance of the Jews of the Persian Empire from Haman's plot to annihilate them, as recorded in the biblical Book of Esther. It is celebrating with dressing up, carnivalesque activity and the giving of gifts of food.
Rosh Hashanah	Literally 'head of the year'. The Jewish new year festival that takes place every year in the autumn.
Semichah	Literally 'support/lean on/lay on [as in hands]'. Term for rabbinic ordination.
Sephardi	Term for Jews who can trace their ancestry from the late fifteenth century expulsions from the Iberian peninsula.
Shabbat	Hebrew term for the Sabbath, lasting from sunset on Friday to Saturday nightfall.
Shoah	Hebrew term for the Holocaust.
Shofar	The horn of a kosher animal, often a ram's or antelope's horn, blown during the Hebrew month of Elul (August/September) and at the synagogue services on *Rosh Hashanah* and *Yom Kippur*.
Shteibl	Literally 'little house'. Yiddish term for a small house of prayer that is less formal than a synagogue.
Sukkah	Usually translated as 'booth/tabernacle'. Temporary structure built for use during the autumn harvest festival of *Sukkot* that follows *Yom Kippur*. Many Jews sleep and eat in the *Sukkah*.
Talmud	The compendium of rabbinic discussion of the 'oral law' dating from the fourth to fifth centuries CE, which orthodox Jews believe was handed down to Moses together with the *Torah* at Mount Sinai. It is the basis for *halachah*.
Torah	The first five books of the Hebrew Bible. In synagogue Jews read extracts from *Torah* scrolls in which the text is written by hand on parchment. The term is also used more generally to describe the whole of the Hebrew Bible.
Yeshiva	Institution for the study of canonical Jewish texts such as the *Talmud*, most of which are orthodox-run. Most are only for men and the female equivalent is the *midrashah*.

Yom Kippur   Literally 'Day of Atonement'. The holiest day in the Jewish calendar marked by fasting and prayer, which takes place ten days after *Rosh Hashanah*.

Index of Names and Institutions

Abrahams, Louis 20
Accord Coalition 105
Adam Science training pro-
    gramme 90
Aish Fellowships programme 65
Aish HaTorah 35, 65–6, 80
Alderman, Geoffrey 6, 19, 27,
    30, 77, 79, 157, 174
All-Party Parliamentary Group
    against Antisemitism 149
All-Party Parliamentary Inquiry
    into Antisemitism 140, 146,
    150, 161
Allen, Woody 118
Alleyne, Brian 174
Alliance for Workers Liberty 149
Al-Qaeda 141
American Jewish Committee
    ᵃ 144, 149
Amiel, Barbara 141, 147, 152
Ancram, Michael 150
Angel, Moses 20
Anglo Jewish Association (AJA)
    21, 22, 23, 25
Anglo Jewish Council of Trades
    and Industry 24
Anti-Defamation League (ADL)
    139, 144
Anti-Nazi League (ANL) 29, 30

Archbishop of Canterbury's
    Commission on Urban
    Priority Areas 30
Arendt, Hannah 57
Ariel, Jonathan 85, 86, 88, 92
Ashdown Fellows programme
    63, 90
Ashkenazi Great Synagogue 2
Assembly of Masorti Synagogues
    3, 78, 84, 96, 99, 100, 102
Association of Jewish Communal
    Professionals 113
Association of Jewish Ex-
    Servicemen and Women
    (AJEX) 28
Association of UK Jewish Culture
    Providers 122
Aviv, Caryn 51

Back, Les 173
Bagguley, Paul 173
Baron, Bernhard 23
Baron-Cohen, Sacha 5
Bauman, Zygmunt 5, 11, 56,
    56–7
Bayfield, Tony 35, 99–100,
    101–2, 106
Beaumont, Peter 153
Beck, Ulrich 175

Beitar 91
Beker, Avi 148
Bekerman, Zvi 50–1
Ben Uri Gallery 118
Benatoff, Cobi 142, 144, 147
Benevolent Societies 21
Bercow, John 4
Berger, Peter 11
Berlin, Isaiah 5
Berman, Lila Corwen 48
Bermant, Chaim 17, 30
Besht Tellers theatre company
    121
Bikkurim 131
Bindman, Geoffrey 155
Black, Eugene 17
B'nai B'rith 26, 144
Bnei Akiva 85, 90
Board of Deputies of British Jews
    3, 5, 17, 21, 22, 23, 24, 25,
    26, 27, 28, 30, 31, 42, 46,
    54, 73, 105, 108, 110, 113,
    114, 121, 123, 132, 133,
    138, 144, 149, 150, 158,
    160, 161, 164, 168
Board of Deputies Community
    Research Unit 40, 42, 54
Board of Deputies Defence
    Committee 29
Board of Trade 20
Boteach, Shmuley 65
Bournemouth Hebrew
    Congregation 66
Boyd, Jonathan 49, 54, 89, 127
Brass, Laurence 161
Brighton and Hove Progressive
    Synagogue 156
British army 21
British Association for Jewish
    Studies 119
British Friends of Peace Now 161

British Israel Communications
    and Research Centre
    (BICOM) 137–8, 149
British National Party (BNP) 149
British Union of Fascists 23
Brodie, Israel 66
Brook, Stephen 9
Brown, Gordon 4, 173
Burg, Avraham 34

Cahan, Abraham 21
Cambridge University 36
Camp Ramah 60
Central Council for Jewish
    Community Services 113
Central Jewish Consultative
    Committee 24
Cesarani, David 6, 17, 18, 22,
    23, 28, 37, 139, 160
Chabad Houses 64
Chabad Lubavitch Centres 64
Chabad-Lubavitch 64–6, 67, 97,
    130
Chaim, Etz 37
Charikar, Shalom 28
Chesler, Phyllis 142, 143, 144,
    146, 147
Chevruta project 127
Chicago University 60
Chief Rabbinate 2, 66, 78, 99,
    108–9, 129, 132, 164,
    168
Chinn, Trevor 5, 73, 114
Christ's College, Finchley 36
Church Lads' Brigade 19
Clinton, Bill 11
Clore Duffield Foundation 122,
    131
Coalition for Alternatives in
    Jewish Education 59
Cohen, Erik 53

Cohen, Stanley 6
Cohen, Steven M. 48–9, 53, 89, 133, 134
Cohn-Sherbok, Daniel 143
Commission Nationale Consultative des Droits de l'Homme (CNCDH) 140
Commission on Jewish Education in North America 44, 59
Commission on Jewish Schools 110, 114, 132
Communist Party 24
Community Security Trust (CST) 114, 140, 149, 150
Conference of Presidents of Major American Jewish Organizations 114
Conference on Alternatives in Jewish Education 125
Cooper, Howard 9
Council for Initiatives in Jewish Education 61
Council of Jewish Federations 40–2
Cousinhood 17–19, 20, 21–2, 23, 27
Cromwell, Oliver 15, 16

Dahrendorf, Ellen 155
Dalyell, Tam 142
Davie, Grace 11
Deech, Ruth 114
Dewey, John 60

Ehrentreu, Dayan 126
Eisen, Arnold 48–9
Ellman, Louise 30
Encounter conference 97–8
Endelman 18
Engage 150

European Institute for the Study of Contemporary Anti-Semitism (EISCA) 149, 150

Fackenheim, Emil 68, 166
Fair Play Campaign Group 150
Federation of Synagogues 2, 3, 78
Finestein, Israel 16, 163
Fink, Deborah 126
Finkelman, Yoel 130
Finkielkraut, Alain 144, 148
Fisk, Robert 126, 153
Fitzsimmons, Lorna 149
Florence Melton adult education programme 90
Fox, Alan 85
Fox, Seymour 59–64, 74, 85, 89
Foxman, Abraham 143, 144, 147, 148, 152
Frankel, William 121
Franklin, Jane 175
Fraser, Jenny 82
Freedland, Jonathan 5, 121, 160
Freud-Kandel, Miri 66, 76
Friedman, Edie 30

Gapes, Mike 149
Gateshead Yeshiva 119
George III 15
German Secret Committee of Public Affairs 15
Gerwitz, Jacob 30
Gilbert, Martin 5
Gilman, Sander 6
Gilroy, Paul 5, 51
Givet, Jacques 139
Goldberg, David 155, 157, 159
Goldberg, J.J. 32
Goldstein, Eric 6
Gorbachev, Michael 65

Graham, David 46
Grant, Linda 121, 157
Greater London Council (GLC)
      29, 31
Greenberg, Steve 75
Grunwald, Henry 150
Gryn, Hugo 78
Gutwein, Daniel 17, 21

Habonim Youth Movement 85,
      90
Hall, Stuart 5
Harris, Clive 174
Harrison, Bernard 153
Hart, Mitchell 6, 47
Henry, Georgina 155
Hertz, Joseph H. 76
Heschel, Abraham J. 37
Hilsum, Lindsay 153
Hirsch, David 154, 158
Hitler, Adolf 23, 24, 68, 138,
      151
Hobsbawm, Eric 156
Hochhauser, Simon 107
Holmes, Kelly 172
HonestReporting.com 144
Hoover Institute 144
Huntingdon Foundation 111
Hussein, Yasmin 173

Immanuel College 103
Independent Jewish Voices (IJV)
      138, 154–60, 168, 169
Ingrams, Richard 142, 145
Institute for Jewish Policy
      Research (JPR) 45, 54, 55,
      105, 110–11, 114, 132, 152,
      155
Institute of Jewish Affairs 28, 45,
      140
Institute of Jewish Studies 119

Interparliamentary Coalition for
      Combating Antisemitism
      150
Israel Ministry of Foreign Affairs
      144
Israel Solidarity 150

J Street 160
Jackson, Colin 172
Jacob Blaustein Institute 144
Jacobs, Lewis 8
Jacobson, Howard 5
Jakobovits, Immanuel 7, 27, 29,
      30, 66, 76, 103, 151, 174
Janner, Greville 5, 30, 42, 49, 114
Jasanoff, Sheila 11
Jeneration 101–2
Jenkins, Roy 29
Jerusalem Fellows programme 61,
      85, 89
Jewdas 123–4, 130, 160, 165
Jewish Agency 34, 61, 115
Jewish Blind Society 113
Jewish Board of Guardians 19
Jewish Book Council 119, 121
Jewish Book Week 121, 122, 129
Jewish Care 4, 81, 113, 114
Jewish Chronicle 16, 20, 23, 24,
      25, 71, 78, 82, 107, 110,
      111, 119–21, 139, 158, 160,
      161
Jewish Community Allocations
      Board 75, 76, 78, 82, 91
Jewish Community Centre (JCC)
      122–3, 128, 131, 134, 171
Jewish Community Secondary
      School 103, 105, 111, 134,
      171
Jewish Continuity 13, 67, 68,
      71–93, 98, 99, 118, 121,
      125, 130, 165

Jewish Cultural and Anti-Racism
    Project (JCARP) 30–1
Jewish Educational Development
    Trust (JEDT) 44, 76, 103–4
Jewish Educational Service of
    North America (JESNA) 35,
    59, 74
Jewish Federations 59
Jewish Film Festival 122
Jewish Friendly Society 21
Jewish Girls' Brigade 133
Jewish Immigrant Aid (JIA) 130
Jewish Labour Council 24
Jewish Lads' Brigade 19, 133
Jewish Leadership Council (JLC)
    35, 103, 114, 115, 132, 138,
    150, 161, 168
Jewish Learning Exchange 65
Jewish Life Education Centre 90
Jewish Museum 118
Jewish Music Institute 122
Jewish National Fund (JNF) 4, 81
Jewish People Policy Planning
    Institute 11
Jewish Quarterly 118–19
Jewish Religious Union 3
Jewish Renaissance 128–9
Jewish Representative Council for
    the Boycott of German
    Goods and Services 24
Jewish Representative Councils
    (JRCs) 21
Jewish Socialists' Group 30
Jewish Theological Seminary 58,
    61
Jewish Welfare Board 113
Jewish Women's Aid 132
Jewish Working Men's Club 19
Jewish Youth Voluntary Service
    groups 28
Jews' College 37, 66–7, 78, 90,
    97, 98, 113, 119, 161
    see also London School of
    Jewish Studies
Jews for Boycotting Israeli Goods
    126
Jews for Justice for Palestinians
    160
Jews' Free School (JFS) 20,
    106–9, 132
JHub 131
Joint Israel Appeal (JIA) 4, 73–4,
    76, 79, 81, 82, 83, 84, 85,
    88, 91
    see also United Jewish Israel
    Appeal
Joshua Venture 131
Julius, Anthony 151

Kahn-Harris, Keith 79, 89, 133,
    134, 168
Kalman, Matthew 119, 121
Kalms, Stanley 5, 43, 44, 67, 78,
    96–7, 113
Kaplan, Mordecai 60
Karpf, Anne 157
Katz, Jacob 56
Kestenbaum, Jonathan 63, 73,
    85, 86, 89
King David School 73, 110
Klein, Emma 50, 52
Klug, Brian 152, 155, 157
Kopelowitz, Ezra 50–1
Kosmin, Barry 41–2, 45–6, 54,
    55
Krauthammer, Charles 148
Kristeva, Julia 122
Kundnani, Arun 173
Kushner, Tony 6

Labour Friends of Israel 149
Laden, Osama bin 147

Lambert, Nick 32, 155, 156
Lamm, Norman 36
Landau, David 145
Lappin, Shalom 160
Laski, Nathan 22
Laski, Neville 22, 23
Laurence, Jonathan 140, 144–5
Lawton, Clive 73–4, 80, 81, 82, 83, 85, 86, 87, 92, 127
Lazarus, Neil 152
L'Chaim Society 65
League of British Jews 21, 25
Leo Baeck College 35, 113, 119
Lerman, Tony 54, 151, 152, 157
Levene, Mark 16
Levy, Michael 5
Lewis, Bernard 144
Lewis, Denise 172
Lewis, Hal 18, 32
Liberal Jewish Synagogue 3, 159
Liberal Judaism 3, 50, 96, 99, 100, 102, 160
Lieberman, Avigdor 161
Liebman, Charles 52
Limmud 78, 86, 90, 125–8, 129, 134, 162, 164, 166
Limmud International 128
Lipman, Maureen 5
Liverpool Education Authority 73
Living Judaism programme 100–1
Livingstone, Ken 29, 31, 154
London Committee of Deputies of British Jews 15
London School of Jewish Studies 90, 119
London University 119
Long-Term Planning for British Jewry Project 45, 46, 54, 55
Lubavitcher Rebbe 67

Lucas, Matt 5

Machon L'Madrichei Chutz La'Aretz 91
MacShane, Dennis 143, 147, 151
Manchester University 54
Mandel Leadership Institute 61, 63, 84, 86, 89
Mandelson, Peter 150
Manhattan Jewish Community Centre 122
Mann, John 149
Marks, Simon 23
Masorti Movement see Assembly of Masorti Synagogues
Matas, David 141, 144
Matisyahu 118
Mayes, Ian 153–4
Mearsheimer, John 142–3, 153
Melitz 34, 85
Melton Research Center for Jewish Education 60–1
Middle East Center for Peach 144
Miller, Helena 104–5, 110
Miller, Stephen 49–50
Milne, Seamus 153
Mitzman, Michael 160
Moishe House for London 123
Montagu, Lily 3
Montefiore, Claude 3
Montefiore, Leonard 23
Montefiore London Semicha Programme 113
Morrison, Paul 9
Mosley, Oswald 138
Movement for Reform Judaism 3, 35, 50, 55, 58, 78, 96, 99–101, 102, 106
Murphy, Jim 149
Mythen, Gabe 11

National Front 29
National Jewish Center for
 Learning and Leadership
 (CLAL) 75
National Jewish Population
 Survey (NJPS) 40–2, 45, 58
National Organisation of Labour
 Students (NOLS) 149
National Union of Students
 (NUS) 120, 149
Netanyahu, Benjamin 150
Neuberger, Julia 36, 160
Neustatter, Hannah 39
New Generation Network 155
New Israel Fund 155, 160, 161
New Jewish Thought project 170
New Moon 119–21
New North London Synagogue
 102
New Statesman 141, 153
Newmark, Jeremy 35, 114
North American Commission on
 Jewish Identity and
 Continuity 40, 59
Norwood 113

Office for National Statistics 46
One Voice 160
Operation Cast Lead 161
Organization for Security and Co-
 operation in Europe (OCSE)
 142
Orzach, Shalom 89
Oxford Centre for Hebrew and
 Jewish Studies 119
Oxford University 36, 65

Padwa, Dayan 78, 121, 170
Palestine Liberation Organisation
 (PLO) 151
Parekh, Bikhu 171

Parliament 16
Pascal, Julia 155
Paulin, Tom 145
Pears Foundation 131
Perl, Benjamin 111, 134
Persoff, Meir 66, 99
Phillips, Melanie 5, 145, 146,
 173
Phillips, Trevor 173
Pikuach 75, 110
Pinter, Harold 5, 156
Poliakov, Léon 139
Popper, Karl 5
Powell, Enoch 28
Preston, Rosalind 36
Project Chesed 124
Pulzer, Peter 152
Putnam, Robert 11

Rackman, Emmanuel 36–7
Raffel, Martin J. 140
Rattansi, Ali 173
Ravenswood 113
Rawidowicz, Simon 56
Rayner, Jay 121
Reconstructionist movement 60
(Reform) Assembly of Rabbis
 105
(Reform) Hebrew Union College
 58
Reform Movement *see* Movement
 for Reform Judaism
Reform Synagogues of Great
 Britain 43
Rich, Danny 160
Romain, Jonathan 105
Ronson, Gerald 30, 114, 134
Rose, Jacqueline 155
Roseman, Kenneth 18
Rosenfeld, Alvin H. 145
Roskies, David 57

Roth, Cecil 138
Roth, Philip 118
Rothschild Foundation Europe
    124
Runymede Trust 172

Sacher, Harry 23
Sacks, Jonathan 4, 13, 36–7, 38,
    41, 42–3, 48, 49, 58, 63–4,
    66, 67, 67–8, 68, 72–3,
    77–9, 80, 84, 85, 98, 106,
    107, 108, 109, 118, 121,
    122, 126, 129, 130, 134,
    145–6, 147, 150, 151, 152,
    165, 166, 170, 172, 173,
    176
Samuel, Louis 22
Sandouga, Yousef 141, 147
Sarah, Elizabeth Tikvah 156
Sarna, Jonathan 115
Schmool, Marlena 46
Schneer, David 51
Schneerson, Menachem Mendel
    37, 64
Schoenfeld, Gabriel 147
Schultz, George 144
Schwab, Joseph 60
Scientology 65
Seed 65
Segal, Lynne 155
Sharansky, Natan 119, 144
Shared Futures project 105
Short, Geoffrey 109
Shukra, Kalbir 174
Sieff, Israel 23
Simon Wiesenthal Centre 144
Simpson, O.J. 65
Sinai League 26
Sinclair, Clive 33
Sinclair, Michael 73–4, 79, 81,
    83, 85, 87, 92, 121

Singer, Isaac Bashevis 118
Slovo, Gillian 157
Socialist Organiser 149
Socialist Workers Party 30
Soloveitchick, Joseph B. 37
Sparks 131
Spiro Institute 119
St John's Wood synagogue 38
Stephen Roth Institute 144
Stop the Boycott 138, 150
Sufi Muslim Council 156
Sugar, Alan 5
Swaythling, Lord 22
Synagogue 2000 programme 101

Tabick, Jackie 36
Taguieff, Pierre-André 140, 142,
    144
Temko, Ned 121
Tent programme 102
Thatcher, Margaret 4, 29
trade unions 24
Tribe 98
Twigg, Stephen 149

UN General Assembly 139
UN World Conference Against
    Racism 141
Unification Church 65
Union of Jewish Students (UJS)
    35, 36, 119, 139, 149, 150
Union of Liberal and Progressive
    Synagogues 102
    see also Liberal Judaism
Union of Orthodox Hebrew
    Congregations (UOHC) 2,
    3, 78
Union of Orthodox Hebrew
    Congregations Beth Din 78
United Jewish Israel Appeal
    (UJIA) 4, 49, 63, 85–6,

88–92, 88–93, 94, 99, 110, 113, 115, 118, 125, 130, 131, 132, 171
United Jewish Protest Committee 24
United Synagogue 2, 3, 19, 22, 35, 43, 55, 58, 65, 66, 67, 77, 78, 96–9, 100, 107, 108–9, 113, 119, 123, 124, 126, 130, 132, 164, 170
United Synagogue Beth Din 66, 77, 78, 96, 98, 99, 126, 132
United Synagogue Council 22, 108–9
University Jewish Chaplaincy 66

Vaisse, Justin 140, 144–5
Vanity Fair 142
Vidal Sassoon International Center for the Study of Antisemitism 145

Wagerman, Jo 36
Wagner, Leslie 84
Walt, Stephen 142–3, 153
Waterman, Stanley 46
Weber, Max 11, 92
Wegier, Michael 89
West London Synagogue 3

Whine, Michael 140
Wiesel, Ellie 144
Wieseltier, Leon 151
Williams, Bill 19, 21, 22
Winehouse, Amy 5
Wineman, Vivian 161
Wise, Yaacov 54
Wistrich, Robert 138–9, 140
Wittenberg, Jonathan 102
Wittgenstein, Ludwig 5
Woocher, Jonathan 35, 74, 84
Workers' Circle 24
Working Party on Race Relations 28
World Jewish Congress 26, 45
World Union of Jewish Students 119
Worms, Fred 44, 72
Wyatt, Petronella 141, 147

Yakar 119
Yavneh College 103, 111
Yeshiva University 58
Yeshivat ha Mivtar 35
Yisrael Beiteinu party 169
Young, David 113
Youth Emergency Council 24

Zneimer, Saul 35, 99